the
BETRAYAL
of the
**URBAN
POOR**

the BETRAYAL of the URBAN POOR

helene
SLESSAREV

Temple University Press

Philadelphia

To the memory of my father, Vsevolod Slessarev,

whose love I will always carry in my heart

Temple University Press, Philadelphia 19122
Copyright © 1997 by Temple University
All rights reserved
Published 1997
Printed in the United States of America

♾ The paper used in this publication meets the
requirements of the American National Standard for
Information Sciences—Permanence of Paper for Printed
Library Materials, ANSI Z39.48–1984

Text design by William Boehm

Library of Congress Cataloging-in-Publication Data

Slessarev, Helene.
The betrayal of the urban poor / Helene Slessarev.
p.   cm.
Includes index.
ISBN 1–56639–542–9 (cloth : alk. paper)
ISBN 1–56639–543–7 (paper : alk. paper)
1. Urban poor—United States. 2. Manpower policy—United States,
3. Social mobility—United States. 4. United States—Economic
policy—1981–1993. 5. United States—Economic policy—1993–
I. Title.
HV4045.S54   1997
362.59 0973—dc21   96–52817

CONTENTS

PREFACE

The Betrayal of the Urban Poor examines the failure of our nation's economic justice policies to create avenues of upward mobility for the urban poor, most of whom are now black and Latino. These policies have been far too limited in scope, making it difficult for them to have a significant impact in rebuilding the basic structures of economic opportunity that are lacking in poor communities. I started this project with the recognition that the civil rights victories of the 1960s had been no more than a first step on the road to racial equality, and that the character of other social mobility policies was often shaped more by political considerations than by a concern for whether the policies would actually alleviate poverty. Organized labor has had a rather mixed historical record on civil rights issues, and therefore I was not surprised by the material that I found in the United Auto Workers' archives concerning the union's resistance to full implementation of the equal employment section of the 1964 Civil Rights Act.

I had also assumed that the civil rights movement's search for equality in access to housing, jobs, and education in the urban North continued to guide modern civil rights leaders and minority politicians. Therefore, governments' failure to enact policies to improve economic opportunities for the poor resulted from a lack of commitment to further racial equality on the part of the movement's former allies, not a change in priorities on the part of black leaders. I remained so firmly convinced that race was the predominant factor shaping the life chances of African-Americans that in 1987 I coauthored a review of William Julius Wilson's *The Truly Disadvantaged* in which we criticized Wilson for his overemphasis of class differences within the black community. Since then, my own experiences in

Chicago politics have taught me that different economic classes within the African-American community now often seek distinctly different goals within the political arena. As a result, the priorities of certain prominent civil rights organizations appear to have changed, becoming more narrowly focused on those issues of interest to the black middle class. I believe that this shift has created new impediments to finding more comprehensive policy solutions to urban poverty.

The discussion of these issues is not intended to belittle the economic progress made by middle-class black Americans, or to ignore the impact that racism continues to have on the well-being of all African-Americans, regardless of economic status. Rather, it is a critique of those black politicians and civil rights leaders who use the symbolism of race to advance either their personal agendas or what are primarily the economic policy goals of their black middle-class constituents. With a few notable exceptions, such as Congressman Bobby Rush, who represents the district in which I live, the majority of Chicago's black politicians have become remarkably silent on the life-and-death issues facing their poorer constituents. For me, it has become difficult to critique the shortcomings of organized labor and the Republican and Democratic policymakers in Washington without also looking at the deficiencies of policymakers much closer to home.

This book weaves together a number of research methodologies. The early chapters include information drawn from primary sources found in the archives of the United Auto Workers, the AFL-CIO, the National Association for the Advancement of Colored People, and the A. Philip Randolph Institute. I have also made extensive use of personal interviews, many of them with friends and coworkers from my years of involvement in Chicago politics. The sections of the book dealing with events in Chicago after 1987 are in part based on my personal experiences as a participant-observer. These sections are not meant to be a comprehensive examination of events in Chicago, but instead are designed to give the reader a stronger understanding of how policies impact at the local level. I have been careful not to violate my own relationships of trust and therefore have chosen primarily to describe events about which there is also documentation in newspapers or other publications. In some instances, I have also been deliberately vague about specific people in order to avoid disclosing sensitive information that is not public knowledge.

Chicago has been my home since 1977. For all but one of those years I have lived as one of very few whites in a predominantly black neighborhood on the city's Southside. My immediate neighborhood is a close-knit community composed of well-kept single-family homes like those found in many middle-class white neighborhoods on Chicago's Northwest side and in the older suburbs that ring the city. Yet, most white Chicagoans are stunned when I tell them where I live. Instinctively, they know that whites simply do not live on that side of the city's invisible but very real color line. My reasons for making that choice are deeply personal. For the last ten years I have been raising my son, who is biracial, as a single parent. This community has been a tremendous source of support for both of us, while giving me a unique vantage point from which to view the increasingly strident anti-black, anti-poor political rhetoric that has found its way into our national discourse. It has also made the epidemic of violence and drug abuse that plagues urban black communities deeply personal, as close friends have lost their children to both.

I first got involved in politics while still in high school in 1960s. After finishing college, I spent six years working, first as a union organizer in Washington, D.C., and then as a community organizer in Chicago, before returning to graduate school. In 1987, while working on my dissertation, I took a full-time job as the economics specialist at the Chicago Urban League, the city's largest race relations organization. At the time it seemed like an ideal position because I was committed to putting my research skills and policy expertise to practical use. While at the Urban League, I participated in the DRIVE coalition and the work of the Affirmative Action Division, both of which are described in this book. During much of 1988 I also worked on Jesse Jackson's presidential campaign as the Midwest volunteer coordinator. Through that experience I developed close friendships with a number of people who had literately grown up in Operation PUSH, had participated in its early boycotts, but over time had become disillusioned by the organization's apparent abandonment of its earlier focus on securing jobs and protecting black consumer rights. This book is in no way intended to disparage the accomplishments of either organization, but to critique the effectiveness of certain aspects of the work they have engaged in during the past ten years and its implications on efforts to find solutions to urban poverty.

In 1989, I took a consulting job with the city of Chicago as the lead researcher in a disparity study documenting the long history of discrimination against minority businesses in Chicago. This evidence was needed in order for the city to justify the continuation of its minority set-aside program in the wake of the Supreme Court's *Croson* decision. I conducted numerous interviews with minority businesspeople whose first opportunities to do municipal contracting resulted from the city's set-aside program. Our research also made it abundantly clear that there are serious flaws in the program that lessen its effectiveness and leave it open to considerable abuse. In 1993, I was asked by Joe Gardner, whom I had come to know during Jackson's 1988 campaign, to serve as the principal policy expert in his campaign for reelection as commissioner of the Water Reclamation District of Greater Chicago. Joe had already decided to run against Mayor Richard M. Daley in the 1995 municipal elections, and as a result we were actually preparing for two elections. The year and a half during which I worked closely with Joe and others on his staff was my most intimate exposure to the inner workings of Chicago-style politics. In January 1996, when the U.S. Attorney's office in Chicago announced that it had been conducting a four-year corruption probe of numerous local politicians, Joe was among those listed as being under investigation. Unbeknownst to all but his closest friends and family, Joe was already in the final stages of terminal cancer and died in May 1996.

Over the years I have also had the opportunity to do consulting work for a number of community-based organizations that provide social services or are involved in community economic development efforts. I currently serve on the board of two such organizations. Along with my time at the Chicago Urban League, these experiences have given me an insider's view into the work of community-based organizations, and again I have drawn on those experiences in writing this book.

ACKNOWLEDGMENTS

I want to thank my family for their support—especially my mother, Helga, who has provided numerous editorial comments on earlier drafts, and my son, Stephan, who has spent many years of his life with this project. I also want to thank the many friends and colleagues I came to know from my work at the Chicago Urban League, Operation PUSH, and in various political campaigns and community organizations. They have been a constant source of knowledge and feedback as I developed my ideas concerning the events and organizations in which we were involved. I hope that those parts of the book that draw on my experiences in Chicago do justice to the innumerable contributions that others have made.

I want to thank Dwight McKee, Steve Saunders, and others for sharing their insights about Operation PUSH, and Jim Blassingame for schooling me in the arts of Chicago politics. A number of people, including Pat Forbes, Ben Kohrman, Buzz Palmer, and colleagues at Wheaton College, have given me input on particular chapters. Several people also contributed their ideas and experiences, including Reverend George Riddick from Operation PUSH, Commissioner Joseph Gardner, and Taylor Cotton from Black Contractors United, who passed away before this book was completed.

I want to thank Wheaton College for encouraging me to continue my community work in Chicago while also serving as the college's director of urban studies, as well as for providing the funds to begin the long process of transforming a dissertation into a publishable book. Finally, I would like to acknowledge the support and encouragement I have received over the years from my community of faith, particularly Reverend Benjamin Johnson, Sr., and his wife, Louise.

the
BETRAYAL
of the
URBAN
POOR

1 | A PARTIAL COMMITMENT TO EQUALITY

This book challenges the notion that excesses in government generosity destroyed the work ethic in poor minority communities and therefore are responsible for the growth in poverty. This gross distortion is driven more by an underlying anti-government political agenda than by any historical accuracy. All rhetoric about equal opportunity aside, the United States has, at best, a partial commitment to equality. The social and economic policies initiated in the 1960s were carefully crafted to minimize their impact on the racial status quo, with the Democratic Party engaged in a delicate balancing act between responding to racial injustice and preserving the often conflicting interests of its other traditional constituencies. Affirmative action policies have been so controversial in large part because they challenge traditional racial boundaries, thereby jeopardizing white male expectations of obtaining the most coveted jobs.

In 1996, after years of minimal funding for urban anti-poverty efforts, both political parties agreed to withdraw the federal government's sixty-year-old commitment to providing financial support for poor women with children. Remarkably, these changes occurred without either party publicly acknowledging the difficult reality that thirty years after the enactment of basic civil rights reforms, economic opportunities remain as limited as ever for poor minorities living in our nation's cities. As of 1990, 43 percent of the nation's poor were concentrated in America's central cities. Living in neighborhoods that are highly segregated by both race and class, poor African-Americans and Latinos are largely cut off from the society's basic structures of opportunity. Decades of racial segregation have left "the economic base of urban black communities uniquely vulnerable to any downturn in the group's economic fortunes."[1] As manufacturing companies left behind their old inner-city facilities during the 1970s and 1980s, segregation quickly triggered a process of neighborhood disinvestment and abandonment. Today, "poor blacks live in communities that typically contain only the rudiments of retail trade."[2] Without an economic base, these communities offer few employment opportunities to the thousands of welfare recipients who will be required to work within the next two years.

Attacking the Poor, Not Poverty

The highly visible growth of urban poverty spawned a virtual cottage industry of academics and policymakers seeking to shed new light on the phenomenon. Conservative writers, who have been the most vocal in their attacks on what they label as liberal welfare policies, have stigmatized poor minorities by arguing that they somehow have "a hidden investment in victimization and poverty."[3] Although these writers correctly identify common attitudes of the poor, their "blame the victim" approach never connects apparent deviant social behavior to the alienation of the poor from the broader society. The conservatives fail to comprehend the link between poverty and powerlessness that leaves poor people constantly having to respond to the actions of others. Life on public aid is the highest expression of such powerlessness because it robs people of the hope of self-advancement through legitimate means. Finding themselves caught between the American myth of equal opportunity and their own inability to achieve their personal dreams, poor people often "internalize their powerlessness as their own fault, rather than as a response to system-wide discrimination."[4] Much of the deviant behavior displayed by members of the underclass has its roots in their sense of powerlessness. Feeling themselves to be outcasts from mainstream society, they do not see themselves as bound by its norms. Indeed, powerlessness leads to a sense of victimization that can become immobilizing. "The oppressed, having internalized the image of the oppressor and adopted his guidelines, are fearful of freedom."[5] They become reluctant to believe in the possibility of change, or that they possess the creative capacity to affect their surroundings.

Martin Luther King, Jr., and others involved in the southern civil rights movement understood that their battle for freedom would be won only if large numbers of black people underwent a personal transformation and became conscious of themselves as purposeful actors infused with a sense of dignity and self-worth. Long years of oppression had beaten them down so badly that they doubted their own capacity to improve their conditions. In the South the strategy of nonviolent direct action became the means by which thousands of ordinary blacks divested themselves of their traditional passivity, breaking forever the image of the "shuffling Negro."[6] Only then could institutional change occur.

Conservatives are oblivious to the continued existence of deep structural barriers that prevent poor minorities from gaining access to the advantages of the dominant society. In *The New Politics of Poverty,* Lawrence Mead simply dismisses poor-quality education, the disappearance of industrial jobs, and the continued presence of racial discrimination, arguing that the existence of powerful social barriers no longer explains why the poor do not work. As he sees it, "motivation is inevitably more at issue than opportunity."[7] Since the social policies of the left and the right have not worked, the fault must lie with the poor themselves. According to Mead, the solutions to poverty lie in the poor becoming "less deviant but more assertive in their own self-interest, especially by working."[8] The often unstated assumption underlying these types of explanations is that all Americans possess equal opportunities for advancement, so that if whole groups of people are falling behind it must be due to their own cultural inadequacies. For example, Nathan Glazer contends that African-Americans have not fared as well because they lack an entrepreneurial spirit and suffer from higher levels of unemployment and social disorganization.[9] Thomas Sowell believes that blacks do not possess the Protestant work ethic required for success.[10] He sees no connection between poor blacks' lack of motivation and their powerlessness, asserting that it is an "arbitrary premise" that the "'disparities' and 'gaps' in incomes and occupations [between whites and blacks] are evidence . . . of discrimination or exploitation."[11]

Closely tied to these cultural arguments are those that place the onus on government social policies, especially those implemented by the Democrats during the 1960s. Supposedly, these anti-poverty efforts were so massive that they made a life of dependency on government aid more attractive than hard work and self-reliance. Charles Murray and George Gilder have both argued that the expanded education, jobs, and welfare programs of the Great Society encouraged laziness and promiscuity and decreased incentive among the urban poor by providing payments to those who chose not to work. According to Murray, "in the late 1960's—at the very moment when the jobs programs began their massive expansion . . . the black youth unemployment rate began to rise again, steeply, and continued to do so throughout the 1970's."[12] The same trends are said to hold for black male labor force participation. Murray blames the liberalization of public aid eligibility for the rise in juvenile delinquency and children born to unwed mothers that occurred in the late 1960s. By making virtually all low-income people welfare recipients, the means-tested programs supposedly robbed them of the social status of working. According to Murray, youths were most affected by this change in the status of work: "In the day to day experience of a youth growing up in a black ghetto there was no evidence whatsoever that working within the system paid off. The way to get something from the system was to be sufficiently a failure to qualify for help, or to con the system."[13]

These authors would have us believe that somehow black inequality was gradually vanishing on its own, rendering any type of government intervention unnecessary. In *Affirmative Discrimination* Glazer presents income and occupational data for the 1950s that show a convergence of black and white incomes, indicating "a virtual collapse in traditional discriminatory patterns in the labor market."[14] Murray goes to considerable lengths in his book *Losing Ground* to prove that during the 1950s and early 1960s black poverty was declining, unemployment was holding steady, and labor force participation rates for blacks were on a par with those of whites from similar backgrounds.[15]

Much of the increase in black income in the 1950s and early 1960s came as the direct result of massive migration out of southern agriculture into industrial employment in the North. Between 1950 and 1970 more than 3 million blacks left the South to replace whites in the industrial labor force, just as new technologies were being introduced that would soon eliminate many of the unskilled jobs on the assembly line.[16] In fact, 1953 was the last year of relatively low black unemployment, 4.4 percent for males and 3.7 percent for females.[17] By 1962, the rates were 10 percent and

9.8 percent, respectively, more than twice the unemployment level among whites, while for black teenagers it was already a shocking 23.6 percent.[18] Those occupations in which unemployment was the highest—for example, laborers, operatives, and "other service workers"—were precisely the occupations in which blacks were most concentrated.[19] Conversely, the occupations with the lowest unemployment rates, such as managers, officials, and proprietors, were those in which blacks were least concentrated. The move from agriculture to industrial labor did not bring the majority of blacks any closer to the center of American economic life. By the end of 1963, at least 750,000 black youth were roaming the streets, out of school and out of work.[20]

It does not take a great deal of complex social science research to conclude that today there are few jobs left in poor minority communities. A drive through streets lined with boarded-up factories, warehouses, and stores will suffice. It has been estimated that between 30 and 50 percent of the employment gap between white and black youth can be explained by differences in job accessibility.[21] A recent labor market study in Illinois found that there are four potential entry-level job seekers for every entry-level job available in the state. In Chicago the ratio was even higher—six job seekers for every available entry-level job.[22] The loss of manufacturing jobs and the high concentration of poorly trained African-Americans and Hispanics has placed the demographics and economics of America's cities on a collision course. Although the overall educational attainment of urban minorities improved during the 1970s and 1980s, these gains were not sufficient to keep pace with even faster rises in the education required to work in the new urban information-based economy.[23] Yet, conservatives would have us think that jobs are plentiful. For example, Mead contends that "since the 1960s, opportunities have grown for the low-skilled. Their education levels as well as the number of jobs have risen. Racial discrimination has fallen, as have welfare disincentives, with the failure of AFDC benefits, since the early 1970's, to keep pace with inflation."[24] The decline in factory jobs was supposedly offset by "an explosion of employment in service trades." Thus, Mead concludes, "Most inner-city poor appear able to find jobs, albeit not of the quality they would like."[25]

Creating Economic Opportunity

A true pledge to alleviate poverty would require a commitment to building structures of economic opportunity. Every economy has such structures, both formal and informal, designed to move each successive generation to a new level of economic security. In poor minority communities, these structures are often nonexistent or in acute disrepair, leaving the majority of residents without any real possibility of economic advancement. Given America's legacy of racial oppression, establishing structures of economic opportunity for people of color would entail more than just competent schools, career training, available employment, childcare, and job referrals. It would require opening up the entire metropolitan labor market, which is now so geographically and occupationally stratified by race and class that poor minorities are confined to only a tiny fraction of the total job opportunities. It would include a commitment to eliminating all remaining forms of racial exclusion, even though they are not legally sanctioned. The lack of access to the mainstream labor market lies at the heart of the urban crisis of poverty. The departure of low-skill manufacturing jobs, continued employment discrimination, and the poor quality of urban education work together to condemn large segments of black and Latino communities to a marginal economic status.

Without special incentives, private capital flows to where the potential for a return on investment is the greatest. Having engaged in a prolonged process of disinvestment from inner-city communities, private businesses are unlikely to be the engine of economic opportunity for the people who live there. It is only through government intervention that such new structures of economic opportunity will emerge. Historically, the majority of public policies have not successfully accomplished this goal. There are several reasons for their shortcomings:

1. The close association between urban poverty and race creates powerful barriers to building broad-based support for strengthening social mobility programs.
2. The development of effective anti-poverty measures requires a redistribution of resources, which has been blocked successfully by more powerful political constituencies.
3. Black leaders, representing the interests of their middle-class sup-

porters, pursue economic policy goals that are no longer directly connected to the enactment of more effective anti-poverty policies.

4. Government economic policies fail to give priority to creating new jobs in poor urban communities, whether through equal access to employment, minority business programs, or support for community development efforts.

The Tangled Web of Race and Poverty

The extent to which Americans have instinctively come to associate urban poverty with people of color has greatly increased the resistance to solutions that would target significant resources to inner-city neighborhoods. Widespread notions of racial inferiority remain one of the most powerful myths in American culture, with many whites, but increasingly also minorities, susceptible to various racially based "blame the victim" explanations for the nation's social ills. Thirty years after the civil rights victories of the mid-1960s, racial antagonism and anger run deep among both whites and people of color. Though often hidden from direct public view or couched in subtle code words, these feelings permeate the discussion of many of the nation's most intractable social problems, such as urban violence, multigenerational welfare, teenage pregnancy, and drug addiction.

As long as the majority of African-Americans were denied the right to vote, politicians had the luxury of simply ignoring black poverty. For decades, it remained almost completely invisible. At the turn of the century, when the profession of social work first came into its own, reformers championed a wide range of causes, such as women's rights, consumers' leagues, child-labor laws, temperance, and prison reform. In all of this, their focus was on the well-being and Americanization of the newly arrived European immigrants. In Chicago, the birthplace of the settlement house movement, Jane Addams and others established sixty-eight such centers from which they sought to minister to the social and spiritual needs of poor immigrants; yet, not a single one was ever set up in a black neighborhood.[26] In 1909, a frustrated W. E. B. Du Bois voiced his concern that "White reformers seemed to be unaware of the Negro problem or refused to admit its existence."[27]

Although poverty was widespread among European immigrants, most of them worked and were poor because their wages were so low. Unions and Social Security benefits eliminated much of that poverty. After several generations in America, the vast majority of European immigrants have gradually assimilated into a common "white American" identity. The economic and cultural gap between early immigrants from northwestern Europe and those arriving later from Southeastern Europe has all but disappeared, so that now "White groups are more like each other than unlike on income, occupation, and education measures."[28]

Blacks were not included in this process of assimilation and its concomitant economic benefits. They were largely left out of the new Social Security programs that are the foundation of the modern American welfare state, even though on the surface those programs appear to be race neutral. In 1935, when the Roosevelt administration enacted the Social Security Act, most blacks were still eking out a meager subsistence under a sharecropping system that bore a striking resemblance to slavery. At the insistence of southern congressmen who feared that government assistance programs would force an increase in rural wages, blacks were largely excluded from the pensions, disability, unemployment compensation, aid to dependent children, and old-age assistance that constituted the original Social Security Act.[29] Initially, farm laborers and domestics, both occupations in which large numbers of blacks were concentrated, were completely excluded from Social Security coverage. Since the old-age pension was set up to resemble an insurance program, only those who had worked long enough at a job covered by the legislation to pay into the system were eligible to receive benefits.[30]

The expansion of industrial unionism during the 1930s did not bring about improvements in black income equivalent to those experienced by whites. Because employers still controlled the hiring process, blacks remained restricted to the "Negro jobs" in segregated departments. Companies also retained the right to pass judgment on a worker's "ability, skill, and efficiency" with regard to promotions.[31] New union contracts often solidified discriminatory job practices such as separate seniority and promotional lines based on race. By overtly or covertly structuring the systems of seniority and promotions on a racially segregated basis, many unions retarded the promotion and wages of black workers.[32] Blacks frequently were prevented from participating in union leadership and often received little help from the union in processing grievances against management.

Black poverty finally surfaced on the public agenda when large numbers of blacks began to migrate to the big cities outside the South. Segregation in the North restricted the areas into which the new arrivals could move. Severe overcrowding transformed once-stable communities into slums, making urban renewal and the construction of public housing top priorities for big city mayors. But it was the fight of southern blacks to gain their basic democratic rights that finally converted black urban poverty into a major national issue. Only with the achievement of these rights could the United States rightfully claim to be a democratic republic. Expansions in democratic representation inevitably led to expansions in public policy. E. E. Schattschneider recognized this dynamic when he wrote, "Broadly speaking, the expansion of the political community has been one of the principal means of producing change in public policy. . . . Every major change in public policy (the Jefferson, Jackson, Lincoln, and Roosevelt revolutions) has been associated with an enlargement of the electorate."[33]

For little more than a year, between 1964 and the middle of 1965, the federal government focused its diverse resources on the growing poverty and unemployment in the nation's black communities. Existing job-training programs were redirected toward the urban poor. In 1964 President Lyndon Johnson enacted his "War on Poverty," a composite of government-supported community organizing and a variety of education and manpower training programs targeted at youth.[34] The bill established Headstart and the Job Corps, two highly successful programs that have since managed to survive numerous budget cuts and reorganizations. Large Democratic victories in the November 1964 elections enabled congressional Democrats to enact a flood of new social legislation, including national health care programs for the elderly and the poor, known as Medicare and Medicaid. Other legislation, such as the Higher Education Act of 1965 and the Elementary and Secondary Education Act of 1965, were aimed at expanding educational opportunities for the poor.[35]

At the same time that poverty and race were becoming inextricably linked in the public mind, the civil rights revolution was finally ending all legal vestiges of slavery in the South. Southern civil rights leaders believed that opposition to equality was not as intransigent in the North, and therefore they assumed that northern blacks would benefit indirectly from the southern struggle.[36] James Farmer, the former executive director of the Congress of Racial Equality, explained that "most of us as leaders didn't have a conceptualization of the race problem. We thought once we'd licked Jim Crow, we'd be over the hump."[37] When the extent of racial segregation and poverty in the North finally became apparent, black leaders called for an opening up of the housing market along with increased public investment in job creation, training, and education. The response from the Democrats in power was minimal. By 1967, shortly before his death, a discouraged Martin Luther King, Jr., lamented the lack of meaningful progress in the North:

> With Selma and the Voting Rights Act one phase of development in the civil rights revolution came to an end. A new phase opened, but few observers realized it or were prepared for its implications. For the vast majority of white Americans, the past decade—the first phase—had been a struggle to treat the Negro with a degree of decency, not of equality. White America was ready to demand that the Negro should be spared the lash of brutality and coarse degradation, but it had never been truly committed to helping him out of poverty, exploitation or all forms of discrimination.[38]

For the many whites, however, the passage of the two major civil rights bills concluded their commitment to racial justice. Further attempts to expand access to better housing, education, and employment were fiercely resisted in the North. The reaction was swift and forceful. By the fall of 1966, after two summers of urban rioting, more than half of the American public thought that racial change was occurring too fast. Among northern whites, the percentage of those who thought the federal government was pushing integration too fast nearly doubled between February 1964 and September 1966.[39] By 1966 a flurry of conservative candidates, including Ronald Reagan, won elective office. Reagan campaigned for governor of

California on a platform that blamed the riots on misguided black leaders, while arguing that government should do less, not more, and that strong civil rights enforcement threatened white liberty.[40] Just as black poverty was finally being recognized as a national problem, the actual commitment to address it was quickly withdrawn.

Throughout the 1970s public support steadily declined for social programs believed responsible for a downward redistribution of benefits to blacks and other minorities competing for increasingly limited government resources.[41] Polling data underscore "the strong connection . . . between racial animosities, on the one hand, and support for the tax revolt and Democratic Party defections on the other."[42] The decline in support was greatest among union households, middle-income Americans, and marginal Democrats. These so-called Reagan Democrats have voted for increasingly strident anti-government politicians committed to dismantling much of the federal structure of the American welfare state. Thomas Edsall and Mary Edsall capture the impact of this reaction when they write, "The intensity of white opposition to government programs associated with the poor and minorities, to rising tax burdens, and to a civil rights regulatory agenda imposing costs on whites had profound consequences for both elective politics and for public policy."[43] The degree to which race determined the boundary between acceptable and unacceptable social spending became quite evident in 1981 when newly elected President Reagan proposed making $32.5 billion in cuts on social spending. While he announced that his cuts would preserve a "safety net" of social programs, they overwhelmingly targeted programs benefiting the poor, thereby disproportionately hurting black women and children. Social Security, a heavily white and middle-class program, was left untouched.

In place of the Democrats' now discredited policies, the Republicans championed a variety of measures designed to punish rather than teach and train. This is a logical outgrowth of their conviction that poverty is caused by individual deviant behavior, not structural imbalances in the larger society. Most of the funding for Reagan's much publicized "War on Drugs" went to law enforcement and new jails; little went to drug prevention and treatment. New welfare reforms at the federal and state levels contained workfare provisions requiring women with children above the age of three to go to school or to work in order to continue receiving benefits. The program floundered because Congress failed to provide adequate funds and facilities for the volume of childcare needed if women on public aid were to go to work. State after state eliminated general assistance for single adults, driving the number of homeless men begging on streetcorners to new heights. With California in the lead, states are now moving to deny "illegal immigrants" access to all public benefits, thereby unleashing a witchhunt against Hispanics in general.

The conservatives' policies have been no more successful than the earlier anti-poverty efforts; if anything, they have contributed to an even greater sense of alienation among poor youth, who feel that they have very few options open to them while they are being blamed for much of what is wrong in our society. The era of punitive policies has seen the unleashing of a gruesome process of self-annihilation among black and Latino youth. The poor have been rendered ever more powerless and stigmatized with fewer resources available to help them move out of their predicament. The current direction of American social policy makes it clear that our goal is no longer to find solutions to urban poverty, but simply to isolate it at a minimal of public expenditure.

Powerful Constituencies Protect Their Turf

It is hard to conceive of a scenario whereby African-Americans, who were among the least powerful groups in American society in the 1960s, exerted such influence over the political agenda that legislation was enacted granting them advantages not possessed by much more powerful groups. Yet, this is what conservative policy analysts would have us believe. Within the political arena, power is manifested through the ability to control the policy agenda and set the parameters of the debate. The dominant political institutions control the scope of conflict by keeping certain issues out of the political arena while allowing others to come to the forefront. As Schattschneider notes, "All forms of political organization have a bias in favor of the exploitation of some kinds of conflict and the suppression of others because organization is the mobilization of bias."[44] The reverse of this is also true, namely, that those people or groups who are powerless lack control over the content of the political agenda.

Power is apparent not only in the character of the policies that are enacted, but also in the decisions that are *not* made. In their classic article "Two Faces of Power," Peter Bachrach and Morton Baratz argue that "to the extent that a person or group—consciously or unconsciously—creates or reinforces barriers to the public airing of policy conflicts, that person or group has power."[45] Power is frequently exercised through shaping the dominant values and political myths of a community, "which tend to favor the vested interests of one or more groups, relative to others."[46]

Poor people have little direct input into the policies that often dramatically affect their lives. The one government-supported effort to mobilize the poor contained in Johnson's War on Poverty legislation met with such vehement opposition from big city mayors that it almost killed congressional support for the whole anti-poverty effort. Although grassroots community organizing has survived, most of the efforts are small scale and piecemeal. Most organizations that work in poor communities are restricted by their not-for-profit status from engaging in lobbying activities. This leaves a handful of public interest groups to advocate before state and national bodies. As a result, the interests of the poor often come to be represented indirectly. For example, public service employee unions such as AFSCME and SEIU, concerned about their own members' jobs, lobby against cuts in state and federal social services. Big city mayors and black congresspeople lobby for more aid to cities, which indirectly provides benefits to the poor concentrated there. The American Hospital Association is one of the leading supporters of Medicaid because those dollars are crucial for many of its member institutions. Even the Children's Defense Fund, one of the strongest anti-poverty lobbying organizations in the country, has for political reasons chosen to focus on kids, thereby helping their poor parents indirectly.

Given that southern blacks only achieved the right to vote in 1965 and had virtually no direct political representation at the time the various anti-poverty measures were enacted, it is much more likely that this legislation was moderated so as to not alienate other, more powerful groups. Thus, a more honest examination of our nation's efforts to address urban poverty requires using the lens suggested by Schattschneider to search out the "biases" contained within those policies designed to grant equality and economic opportunity to the least powerful in modern American society.

Reestablishing structures of opportunity in poor minority communities would necessitate a significant redistribution of resources away from both of the major political parties' favored constituencies. Political leaders whose primary interest is reelection to office are most attuned to those constituencies that contribute to that goal either through financial or organizational support. In a capitalist economy where money is the basic medium of wealth and power, those with little income lack the basic resources needed to control their own destinies, let alone the priorities of the larger society. Lack of money, information, and social contacts leaves the poor disconnected and alienated from a political process in which they find it difficult to function as purposeful, self-directed actors.[47] With voter turnout and interest group membership heavily skewed toward the middle- and upper-income brackets, few politicians are likely to place the interests of the poor uppermost on their legislative agendas.

Despite all the current rhetoric about the evils of welfare, it has been the favored policy choice of Democrats and Republicans alike. Although long-term dependency on public aid is clearly detrimental to its recipients, from a political standpoint providing a minimal income to the poor is more palatable than the alternatives of creating new jobs and functional educational systems. By simply removing a large segment of poor adults from the labor force, policymakers avoid having to tackle such thorny issues as shrinking central city job markets and poor-quality public schools. Between 1961 and 1976, the share of the federal budget devoted to education, training, or other services designed to enhance the earning capacities of the poor directly never amounted to "more than 1 percent of full-employment GNP or 5 percent of the budget."[48] The largest increases in cash benefits took place in Social Security and unemployment compensation, neither of which is aimed at the poor. Shortly after the November 1994 Republican congressional victories, the *New York Times* reported that direct government aid to the poor totaled about $140 billion a year, roughly the same amount spent on Medicare, noting that "payment to the poor adds up to less than the three largest tax breaks that benefit the middle class and wealthy."[49]

Policymakers have routinely sacrificed the interests of poor minorities in an effort to provide advantages to other more powerful groups in society. Throughout the years during which the Democrats held the federal policy initiative, every policy designed to promote economic mobility, whether it was a civil rights bill or a job-training program, was carefully crafted to protect the vested interests of organized labor. At the local level, big city politicians sought to insulate their labor allies from the effects of increased demands for municipal employment and minority access to the craft unions. The unions were the party's organizational backbone in the industrial centers of the North and therefore held considerable power in determining the success of big city Democrats. Labor's political muscle successfully prevented most structural solutions to poverty from entering the political agenda. Labor left its imprint on equal employment legislation, job training, full-employment legislation, and even minority business development policies. The powerful building trade unions have used their substantial organizational and political muscle to sabotage the implementation of affirmative action mandates in the industries over which they have control.

Only policies that worked within the northern racial status quo were considered politically feasible, leaving Democrats willing to implement only a limited number of policy options. As a result, many of the remedial education and job-training programs that lay at the heart of the Democrats' anti-poverty agenda were set up to work within the context of larger institutions or economic arrangements that were increasingly harmful to the well-being of poor urban minorities. For example, remedial education efforts were grafted onto segregated school systems that had never been designed to prepare students for college or skilled employment, while job-training programs were designed to serve a limited number of people in a labor market where the job growth was occurring in distant suburbs, unreachable on public transportation.

The result of this approach has been devastating, both for the urban poor and for the Democratic Party. To borrow from the famous leadership guru Stephen Covey, the Democrats created a lose-lose scenario. In hindsight, it is apparent that the Democrats were unsuccessful in holding onto their traditional constituencies. It is also clear that where they had control over events, Democrats sought to slow the pace of racial reform to accommodate whites who felt threatened by increased competition for jobs and education. It is not surprising that the most pro-active efforts to end employment discrimination emerged from the courts, which are much more insulated from the pressures of maintaining an electoral majority. Yet, by not investing in more comprehensive solutions, the Democrats' efforts did little to alter the structural conditions that were creating increasingly isolated poor urban communities. When the Republicans took control of the White House in 1968 they abandoned any semblance of an urban policy agenda and instead promoted programs to help minority businesspeople. Since that time, the federal government has consistently emphasized trickle-down policies, claiming that aid to minority businesses would uplift whole black communities. In reality, they have had little impact on urban poverty. Much of the money awarded in special loans and contracts has gone to minority firms located far outside of minority communities. Instead, such policies have contributed to the expansion of a black elite and to a growing social distance between middle-class and poor African-Americans. Michael Dawson has identified this as "a 'pulling away' of the African-American class structure at both ends as the top becomes a mainstream bourgeoisie and the bottom is condemned to 'ever-widening poverty.' "[50]

For the Republican Party, which reaped the benefits of the white backlash against civil rights, the great advantage of minority business development policies is that they seldom challenge the boundaries separating whites and blacks. In fact, the originator of black capitalism, Booker T. Washington, publicly discouraged his followers from early involvement in the struggle to overturn Jim Crow laws in the South. Those social programs that did challenge the racial status quo quickly became highly unpopular. Public housing construction for families came to a virtual halt after the 1968 Fair Housing Act mandated that any new construction support housing integration. Political opposition to the prospect of poor minorities moving into all-white neighborhoods was so intense that in 1981 Congress supported the almost complete elimination of funds for the construction of new family units.

Republicans, who have been ideologically committed to private-sector solutions, have never supported pro-active social mobility programs. Nonetheless, they discovered the political advantage that could be gained by criticizing even the mild efforts made by their opponents. With the election of Reagan in 1980, they launched their first broadside attack on the Democrats' anti-poverty measures. The 1981 federal budget called for the elimination of whole programs and deep cuts in others, including job training, subsidized housing, and Medicaid. The programs that managed to survive were those that had developed powerful constituencies with the resources to launch all-out lobbying campaigns on their behalf. For example, although Reagan proposed deep cuts in the federal share of Medicaid, doctors and hospitals whose revenues were closely tied to receipt of the federal dollars unleashed a vigorous effort to persuade Congress to reject the cuts. Other programs that did not have similar clout, such as new public housing construction and public service employment, vanished from the federal budget.

Black Leaders Focus on Middle-Class Issues

Martin Luther King, Jr., and the movement he led transformed American race relations by forcing people to recognize southern racism as a great moral failing. With the death of King and of Malcolm X, that kind of moral leadership has largely vanished. In their place, a new generation of leaders has emerged whose success is too often marked not by their ability to empower others, but through their personal advancement and enrichment. To quote Cornel West, "Most present day black leaders appear too hungry for status to be angry, too eager for acceptance to be bold, too self-interested in advancement to be deviant."[51] By functioning as their communities' arbiters and dealmakers, these leaders control a large portion of the legitimate resources that flow into those communities. Just as is often the case with international humanitarian aid, they also skim off a significant share of those resources for their own use.

Although class distinctions existed within black communities prior to the civil rights reforms, widespread racial exclusion created a commonality of interest regardless of income. As William Julius Wilson notes, as late as the 1960s, segregated housing patterns created "a vertical integration of different income groups as lower-, working-, and middle-class professional black families all resided more or less in the same ghetto neighborhoods."[52] The lowering of racial barriers gradually eroded those bonds, as better-educated blacks moved into professions from which they had once been excluded, leaving their old neighborhoods behind. Today, 30 percent of all African-Americans live in the suburbs. Improvements in the living standards of middle-class African-Americans have widened their distance from those still locked in poverty, diminishing support for anti-poverty measures among black leaders.

Beginning with the Republican ascendancy in the 1968 elections, the emphasis of national urban policy shifted toward assisting those who required the least help, while neglecting those in greatest need. New government policies incorporated much of the civil rights agenda of an expanding black middle class by opening up avenues of advancement for those minorities who possessed the skills and education needed to propel them into the mainstream once the artificial barriers of segregation had been lifted. For the first time, government intervention empowered the black middle class. The institutionalization of the civil rights movement and the rapid expansion in the number of black elected officials created a generation of leaders committed to further expanding benefits to blacks. Yet, more than ever, these leaders focused on meeting the demands of middle class, not those of the very poor. Even those minority politicians who directly represent predominantly low-income communities often display little enthusiasm for addressing the needs of their poor constituents. This shift was in part a reaction to the racial backlash that occurred among whites and the institutions that represented them. As progress slowed and white supporters withdrew, black leaders turned inward. Increasingly, they solicited financial support from black businesspeople and professionals, who in turn exerted greater influence on the choice of issues. Under these conditions, black leaders found it in their interest to support the creation of black wealth, knowing that some of those dollars would in turn be used to support them.

The high concentration of African-Americans (and, to a lesser extent, Latinos) in contiguous urban neighborhoods, coupled with the requirements for political representation contained in the Voting Rights Act, has greatly expanded the number of minority elected officials at the local level. Many of these politicians mobilize their constituents on the basis of familiar calls for racial solidarity, making vague promises of community improvements but frequently delivering little once in office. In a racially homogeneous political district, this is an easy formula for electoral success. Once elected, these leaders function as their community's representatives to the larger society, with little accountability toward the majority of their own constituents. Increasingly, their constituents, seeing through the empty promises, are choosing not to vote at all.

Although a number of black congresspeople do actively represent their low-income constituents in national policy debates, many black leaders at the local level focus on securing contracts, either for their personal gain or for that of an organization they represent. They have sought to tag minority set-asides onto all sorts of projects, even though there often are not enough legitimate minority businesses to do all the work. Set-asides were initially a response to long-standing discriminatory practices in the awarding of public contracts that excluded all but a few politically connected firms; however, they have resulted in the creation of a new group of insider firms, many of whom are brokering contracts rather than actually doing the work. The set-asides are rarely tied to any requirements that minority firms receiving the benefits either hire from or invest in poor communities. That is left entirely to the conscience of the individual entrepreneur. Furthermore, since much of the work is either in construction or professional services, very few of these firms create low-skill jobs that could reasonably be done by community residents.

In poor communities, social services are big business, filling the void created by the departure of private-sector jobs. Many poor people's whole lives revolve around their interactions with a vast network of agencies. These agencies have become a major source of income, not only for the recipients, but also for the staff and managers. In response to earlier demands for community control, most of the public and not-for-profit institutions that service exclusively minority clients now have predominantly minority managers and staff. Although many very dedicated staff members work within them, these institutions are often deeply flawed, with little commitment to providing the best possible services to their clients, whether they are school children, public housing residents, or substance abusers. Instead, they have become a source of wealth creation for a handful of top managers and outside contractors. It is not unusual to find the CEOs of larger social service agencies commanding six-figure salaries along with other perks generally associated with corporate America, while their line staffs receive such meager salaries that only the most committed remain in the job for very long.

Many social service providers have monopoly control over their clients, who are restricted from obtaining services on the private market either because of a lack of income or because they are on public aid. Since these clients cannot choose to go elsewhere, there is little incentive to provide quality services or to innovate. The agency's funding is almost always guaranteed, unless an audit reveals flagrant misuse of funds. Grant amounts are generally determined by the number of clients served, not whether those services were actually effective. Inevitably, the top managers come to develop an aversion to any change that threatens to disrupt their status quo. Trying to protect their monopoly positions, they fear the possibility of increased competition. They also have little incentive to support systemic solutions to poverty, because their own livelihood rests on its continued existence.

There is a virtual conspiracy of silence among minority leaders when confronted with these kinds of abuses of authority and mismanagement. Minority leadership circles are relatively small, and people are likely to have long associations with each other that makes them reluctant to speak out. State and federal departments that supervise most urban social service providers view funding in political terms, in which a certain amount of money is distributed to black agencies, a certain amount to Hispanics, and some to Asians. They have little incentive to disrupt that political balance by raising questions about effectiveness.

Jobs Disappear from the Political Agenda

One of the most remarkable aspects of the 1995–96 debate over welfare reform has been the absence of any serious discussion on the need to expand the pool of livable wage jobs even as states are being required to place 50 percent of their welfare populations into jobs by the year 2002. Policymakers appear to be so thoroughly convinced that welfare recipients could work if they wished to that they minimize that absence of employment opportunities in urban communities. Government-supported job creation has always been controversial in the United States. The federal government's last involvement in directly funding the creation of jobs ended with the 1981 elimination of the Public Service Employment (PSE) component of the Comprehensive Employment and Training Act (CETA). Since that time, government-sponsored job creation has all but vanished from the national political agenda. Recently, even the value of job training for the poor has been called into question, as state level welfare reforms emphasize "work first" for welfare recipients.

Although Republicans historically have been reluctant to support direct government funding for job creation, they have long championed a variety of pro-business economic policies that supposedly would be more effective job generators. Ranging from cuts in the capital gains tax to support for minority businesses, these programs represent costs to the government even though they often do not involve direct outlay of funds, as was the case with programs such as PSE. Yet, despite the claims of conservative policymakers, these policies seldom contain explicit mechanisms for creating new jobs, let alone jobs accessible to the urban poor. Furthermore, since the Nixon administration, policies passed off as federal urban initiatives have not contained any specific job-generation mechanisms targeting the poor and long-term unemployed. At its height, PSE primarily functioned as a subsidy to local governments, who used the funds to shift their public employees onto the federal payroll. Minority business set-asides, which are frequently justified as a means of creating more jobs accessible to minority workers, seldom contain any explicit requirements that the businesses locate in areas of high unemployment or that they hire from poor communities.

In the meantime, state and local governments have made use of a wide variety of business incentives, many in the form of tax subsidies for businesses locating in their jurisdictions. Again, these are generally tied to vague promises on the part of the businesses that they will create new jobs, but there are no sanctions against companies who fail to make good on these pledges. Community-based economic development efforts, which in many cases are the principal generators of new investment in poor urban communities, have up until very recently focused almost entirely on constructing and rehabbing housing, which is not a significant source of new employment for community residents. Despite the glaring need for jobs to buttress any efforts to revitalize the housing stock of these communities, publicly supported financing mechanisms have been geared toward housing, not jobs.

The Book's Strategy

This book focuses on economic mobility policies as one large component of what is needed to create structures of economic opportunity. Recognizing that for minorities mobility is determined by a combination of achieving racial equality and gaining the necessary education, skills, and capital, the book traces policies aimed at both. Certainly there are numerous other policies influencing urban poverty, such as segregated housing patterns and poor quality schools, that are not treated in this book. I have chosen to take a historical approach, examining the flawed nature of federal anti-poverty and civil rights policies at their origins in the 1960s. These are the foundation upon which all subsequent policies have been built, and they continue to be the symbol of government excess for Republicans who wish to dismantle existing economic mobility policies.

Subsequent chapters examine the biases incorporated into three distinct categories of economic mobility policy—equal access to employment opportunities, job creation and training, and small and minority business development—that have prevented them from more effectively serving those most in need. Although this book primarily addresses national policy choices, it is also about local implementation. Because much of what goes on in national politics is rhetoric and public posturing, various actors' true commitments are often revealed more fully in their actions at the local level. For that reason, several of the later chapters examine the dynamics of civil rights enforcement, minority business programs, and community economic development in Chicago.

Chicago is a city of stark contrasts. Its wealth and resources are spread very unevenly, with some communities doing extremely well while others are descending into abject poverty. The Northside community of Lincoln Park has an average family income of $114,000, while in Oakland on the Southside the average family income is only $11,500. Today, more than one-third of all children in Chicago are growing up in poor families. The city's legacy of segregation has created whole communities made up almost entirely of poor people, without hope, without jobs, with collapsing infrastructures, and schools that cannot cope. Much of the nation's understanding of urban poverty has been defined by several books written about Chicago, including William Julius Wilson's *The Truly Disadvantaged,* Nicholas Lemann's *The Promised Land,* and Alex Kotlowitz's *There Are No Children Here.* As the third largest city in the country, it has one of the highest concentrations of poor people.

Although not as commonly known, it also has one of the largest black middle classes in the country and is a leading center of black business. Several nationally prominent black businesses are headquartered in the city, including Soft Sheen, Johnson Publications, and Johnson Products. Black political activism has a long and colorful history, dating back to 1928, when Oscar DePriest was elected as the first black congressman since the end of Reconstruction, and culminating in the election of Harold Washington as the city's first black mayor.

Chicago also holds the distinction of being one of the most segregated cities in America. King chose the city as the site of his first and only attempt to organize blacks against the northern manifestations of racial oppression. His efforts were largely frustrated by Mayor Richard J. Daley, who accommodated the minister long enough to get him out of town, but did nothing to remedy the gross inequities in public jobs, services, and schools. The city has been the scene of some of the most violent confrontations between black workers and the building trades unions over access to construction jobs. Years of agitation have resulted in minimal accommodation in a sector of the local economy rich in well-paying jobs.

Chicago is an extremely political town, where the long reign of machine politics has made local government primarily a provider of jobs, services, and contracts, not a policy innovator. Although no longer the monolith it was under Richard J. Daley, the Democratic Party still controls the flow of public dollars that come into the city. Chicago is also characterized by a long history of grassroots political mobilization that has served as a counterbalance to the machine's stranglehold on local government. Saul Alinsky, the father of modern community organizing, built two of his most successful community organizations in the city, setting a precedent for a rich tradition of confrontation between City Hall and neighborhood representatives. Residents' strong identification with the specific neighborhoods in which they live has also made it fertile ground for community-based economic development efforts. Given that Chicago is not a typical city, it cannot be assumed that local policy implementation would occur the same way elsewhere; however, some similarities are bound to exist.

Chapter 2 examines the limitations that were built into the federal anti-poverty and equal employment policies at the time of their inception. Chapter 3 focuses on the resistance to implementing an active labor market strategy that would include extensive job training for the long-term unemployed and direct government job creation. Chapter 4 looks at organized labor's repeated efforts to narrow the impact of the equal employment provisions of the 1964 Civil Rights Act. In Chapter 5 the books shifts to Chicago to examine the long-standing conflict over access to skilled trades jobs that has limited opportunities for minority males in an important sector of the urban economy.

Chapter 6 traces the Republicans' embrace of minority business programs as their version of an urban economic strategy and the subsequent expansion of minority set-aside programs. Chapter 7 looks at how civil rights and black political leaders in Chicago have benefited directly from the expansion of minority set-asides and other minority business policies. Chapter 8 is a look at the proliferation of business tax subsidies at the local level and the constraints faced by economic development efforts in poor urban communities.

2 | CONCESSIONS FROM THE START

Although they were heralded as major new initiatives that would end slums and racism, neither the anti-poverty nor the civil rights legislation enacted in 1964 were comprehensive solutions to black poverty, disenfranchisement, and discrimination. Rather, they were tentative first steps. These two pieces of legislation, passed within a month of each other, established the now inextricable link between poverty and race. Their content was shaped by a variety of Washington insiders—lobbyists, members of Congress, and bureaucrats in the Kennedy and Johnson administrations—with little direct input from the people whose lives they were going to affect. The majority of African-Americans had no political representation in Washington at the time. The array of public interest advocacy and lobbying organizations that now work on behalf of poor people did not yet exist. The scope of both pieces of legislation was circumscribed by the political alignments of the time, a limited understanding of the pervasive nature of northern racism, and an unwillingness to commit to significant new expenditures. Their limited nature assured that neither initiative would have a significant impact on opening up opportunities for the urban poor, whose lack of skills and geographic isolation made them marginal in a labor market that was being rapidly transformed by the advent of new technologies and the move to suburbia.

Kennedy: The Reluctant Reformer

President John F. Kennedy, the originator of both pieces of legislation, began his brief tenure in office as a policy conservative. His initial response to postwar record levels of unemployment was to go further than most Republicans in his overtures to business.[1] His administration's principal employment strategy was to rely on aggregate demand measures such as tax cuts and increased government spending to help stimulate the overall economy. This was supplemented by a variety of aid programs for education and training, all under local control.[2] Kennedy refused to consider any direct job-creation programs. When the economic recovery of 1961–63 added $28 billion to the economy, yet unemployment dropped by only 1 percent, Kennedy's Council of Economic Advisors recommended increasing the funding for job retraining, relocation, and basic education programs, but the proposed budget exceeded what Kennedy was prepared to spend.[3]

Kennedy's stance toward civil rights was equally cautious, even though African-Americans had supplied him with a critical margin of support in his narrow victory over Richard Nixon. At the time of his election the country was in the midst of unprecedented racial change. A peaceful movement for black civil rights was sweeping across the South, aimed at ending the last legal and social vestiges of the old slave system. The massive migration of blacks to the North, where they had the right to vote, had established them as a large enough voting block for politicians from both parties to make new efforts to gain their support. Northern Democrats began courting the black vote by promising civil rights reforms in the South.[4] In 1960 the Democrats included a strong civil rights plank in their platform, promising to force congressional passage of a civil rights package that was defeated several times during the Eisenhower years.

Nonetheless, Kennedy chose to move slowly, fearing that any significant change in the racial status quo would antagonize the southern wing of his own party, which still represented a very powerful voting block in Congress. Southern Democrats occupied more than half of all committee chairmanships in both the House and the Senate. In the House, the Rules Committee, under the leadership of Congressman Judge Howard Smith (D-VA), had long been the burial ground of a great deal of progressive civil rights and social legislation. If antagonized, the southern delegation had the power to block the president's tax reform and foreign trade bills, which were more central to his legislative agenda.[5]

Southern congressional strength rested on the virtual disenfranchisement of the region's black population, who as a result were woefully underrepresented in the nation's leading legislative body. In 1964 there were only six black congressmen in the House of Representatives, all of whom represented northern districts.[6] The senior black congressmen were Adam Clayton Powell (D-NY) and William Dawson (D-IL). Although Powell was outspoken on race issues, Dawson remained a loyal member of the Chicago political machine. The small number of black congressmen meant that there were few representatives likely to regard issues of importance to blacks as one of their top legislative priorities.

Under the circumstances, Kennedy was unwilling to introduce any new civil rights legislation, even though he had promised to do so during his campaign. According to Roy Wilkins, "Within ten days of his election, came word that he was positively not going to advocate any new civil rights legislation in the new Congress . . . because he did not want to split the party."[7] When Congressman Emmanuel Celler (D-NY) and Senator Philip Clark introduced legislation in 1961 that Kennedy had endorsed as a candidate, the president disavowed it. When the Civil Rights Commission in a series of five reports made more than a score of legislative recommendations, Kennedy ignored most of them. Nor did he support efforts by the Senate's civil rights block to reduce the majority needed for cloture (the decision to end extended debate in the Senate) from two-thirds to three-fifths, and that measure was defeated as well.[8]

Kennedy did use his executive powers to appoint more blacks to federal judgeships and executive positions within the federal government than any previous president. He also provided rhetorical support for black equal rights and consciously set about liberalizing the Civil Rights Commission. Early in his tenure he signed an executive order requiring federal contract compliance with nondiscrimination policies, which for the first time mandated that employers implement affirmative action efforts in hiring minorities.[9] The President's Committee on Equal Employment Opportunity, charged with enforcing the executive order, was given the authority to terminate any government contract or refrain from entering into one with any employer who had a record of discrimination. However, little use was made of these enforcement powers.

Kennedy's initial job-training legislation was the completion of the Democrats' unfinished employment policy agenda from the previous decade, not a bold new initiative aimed at urban unemployment. It had already become apparent during the mid-1950s that the ongoing restructuring of the American economy was creating pockets of poverty amid the nation's growing wealth. Policymakers initially focused their attention on poor rural areas, proposing a variety of incentives aimed at reinvigorating local economies, such as public works spending, long-term credit for new industry or businesses, technical assistance, retraining of workers, and allowances equivalent to unemployment benefits for workers undergoing retraining. The Depressed Areas legislation, introduced in 1955, had wound its way through six years of hearings and debate. President Dwight D. Eisenhower vetoed it twice.[10] Kennedy finally passed the bill, along with legislation aimed at combating the rise of juvenile delinquency, which some policymakers had come to recognize not just as an individual pathology but as the result of growing youth unemployment.[11]

Kennedy's Manpower Development and Training Act (MDTA) focused on retraining workers displaced by automation, not on urban unemployment. Barely a year after MDTA was passed, even its supporters had to acknowledge that the program was not reaching the chronically unemployed. Twenty percent of the country's unemployed had less than an eighth-grade education, but only 3 percent of MDTA trainees came from this group. Among unemployed blacks, 44 percent had never finished eighth grade, yet only 5 percent of the black participants came from this group. In response to these shortcomings, Kennedy proposed that MDTA be expanded to allow for literacy and basic skills training in addition to the occupational training already taking place. The maximum period for training allowances was extended from fifty-two to seventy-two weeks. Signaling a shift in his vision of the intended beneficiaries of job training, Kennedy announced these proposals in a message on civil rights and job opportunities for blacks sent to Congress in June 1963. Kennedy also expanded the earlier programs aimed at reducing juvenile delinquency by awarding $30 million worth of grants to organizations working with youths in dozens of cities.[12]

The Southern Movement Forces National Action

By 1963 the southern civil rights marches forced Kennedy into action on both civil rights and urban poverty. Demonstrations were rocking the South. As long as Kennedy refused to seek a federal solution, protesters could only achieve change locality by locality. Nonviolent mass action increasingly threatened to erupt into open racial warfare as frustrations over repeated defeats mounted. In the week of May 25, 1963, alone, there were civil rights demonstrations in thirty-three southern cities, not all of which remained peaceful.[13] The demonstrations were drawing ever larger numbers of southern blacks. A *Newsweek* poll in July 1963 revealed that 40 percent of all blacks had taken part in a sit-in, march, or picket.[14] The northern press had begun to raise a cry for new civil rights legislation. In six of eleven national opinion polls done between 1961 and 1965, civil rights was identified as the country's number one problem by the majority of respondents.[15] Increased support among northern whites for racial change in the South gave northern Democrats more maneuverability in Congress. It also increased the political pressure on the national Democratic leadership to initiate serious civil rights reforms. In little more than a month, beginning in mid-May 1963, more than 127 civil rights bills were introduced in the U.S. House of Representatives.[16]

While publicly silent, the nation's civil rights advocates continued to press Kennedy behind the scenes. In April 1963, just two months before Kennedy finally introduced his civil rights bill, the Leadership Conference on Civil Rights, the movement's lobbying organization, criticized the president in an internal memo for his message to Congress on civil rights, which they believed fell "woefully short of meeting the needs that exist." Concerning the lack of any legislative proposals for fair employment, the conference wrote that "it was surely to be expected that the President would have proposed 'federal legislation establishing a Fair Employment Practices Commission . . . ' as pledged in the 1960 Democratic Party platform."[17]

The Leadership Conference on Civil Rights was a coalition of seventy-four organizations with strong ties to the Democratic Party's northern wing. Their commitment to civil rights stretched back to the 1946 fight for a permanent Fair Employment Practices Commission (FEPC). Among its prominent members were the National Association for the Advancement of Colored People (NAACP), the mainline Protestant denominations, the Catholic Interracial Council, the National Council of Churches, the American Jewish Committee, the American Jewish Congress, and the

Jewish Labor Committee. The newer civil rights organizations, such as King's Southern Christian Leadership Conference (SCLC) and the Student Nonviolent Coordinating Committee (SNCC), born in the struggle for equality in the South, were not as involved in the conference. In contrast to the older organizations such as the NAACP and the National Urban League (NUL), these organizations were grassroots activist in their orientation, having little involvement in national politics prior to the 1960s. Both the SCLC and SNCC were rooted in the South, coming North mainly to do fundraising and recruit volunteers. The NAACP and the NUL were both based in New York City and had a mostly middle-class constituency in the North. They focused on influencing the nation's elite by lobbying corporate executives to open up new jobs to blacks, serving as presidential advisors on racial matters, and pursuing carefully crafted legal strategies to challenge segregation. During the 1930s, the NAACP had come under considerable internal pressure from a group of young militants who wanted the organization to reorient itself more toward the economic issues facing the black working class. These militants believed that "the colored masses were more plagued by economic problems than were the Negro business-professional classes, who wanted the NAACP to retain its traditional emphasis on political-civil equality, because racial discrimination in these areas especially affected them."[18]

It was only after the outbreak of serious violence against civil rights marchers in Birmingham, Alabama, that President Kennedy finally called for the enactment of national civil rights legislation that with one sweep could establish a new order in the changing South. His first draft of what would later become the Civil Rights Act of 1964 only addressed the desegregation of public facilities, authorized the federal government to participate more fully in lawsuits against school segregation, and gave the federal government a greater role in protecting voting rights. However, the proposed bill did not even cover all public facilities.[19] For example, it exempted public swimming pools and bowling alleys that did not serve food.[20] The initial bill did not include a section banning employment discrimination because Kennedy felt it was too controversial and that southern opposition to it could endanger the success of the entire bill.[21]

Although the Democratic Party had included fair employment in its party platform since 1948, civil rights supporters in Congress had seen more than two hundred fair employment measures defeated between 1946 and 1963. While the issue lay dormant in Congress, thirty-four states in the North and West had enacted their own versions of a fair employment law. By 1960, Illinois was the only major industrial state without one—the rest were all southern states. However, these state laws were all weakly enforced. In a number of states FEPCs could issue cease-and-desist orders forcing an immediate end to discriminatory practices, but they had to go to court to have them implemented. Not surprisingly, state commissions rarely used these powers. A 1961 Senate study found that in twelve states somewhat more than nineteen thousand cases had been opened since the date that state's law had been enacted, and out of these only twenty-six cease-and-desist orders had been issued.[22]

Most of these state laws had little impact on workplace discrimination. The commissions' work was mostly educational. Conciliation was their primary means of resolving cases of employment discrimination, most of which never received a formal hearing. State commissioners' reluctance to make full use of their powers led them "to settle many cases on extremely poor terms."[23] In New York State, 99 percent of the cases were settled with the discriminators promising to mend their ways. Back-pay awards or even requirements to hire the victim of discrimination were rare, so that discriminators had little incentive to change their employment practices.[24] According to Herbert Hill, who for thirty years served as the NAACP's labor director, the state fair employment practice laws viewed "racial discrimination in employment as a consequence of individual acts of bigotry, with the result that only extremely limited relief was provided for the victims."[25] Their poor record notwithstanding, these state laws became the model for the national legislation.

Washington Insiders Design the Legislation

Just as it had moved civil rights to the forefront of the national agenda, the southern movement brought black urban poverty into the national consciousness. In 1963 the administration's scattered efforts at retraining and youth skills development were merged into a unified focus on the nation's black ghettos. Policymakers who had thus far attacked the problem piecemeal came to recognize the need for a broader assault on poverty and unemployment. In the employment arena, this shift occurred after the more experienced unionized workers who had been the targets of the first manpower programs were peeled away by economic recovery so that "the concentration of unemployment and poverty, . . . became more apparent. While unemployment had long been a constant feature of ghetto life, by the 1960's the problem had become much more pronounced. At the same time, rising Negro militancy that began with a quest for equal access to public facilities was swinging to demands for equal economic opportunities and results."[26]

Although the architects of the War on Poverty were working against the general backdrop of heightened civil rights consciousness, the programs were conceived and implemented with no real input from civil rights leaders, who were still focused on attaining basic democratic rights in the South. The federal manpower experts in the Department of Labor and the economists at the Council of Economic Advisors who designed the antipoverty programs regarded the causes of black poverty and unemployment as essentially the same as those found among whites. They did not comprehend the degree to which black poverty was the result of racial inequalities in education, employment, and the housing market rather than simply a lack of education and skills. Their new programs were based on the theory of human capital development, which held that differences in employment earnings were directly related to differences in length of education. Increased education was seen as an investment that would pay off with higher earnings over the lifetime of the individual. Following this logic, the key to improving blacks' economic condition lay in improving their education and job skills.[27] There was no understanding of the degree to which racial barriers prevented even well-educated blacks from moving into professional jobs that were open to whites with the same level of education. Since segregation restricted the range of professional and technical jobs open to better-educated minorities, their income actually tended to decline as a percentage of white income.[28]

The final version of the Civil Rights Act was also largely shaped by politicians and lobbyists who were not directly involved in the civil rights struggle. Although the Congress of Industrial Organizations (CIO) had been a long-time supporter of fair employment legislation, the American Federation of Labor (AFL) had previously been opposed. Now for the first time, the merged labor federation declared its willingness to support a comprehensive bill that would cover unions as well as employers. The AFL-CIO finally consented because "they had just been so beaten for their racism they wanted a bill, and then they could blame it all on the bill if it wasn't enforced."[29] In his testimony before the House Committee on the Judiciary, George Meany, president of the AFL-CIO, admitted that the federation had been unable to break down discriminatory employment barriers within its own member unions.[30] Organized labor's track record in eliminating racial exclusion within its ranks was dubious at best. There were only two blacks among the twenty-seven vice presidents on the federation's executive council. The national organization had refused to sanction unions that permitted segregated locals, and consequently such practices continued. In the early 1960s it had shied away from any major campaigns to unionize the South because they would have required involving blacks on an integrated basis, thereby inevitably alienating southern white trade unionists.[31] Meany's testimony and his verbal commitments to support the fair employment legislation were crucial in convincing the administration that Title VII (the fair employment section of the Civil Rights Act) had enough support to overcome southern opposition. "It was through the help and support of the trade unions that Title VII became part of the bill."[32]

Labor played a central role in securing passage of the bill. Two weeks after Kennedy announced his civil rights proposals, the United Auto Workers (UAW) donated $5,000 to the Leadership Conference to cover the start-up costs of the campaign. Walter Reuther, president of the UAW and head of the AFL-CIO's Industrial Union Department, lent office space owned by the department to the Conference lobbyists.[33] Three out of five of the chief lobbyists for the Conference had strong labor connections: Joseph Rauh, who served as the UAW's general counsel and was also the vice president of Americans for Democracy; Andrew Biemiller, a former Wisconsin congressman who now worked as the legislative director for the AFL-CIO; and Jack Conway, a staff member of the AFL-CIO's Industrial Union Department. Much of the office staff was also on loan from Reuther's Industrial Union Department.[34]

Kennedy finally acquiesced to demands that he support a comprehensive bill following the bombing of a black church in Birmingham in which four little girls were killed. Title VII was added to the bill, creating an Equal Employment Opportunities Commission (EEOC) with full cease-and-desist powers. He also extended coverage of his desegregation title to all public facilities, forbade federal aid to any activities practicing discrimination, and established federal administrative procedures for voter registration.[35]

By the fall of 1963 there were two versions of the civil rights bill, one written by a subcommittee of the House Judiciary Committee that civil rights leaders considered their "dream bill," the other written by the White House. In order to get their bill reported out of the full House Judiciary Committee, civil rights advocates were forced to accept a crucial compromise—removing the Commission's cease-and-desist powers, thereby stripping it of a powerful enforcement tool. Arnold Aronson of the Leadership Conference reported that the final House bill was "a compromise hammered out by the Administration and House Republicans and fairly forced upon Democratic and Republican liberals. . . . Although the subcommittee bill was attacked as 'extreme' and its supporters as 'extremists' there was nothing in it that went beyond the Democratic platform of 1960."[36]

War on Poverty Provides the Poor Training without Jobs

The final version of what became the Economic Opportunity Act welded together two very different solutions to urban poverty—the concept of community action and a variety of education and manpower training programs.[37] The community action component rested on the recognition that poverty and powerlessness were tightly interwoven. Therefore, the legislation sought to use federal resources to empower poor people to take greater control over their lives and their communities. This was the first time that a piece of federal legislation had ever sought directly to empower poor people and earmarked funding specifically for that purpose. It marked a major departure from the traditional social service approach in which the poor are the passive recipients of an array of services deemed necessary by a set of "experts" from outside of the community. Too often, those experts have preconceived notions about what poor people supposedly need to stabilize their lives.

Funding for the community action programs went directly from the federal government to local community organizations in poor neighborhoods. It completely bypassed the local political establishment, who soon found themselves the target of grassroots protest movements. Federal funds were used to hire community organizers, who mobilized poor residents to protest the lack of city services in their neighborhoods, the existence of widespread building code violations, inadequate recreational opportunities, and poor schools, all of which local government was responsible for providing. Even though program officials in Washington sought to strike a balance between contending local interest groups— public officials, the private sector, and representatives of the poor—the grassroots community action agencies were quickly engaged in serious confrontations with the local power structure. Not surprisingly, community action became highly controversial.[38] Under fire from a constituency that they had long been able to ignore, local politicians reacted swiftly. As early as the spring of 1965 a group of mayors, led by Chicago's Richard J. Daley, a major powerbroker within the Democratic Party, met with Vice President Hubert Humphrey to protest what they saw as federal funding of local opposition groups. When forced to choose, both Humphrey and Johnson sided with the powerful local party chieftains and instructed the Office of Economic Opportunity to reduce the role of the poor in policy planning.[39] The curtailment of the community action component returned control to the local political elite, guaranteeing that solutions to urban poverty would conform to a social work model focusing on individual pathologies. An assault on the local economic and social institutions that perpetuated poverty had been ruled as out of order.

Aside from the community action component, most of the War on Poverty programs targeted youth education and training, showing their programmatic origins in the earlier efforts to prevent juvenile delinquency. The Job Corps, modeled on the New Deal's Youth Conservation Corps, established large urban training and remedial education residential centers rather than rural camps. By removing youth from detrimental home situations, and by offering needed education and work experience, the Job Corps hoped to become a major force in breaking the link between poverty and idleness.[40] The Neighborhood Youth Corps (NYC) was to be a prevocational training program for both in-school and out-of-school youth. The NYC was not intended to provide training for specific occupations; rather, its goal was to give low-income youth the support they needed to finish high school, along with the motivation, basic work habits, and understanding of the world of work necessary to participate in more advanced skills training.[41] The bill also set up what would become known as college work-study to assist college students in earning their way through school.

In sum, the War on Poverty was essentially a youth preemployment training program designed more to promote positive attitudes toward work than to provide specific job skills. During the early planning process for the bill, Secretary of Labor Willard Wirtz, had submitted a proposal calling for a job-creation component with a focus not on youth but on adults. Wirtz's proposal had a $3.5 billion price tag, far more than President Johnson was prepared to spend. Furthermore, organized labor, whose support was crucial to the passage of any social program sponsored by the Democrats, disliked the idea of government-created jobs that might compete against union labor. Thus, the idea was rejected, only to resurface during congressional hearings.[42] A job-creation component was also contained in the recommendations made by the Senate Subcommittee on Employment and Manpower chaired by Senator Joseph Clark (D-PA).[43]

The final version of the bill left the task of job creation completely in the hands of private industry. According to Garth Mangum, this omission was due to the prevailing image of government-sponsored employment as "leaf-raking," a stigma that had been attached to many of the earlier New Deal employment programs.[44] The administration assumed that its impending tax cut would encourage private investors to create the needed jobs. The poverty programs were designed to prepare the poor to take those jobs.[45] Little thought was given to the impact that capital flight would have on poor inner-city residents who were becoming geographically isolated from the suburban areas of job growth. Without some form of intervention or special incentives, the process of disinvestment is nearly impossible to reverse. By tying the success of the new job training programs to the willingness and ability of private employers to create the necessary jobs, federal policymakers almost guaranteed that they would have only a limited impact in alleviating concentrated unemployment.

President Johnson had given the drafters of the anti-poverty legislation two very specific guidelines: (1) the program was to provide rehabilitation, not income, and (2) it must not cost much money.[46] The final price tag was set at $962.5 million, of which $500 million was diverted from Defense Department economies and the rest was taken from existing poverty programs.[47] The same Clark committee that had called for a job-creation component recommended $5 billion in annual expenditures for the program. Yet, Johnson viewed any large new expenditures for social programs as incompatible with the goals of his intended tax cut. The program's meager funding meant that it was never able to serve more than a small proportion of those eligible. Writing in response to the NAACP's criticisms of the NYC, its administrator explained that there were 1.8 million youth whose incomes made them eligible to participate, but funds were available to train only 20 percent of them. He added, "We have yet to run out of eligible applicants for the program." [48] Many poor youth and adults went untouched by the War on Poverty.

The negative consequences of the limited funds was further compounded by a distribution formula that dispersed the precious dollars rather than targeting them on those cities with the highest concentrations of poverty. Within a year after its enactment, War on Poverty money was funding five hundred agencies across the country. A new community action agency had been located in almost every congressional district, while new Job Corps programs were also spread across the country, even in places far removed from urban youth.[49]

Despite all the rhetoric about community action, the majority of War on Poverty programs provided traditional social and educational services.[50] Contrary to their overwhelmingly negative image, according to evaluation studies these early efforts to train poor inner city youth showed mixed results. Those participants who remained in the residential Job Corps program for more than six months showed clear improvements in school attendance, high school completion, employment rates, and wages. The strong positive improvements made by Job Corps participants demonstrated the value of long-term intensive training for educationally disadvantaged youth. The downside of Job Corps was its high cost, which has always limited its political support. In contrast, the work experience programs funded through the NYC were found to often have a negative effect on school enrollment and graduation. Part-time work disrupted the academic performance of some less able youth, with the result that NYC participants were actually less likely to graduate than youth who did not participate. In the mid-1960s, it was already evident that the complexities of the high school dropout problem could not be solved by short-term quick-fix programs.[51] A turnaround in the life chances of troubled youth would require a serious commitment of resources. Certain Office of Equal Opportunity programs, especially the community action projects, Legal Services, and Job Corps, came under almost constant political attack from conservative members of Congress. Yet, most survived, even after the Office of Equal Opportunity was abolished under the Nixon administration and the individual programs were integrated into the various departments.

The enactment of the anti-poverty measures coincided with massive urban renewal projects that in many cases destroyed existing communities and created artificial new ones with little economic infrastructure. As unemployment climbed, more people turned to public aid as a source of temporary income. The limited dollars set aside for education and retraining restricted access to these crucial social mobility programs, condemning many people to a state of permanent subsistence income. These small-scale programs were expected to bear fruit without ever challenging the large segregated institutions that perpetuated black poverty. Since private employers retained control over hiring and job creation, the continued presence of widespread racial discrimination in the workplace meant that blacks, no matter how well trained, would not have access to the same jobs as whites. The small remedial education efforts could not possibly compensate for the failures of segregated school systems in which black children received a markedly inferior education to that of white children. Only a full-scale assault on these racial barriers would have created the social space in which job training and remedial education could successfully transform lives. This was the challenge of the new civil rights laws.

Equal Employment Designed to Have Limited Impact

Since the chief opponents of the civil rights bill were the southern members of his own party, President Johnson had no choice but to turn to the opposition party to secure the bill's final passage. To gain the remaining votes, Johnson accepted another series of compromise amendments offered by Senator Everett Dirksen (R-IL), the minority leader in the Senate. Without Dirksen's cooperation, the bill's sponsors could not have enlisted the support of the moderate Republicans, whose votes were needed to balance off the southern Democrats. In exchange for Dirksen's vote, the Democrats agreed to a further weakening of the EEOC's enforcement powers. In Dirksen's version of Title VII, the EEOC was left with only the power to conciliate. The EEOC could recommend to the U.S. attorney general that a lawsuit be filed by the Justice Department. If the Justice Department was persuaded that an employer or union had engaged in a "pattern or practice of resistance" to fair employment, then it had the right to initiate a court suit on behalf of the plaintiffs.[52] The new draft also required that in states with existing fair employment commissions all complaints first be forwarded to the state agency. Only if they could not be resolved on that level would the EEOC investigate the charges. A May 1964 *New York Times* editorial about the Senate compromise commented that "the question the country cannot yet answer is whether, in the interest of marshaling enough northern and western votes . . . concessions have been made that would gravely weaken the bill's enforcement powers in key areas of fair employment and access to public accommodations."[53] In the midst of a highly volatile political crisis, the goal was to pass a bill that at least gave the appearance, if not the substance, of change.

The Dirksen amendments made the EEOC the only federal regulatory agency without its own enforcement mechanism. An analysis of the results written at the time stated, "Society's greatest gain from the work of regulatory agencies is the extent to which the agencies prevent violations of their respective statutes. . . . Society's greatest gain from an EEOC would be the EEOC's prevention of unfair employment practices, not the rectification of such practices after they had been committed."[54] In the bill's final form, the EEOC's investigatory powers could only be initiated after a specific complaint was filed.[55] Unlike the National Labor Relations Board, the Federal Trade Commission, and the Securities and Exchange Commission, the EEOC could not issue cease-and-desist orders to bring discriminatory practices to an immediate halt or initiate legal action in the federal courts. Even the sanctioning powers given to the secretary of labor by Johnson's Executive Order on Contract Compliance were more severe than those given to the EEOC. The legal framework established by Title

VII was much weaker than the one established to remedy school segregation that was a part of the same 1964 Act. Its powers were weaker than those of many of the state FEPCs, even though their experiences had already shown that a commission that could conciliate but not compel was largely ineffective. The history of the state commissions had also shown that most victims would never come forward with complaints, so without the EEOC's power to initiate its own investigations many cases of discriminatory practices would go undetected.

By minimizing the EEOC's enforcement powers, the Republicans were protecting the nation's employers, who opposed any government intrusion into what they regarded as their management prerogatives. In its final form, Title VII was quite acceptable to members of the business community. Their attitude was captured in the following remarks made by Charles Kothe, vice president of industrial relations for the National Association of Manufacturing:

> It is important that we recognize at the outset the law imposes no great or unusual burden on the employer. As a matter of fact, the level of its requirements is far below most of the self-imposed standards of most enlightened businessmen. The law requires no affirmative action as such. No one is obligated to change the present complement of employees or to set out to establish a social or racial mix on the basis of a formula or quota. To the contrary, any such effort might conceivably become a violation, for the law specifically prohibits quotas. . . . The law is adjudicative in nature. It makes no reference to substantive rights. In other words, it is designed principally as a procedure to redress claims of prejudice. . . . The EEOC, unlike the NLRB, has absolutely no judicial or even quasi-judicial power. It cannot issue orders or findings of fact.[56]

The final version of the bill granted the right to file a private lawsuit in federal court, but the plaintiff could not be sure what relief victory would bring or how much it would cost. The lack of EEOC enforcement powers placed much of the burden of enforcement on individual workers, who in most cases would have to seek help from one of the civil rights organizations or public interest law centers to pursue their case. But private citizens and civil rights organizations did not have the vast resources required to eliminate the extensive patterns of discrimination that still existed throughout the economy. Only the government had the wherewithal necessary to accomplish that.[57] By giving the EEOC only the power to be reactive, not pro-active, Congress ensured that it would not be a vehicle for opening up those sectors of the economy in which minorities and women were greatly underrepresented. Individual lawsuits against discrimination were most likely to be filed in areas of the economy where there already were significant concentrations of aggrieved workers. This meant it would have its most immediate impact on blue-collar industrial occupations, while other sectors of the economy would be affected more gradually. Those were the very jobs in which the existing workforce was best organized to resist any perceived threat against their traditional prerogatives.

Organized Labor Protects Itself

Organized labor used its strategic position as a powerbroker within the Democratic Party to blunt the impact of the legislation on the unionized workforce. The AFL-CIO's primary concern was to protect the job status of its core constituency of white males. It sought to assure that the bill's passage would result in no immediate changes in existing racial hierarchies in the workplace. According to Herbert Hill, "The AFL-CIO and its affiliate unions supported Title VII, but only at a price. That price was Section 703(h), where they attempted to postpone for a generation justice for black workers. That's the seniority clause, which unions interpreted to mean that nothing in the Act shall be construed as requiring any alteration of established seniority systems."[58] The insertion of Section 703(h) elevated the sanctity of labor–management contracts above a commitment to racial justice. Past patterns of discrimination were exempted, so the new law would bring little relief to those who for years had been locked into inferior jobs. Only new employees would be able to challenge the inequalities that remained widespread throughout industry.

During the congressional debates, the enemies of civil rights sought to portray Title VII as a threat to existing seniority rights, raising the specter of reverse discrimination against whites.[59] In a speech on the Senate floor aimed at weakening labor's support for fair employment, Senator Lister Hill

(D-AL), an ardent segregationist, claimed that the pending bill would be "a blow to labor union freedom" and would "undermine a basic fabric of unionism, the seniority system and would make it possible for labor unions to be denied their representation rights under the National Labor Relations Act and the Railway Labor Act."[60] Similar charges were made as part of anti–civil rights propaganda mailed out to unions by the Coordinating Committee for Fundamental American Freedoms, a southern anti-civil rights organization.[61] Many of the same individuals and groups who were now crying the loudest about how fair employment legislation threatened the integrity of organized labor had in the past been among labor's most strident opponents.

The AFL-CIO was so confident in the limited impact of Title VII that it responded by arguing that its passage would actually strengthen organized labor by making nonunion employers subject to the same nondiscrimination requirements as unionized employers. The federation insisted that "the Bill does not require 'racial balance' on the job. It does not upset seniority rights already obtained by any employee. It does not give any race preferential treatment in hiring or in terms of employment."[62] Furthermore, "The AFL-CIO does not believe in righting ancient wrongs by perpetrating new ones. . . . [The civil rights bill] will take away nothing from the American worker which he has already acquired."[63] Similarly, an AFL-CIO press release concluded by saying, "In short, the proposed legislation would not alter a union's present substantive obligations under federal law and under the AFL-CIO policy."[64] In a similar vein, the Industrial Union Department issued a legislative alert in May 1964 saying that "there is nothing in the bill requiring racial quotas on jobs. It has nothing to do with day to day operations of business firms or unions or with seniority systems."[65] The statements go to great length to downplay the existence of discrimination, calling it an "ancient wrong" while insisting that the status quo would remain intact.

The AFL-CIO cited its experiences with the state FEPC laws and federal executive orders as further proof that little would change. In a letter to Senator Hill, Reuther wrote that "none of the numerous state FEPC laws and none of the Presidential regulations covering millions of employees, have undermined the rights of organized labor or resulted in the kind of chaos and disruption which you predict as the result of the pending Federal law." Reuther saw the law applying to only the most extreme cases.

Your principal concern appears to be that the pending law will require a mathematical apportionment of jobs on a "one white"–"one Negro" or other similarly rigid basis. This, however, is not the construction of FEPC which has been employed heretofore, and we do not believe it to be the import of the pending federal measure. The preponderance of cases involve a "100% white" situation, where employers have refused to hire or promote a single Negro worker, or unions have barred Negroes from entering a craft or achieving apprenticeship training. In other cases there has been "token" integration only, to provide the pretense rather than the reality of non-discrimination. It is these situations which are the principal focus of the pending law.[66]

The Democratic leadership also sought to minimize the impending changes.

Contrary to the allegations of some opponents of this Title, there is nothing in it that will give any power to the Commission or any court to require hiring, firing, or the promotion of employees in order to meet a racial "quota" or to achieve a certain racial balance. In fact the very opposite is true. Title VII prohibits discrimination. . . . Title VII is designed to encourage hiring on the basis of ability and qualifications, not race or religion.[67]

The Democratic Party's leadership believed that the law would mainly affect southern states that had no FEPC laws of their own. A national law would "impose no substantial new obligations on states that already have a law."[68] On the whole it was viewed as a moderate and constructive attempt to eliminate discrimination. Officials in the Johnson administration echoed these interpretations. In August 1964, Wirtz, speaking at a businessmen's conference, reassured the audience that "in no way, does this [Title VII] mean that the government will set racial 'quotas' or job preference rules." He warned that "the worst thing would be to try to take a shortcut across the quicksands of quotas."[69]

As is so often the case, the process of building a congressional majority in support of a highly controversial bill had given significant leverage over its final content to key constituencies that perceived themselves to be at risk of losing existing privileges. The final version was written in such a way as to protect those prerogatives, thereby successfully minimizing the potential impact of the legislation in opening up employment opportunities for unskilled minorities. Both organized labor and the Democratic leadership went to great lengths to appease the fears of their white constituents. Civil rights advocates were displeased with the results, but regarded the outcome as a breakthrough nonetheless. For them, it was a law borne of great sacrifices. They intended to seek future amendments that would remedy its weaknesses.

Although powerful social upheaval can bring the demands of otherwise disenfranchised groups to the forefront, the people involved in the struggle will not necessarily determine the character of any policies that result from it. Once it is in the hands of the institutional actors in the political arena, the normal process of bargaining and trade-offs takes place. Whoever holds the power in that setting will determine the legislative outcome, which in the long run will stand as the fruits of the struggle. The civil rights movement provided the impetus for both the War on Poverty and the new civil rights laws, but the content of each was determined by the Washington-based policy experts, lobbyists, and the political leadership of both parties.

In both cases the Democrats sought to treat racial oppression in regions outside of the South as isolated incidents of wrongdoing, not systemic patterns of injustice. Congress was willing to pass legislation that corrected racial inequities, but only to the degree that other constituencies were not adversely affected. Yet, the very nature of the racial oppression that limited earnings, educational opportunities, and housing choices for minorities also created undue advantages for whites. Johnson was eager to enact antipoverty legislation, but reluctant to commit the fiscal resources needed to make a significant improvement in the lives of those most disadvantaged by the dying racial order.

While it is in the nature of a pluralist democracy to compromise, policymakers will do so more easily on those issues in which they do not have a direct vested interest. Given that the urban poor have few assets that are significant in the eyes of politicians seeking reelection, it becomes expedient to initiate policies claiming to end poverty and injustice while not fully providing the tools needed to make those proclamations a reality. However, it becomes mean-spirited when three decades later politicians blame those still left in poverty for the failure of programs that were never intended to be fully effective.

3 | THE POOR GET TRAINING BUT NO JOBS

By shunning all job-creation proposals, the War on Poverty left out a crucial component of a viable structure for economic opportunity. As long as the prospect of securing a stable job appears limited, there is less incentive for an unemployed person to enter training. This is particularly true for those who are marginalized because of poverty and the color of their skin. The jobs Lyndon Johnson predicted the private sector would make available to the urban poor largely never materialized. Throughout the entire post–World War II era, the nation's cities experienced a steady loss of jobs. In 1948, 68 percent of all jobs in the twenty-five largest metropolitan areas were located in the central cities. By 1963, only 60 percent remained in the city.[1] The outmigration of jobs and capital accelerated following the urban riots of the mid-1960s. Black men bore the brunt of the resulting increases in unemployment—their labor force participation rates fell from 85 percent in 1954 to 71 percent in 1977.[2] The grim job prospects for African-American men are captured in this 1969 assessment: "Changes in the composition of jobs within central cities bode badly for the Negro male in the ghetto who aspires for a high wage 'regular' blue collar job. If present trends continue, i.e., Negroes remain heavily concentrated within the central city, it is likely that the Negro female will become even more important as an earner in the typical urban Negro family."[3]

The shrinking pool of manufacturing jobs placed those workers lacking basic educational and vocational skills at a competitive disadvantage. With a smaller number of jobs available, employers inevitably hired only the most experienced and job-ready applicants. Young black men who were the products of segregated schools frequently found themselves without the skills needed to gain a foothold in a more competitive labor market. Many of them had been educated in the South, where states typically spent half as much per black child as they did per white child, paid white teachers 30 percent more than black teachers, and invested four times as much in white school facilities as in black ones.[4] Northern states did not do much better. As long as a racially divided labor market restricted blacks to the least-skilled jobs, there was little need to create quality schools in black neighborhoods. Not surprisingly, in the early 1960s more than half of all adult black men had less than a grammar school education, compared to only 21 percent of white men.[5] Illiteracy was four times higher among blacks than whites, and one out of every ten black men was completely illiterate.[6]

Under these circumstances, an active labor market policy, wherein the government spearheads the creation of new jobs and retraining of workers, becomes a crucial element in a commitment to racial equality and social mobility. Although successive generations of job-training and remedial education programs have existed since the 1960s, on the whole they have been too small and unfocused to keep pace with rising urban dropout and unemployment rates. When Congress finally did create a public employment program during the recession of the 1970s the jobs went mostly to workers recently laid off municipal payrolls, not to the urban poor. In the conservative resurgence that followed, the concept of government-supported job creation all but vanished from the policy agenda. Complete reliance on the private sector for job creation became the accepted norm.

Those training programs that have survived increasingly reflect private-sector priorities. There has been a positive recognition that training must be geared toward the actual employment needs of business, but there has also been an accommodation of corporate biases against minority and women workers. Corporations have secured large amounts of public dollars to cover their training costs while retaining full control over hiring and firing decisions. The structure of financial rewards leads training agencies to admit only the most job-ready from among their large pool of unemployed applicants. Even though countless evaluation studies point to the value of long-term training, chronic underfunding has led to a predominance of short-term, minimalist approaches.

Much of this nation's future hinges on its ability to deliver quality education and training to its youth. However, a segregated housing market almost guarantees that most minority children will be educated in all-minority schools where the quality of the resources, teaching, and curriculum is substandard. These schools become a microcosm of the larger communities in which they are situated, beset by violence, teen pregnancy, and high dropout rates. Under these conditions, many urban youth reach adulthood without the skills needed to hold down a secure job. For them, effective job training could offer the possibility of a second chance. Yet, in their communities, the federal government's only job-training program, the Job Training Partnership Act (JTPA), is almost invisible, offering little hope to the vast numbers of unemployed poor.

Civil Rights Leaders Link Equality to Jobs

At the height of the southern phase of the civil rights movement, there was already a recognition that racial equality could not be achieved without also addressing the need for jobs. During the 1963 protests in Birmingham, Alabama, the most industrialized city in the South, the single demand for an end to segregation gave way to a broad call for advances in employment, school integration, and better police protection.[7] Organizers of the historic March on Washington in 1963 adopted the call for jobs as a dual demand. Many of the marchers carried signs that read "Jobs Now!" That same year, Whitney Young, president of the National Urban League, called on the government to initiate a massive domestic Marshall Plan that would involve a ten-year federal commitment to eradicate what he called the "discrimination gap."[8]

In the last years of his life, as Martin Luther King, Jr., turned his attention to the depressed living standards of African-Americans in the North, he realized that their poverty was structured into the economic system in the United States.[9] As rioting broke out in city after city, King attributed the increasingly angry mood of urban blacks to the lack of progress in securing jobs. He anguished over his inability to stem the tide of violence: "I can't stop a riot unless I can give people jobs. Industry is playing games with us. Even a long-standing ally like organized labor tolerates building trades unions that won't allow Negroes in them."[10] Believing that the country was sacrificing its commitment to end poverty in order to wage war in Vietnam, King became an early critic of President Johnson's decision to send combat troops into action. Even though Johnson deliberately downplayed the significance of military escalation, Vietnam quickly became the central issue facing his presidency and his administration began to evaluate all domestic spending in terms of its impact on the war effort.

In 1967, King decided to undertake a major new national campaign that would mobilize thousands of poor to converge on Washington and demand that Congress to enact comprehensive anti-poverty legislation. The Poor People's Campaign called for creating economic opportunity by providing adequate jobs for the unemployed, a guaranteed annual income, a decent minimum wage, adequate housing, and the repeal of the federal freeze on state welfare rolls.[11] It was the most far-reaching anti-poverty proposal to emerge from the civil rights movement, the administration, or congressional Democrats. It specifically made the poor the beneficiaries of job-creation policies and would have required a redistribution of income from the wealthy to the country's poor. King was convinced that only such a bold initiative would defuse the urban time bomb, halt the racial backlash, and make Vietnam too great a political and fiscal liability for the Democrats to carry into the 1968 presidential elections.[12] King was assassinated just weeks before the campaign was scheduled to commence. The Southern Christian Leadership Conference decided to proceed with the plans, but the campaign turned into a debacle, leaving Congress unmoved and possibly even more hostile to the poor.[13]

The only other anti-poverty plan to approach the scope of King's proposal was the "Freedom Budget" developed by A. Philip Randolph, the veteran civil rights leader and president of the Sleeping Car Porters Union. Randolph chose to make job creation the central focus of his work following the passage of the 1964 and 1965 civil rights legislation. He made the enactment of a national full-employment budget the top priority of his newly formed institute. Founded in 1965, the A. Philip Randolph Institute was almost completely funded by the AFL-CIO. Given his strong labor ties, Randolph tended to view the twin goals of equal employment and full employment as alternate policy choices, rather than as complementary to each other. Organized labor hoped that a focus on poverty and unemployment would deflect attention away from the highly divisive issues of affirmative action and access to jobs. Randolph incorporated his employment concepts into the Freedom Budget. Aimed at a broad audience, the Freedom Budget was purposefully designed not to be redistributive, but instead to "benefit all Americans."[14] Randolph did not want it to appear as "simply a special plea on behalf of the narrow self-interest of a minority."[15] Leon Keyserling, the economist who wrote the budget's first drafts, objected to a proposed cover for the pamphlet version because the "pictures of four people who are manifestly deprived, harassed, and poor shrink the whole concept of the Freedom Budget." In Keyserling's view, "It is indeed the core idea of the whole text, that this is not just a 'Freedom Budget' for Negroes or for poor people but for the benefit of all Americans."[16]

In an attempt to make the Freedom Budget acceptable to the Johnson administration, Randolph constructed it so as to make increased social spending compatible with the large increases in defense spending brought on by the war in Vietnam. The budget was to prove that the "country is economically and financially capable of eliminating poverty, whatever its international commitments may be."[17] Its strong pro-war stance was undoubtedly the result of the institute's close ties to the AFL-CIO as well as Randolph's own anti-communism. Keyserling explained the acceptance of military spending as a tactical move: "We do not believe that a maximum coalition can be obtained in support of the domestic priority objectives of the 'Freedom Budget,' if this coalition is limited to those who, for all practical purposes, act upon the assumption that these domestic purposes are unattainable unless there is a very drastic change with respect to military and space."[18]

Many in the civil rights movement were skeptical of the Freedom Budget for the very reasons that the Randolph Institute championed it. For example, Joseph Rauh of the Leadership Conference on Civil Rights viewed the Freedom Budget as "a fake. . . . It was an effort to make the Vietnam War look good. . . . All this period Bayard [the executive director of the Randolph Institute] was fighting against King talking against the Vietnam War. As an agent of the labor movement they were trying to stop King."[19] The Congress of Racial Equality (CORE) endorsed it, while disagreeing with the premise that the country could afford "guns and butter."[20] The National Association for the Advancement of Colored People (NAACP) felt it ought to be consolidated with several other budget proposals in existence at the time.[21] The Freedom Budget was never formally introduced in Congress, not because civil rights organizations failed to support it, but because the AFL-CIO's legislative director was unenthusiastic about submitting it as a package. Organized labor "never really focused on introducing something as comprehensive as the Freedom Budget."[22]

Democrats Tilt Jobs Policy to the Newly Unemployed

Having been forced by the momentum of the mass movement in the South to enact two major pieces of civil rights legislation within a year's time, the Johnson administration searched for a means of gaining control over the civil rights movement. Heightened conflict over minority access endangered the future electoral viability of the Democratic Party. Many southern Democrats were abandoning the party, alienated by the racial reforms of 1964 and 1965 and their subsequent loss of congressional power. Racial conflict in the North now threatened to dismember the party even further. The administration became convinced that a shift toward poverty issues would merge the civil rights movement with the poverty movement, which had originated within the administration and was under its control.[23] Johnson drew upon the findings of an unpublished report written by Daniel Patrick Moynihan, then a staff member at the Department of Labor. The report argued that many blacks would be unable to take advantage of the new opportunities because the "Negro social structure, in particular the Negro family, battered and harassed by discrimination, injustice, and uprooting, is in the deepest trouble."[24] According to Johnson, the breakdown of the black family structure made the nature of black poverty unique, because "it flows from centuries of oppression and persecution of the Negro man."[25]

Johnson hoped that a focus on the plight of the black family would serve as the basis for a new consensus between the administration and the movement while evoking sympathetic support from whites. His goal was to leapfrog over the movement and rechannel it "away from the mere passage and implementation of legislation into the area of social and economic change, thereby, reducing the conflict with the movement by co-optation."[26] The president's plan fell apart after the public release of the

Moynihan Report created such a furor that it became another wedge driving blacks further away from the administration. Many were outraged by references to the "plight of the black family," as though all black families were in danger of disintegration. The issue touched too closely upon long-held negative stereotypes of black families, so that black leaders could not accept the early warnings of an emerging social crisis among poor urban blacks. The focus on poor families also reinforced a social service approach to addressing poverty, rather than one emphasizing economic development and job creation.

Despite his rhetorical support of the urgent need to eliminate poverty, Johnson refused to support any major new domestic expenditures. This was largely due to the costs of the war in Vietnam. By the end of 1966, spending on the war had reached $20 billion and the federal deficit was approaching $10 billion instead of the projected $1.8 billion.[27] In response, Johnson's 1967 domestic budget actually contained deep cuts in the anti-poverty, education, and economic development programs he had initiated just two years before.[28] When the Senate proposed allocating $1 billion for an Emergency Employment Act that would create 200,000 meaningful public service jobs in areas of high unemployment in 1968 and another 250,000 in 1969, the administration launched an all-out effort to defeat it. The bill had been endorsed by many local governments and by every important presidential task force appointed since 1965.[29] The following year, the Senate was again frustrated in its attempt to add a public service employment provision to the extension of the Manpower Development and Training Act that would have created 600,000 jobs over the following two years.[30]

Throughout his tenure as president, Johnson opposed all forms of emergency public service employment, continuing to emphasize the need to involve private employers in the training and employment of the jobless. Johnson's solution to the need for more jobs was to sponsor a new manpower program called JOBS (Job Opportunities in the Business Sector), which relied heavily on private-sector job creation. Initiated in 1968, the program awarded subsidies to employers who agreed to hire and train the disadvantaged. This was the government's first concerted effort to bring the private sector into the process of job training. The businesses who participated tended to be larger ones who could more easily absorb less-qualified employees in their workforces. When those industries were hit hard in the 1970–71 recession, the JOBS program went into decline.

In 1969, what was by then the standard public service employment bill was again introduced on Capitol Hill, even though President Richard Nixon's attitude toward it was no more favorable than Johnson's had been.[31] The notion of public service employment remained an intensely divisive ideological issue, haunted by the old image of dead-end, make-work jobs. Yet, the deepening economic crisis made jobs legislation more important to the Democrats and more attractive to some Republicans. By mid-1971, organized labor, concerned with the effects of rising unemployment on its own membership, finally mobilized in support of jobs legislation. The result was the Emergency Employment Act (EEA), which allocated $2.5 billion to create roughly 200,000 jobs for two years, less than half the number contained in earlier proposals.[32] It was designed as a countercyclical program, aimed at workers who had just recently been laid off, not at the long-term unemployed. The bill's focus was on veterans, laid-off aerospace workers, minorities, and others, but not on those with the weakest education or jobs skills. The jobs were designed to be temporary, locally controlled, and a transition to regular employment, giving the program broad political appeal.[33] Local control gave the EEA an automatic constituency, making it the first popular jobs program since the New Deal. The Democrats and organized labor liked its broad eligibility and its lack of federal oversight. Local elected officials liked it because they saw it as a means of relieving local fiscal strains.

Although supportive of the new program because it created additional public-sector jobs, labor worried that it could take employment away from its members if local governments were to lay off regular employees and then use the federal dollars to hire the unemployed into the same job slots. To assure their members' jobs, the unions made certain that the program targeted recently laid-off workers rather than those with no previous employment experience. The unions also wanted the jobs restricted to entry-level positions. Seeing public service employment as a way to protect their members' jobs, the unions made the program more restrictive at the local level. In all cities studied as part of a 1973 program evaluation, city planners had acquiesced to the unions' desire that only entry-level jobs be offered through the program.[34]

The 1972 Democratic Convention nominated George McGovern as presidential candidate and adopted a platform calling for a "guaranteed job for all" as the party's "primary economic objective." Unlike previous Democratic conventions, the 1972 delegates had been selected on the basis of a new set of rules that purposely excluded party regulars and the AFL-CIO. The new delegates reflected the growing participation in the party's affairs by blacks, Latinos, and women, for whom job creation was a much more salient issue. Furthermore, without the AFL-CIO present at the proceedings, the usual objections that public jobs would rob union members of employment were not heard. Having been pushed aside, the old guard chose to sit out the election, dooming the party to defeat and permanently stigmatizing the call for guaranteed jobs as a fringe issue.

Following the election, congressional liberals introduced a bill calling for the creation of over a million new jobs. The proposal was defeated, largely because forty-four southern Democrats voted against it.[35] The Republicans still operated on the old assumption that the poor were unemployed because they lacked basic skills, not because of a lack of employment possibilities.[36] For Republicans, local control, not public jobs, was the key to an effective jobs policy. A compromise was reached, with the Democrats agreeing to local control over the old Manpower Development and Training Act (MDTA) and War on Poverty training programs in exchange for a small public employment component. The new program, known as the Comprehensive Employment and Training Act of 1973 (CETA) gave local governments a lump sum of money they could spend on a wide range of training activities as long as they followed federal guidelines on eligibility and allowable program activities.[37] For ten years CETA was the centerpiece of America's jobs policy.

Shortly after CETA's passage, a greatly enlarged public service employment (PSE) component was added. Within six months, it employed 250,000 people, quickly overshadowing CETA's training components in terms of funding and visibility. At its height, the training programs amounted to less than one-fifth of total CETA dollars. The program never guaranteed a job to everyone who wanted one, offering less than a million slots a year. Its only eligibility requirement was that a person be unemployed for fifteen days.[38] Until the program was reformed in 1978, most of the jobs were given to adult white males with at least a high school education, who were more employable than the general workforce.[39] The Democrats were particularly sensitive to the disaffection of this group of traditional party voters, many of whom had defected to the Republicans in the 1972 election.

PSE quickly became a powerful political asset in the hands of local politicians who controlled the distribution of jobs in their areas. The plans for use of the money were set by local elected officials or their immediate staffs, not the local CETA offices. CETA planning councils had virtually no role with regard to PSE. Localities with the worst budget crises used PSE dollars to rehire laid-off public employees.[40] The greater the fiscal needs of the jurisdiction, the more likely local politicians were to exercise complete control over the program.[41] Between 1974 and 1978, PSE jobs rose from 1 percent to more than 7 percent of all state and local government employment.[42]

In response to a flood of criticisms against CETA for waste and inappropriate use of money, Congress passed a set of reforms in 1978 that tightened up eligibility. For the first time, the PSE component was targeted to the long-term unemployed. The length of a PSE job was restricted to eighteen months, after which a participant was expected to get a job in the private sector. The amendments also placed new restrictions on the extent to which municipal governments could shift regular employees onto the CETA payroll. PSE jobs were now required to be community oriented. Congress wanted to make sure that PSE dollars were funding new jobs rather than replacing regular positions in state and local government. The amendments also reduced the number of jobs by 100,000, reversing the trend within CETA of placing the main emphasis on PSE rather than on job training. Once the program targeted the poor and long-term unemployed and municipal jobs could no longer be transferred to the federal payroll, CETA became much less popular among local politicians. They lost interest in it, making it vulnerable to conservative attacks as a counterproductive program.

Throughout much of the 1970s, as urban jobs disappeared and welfare rolls grew, the crucial social mobility component of the nation's jobs policy was largely neglected in favor of providing jobs for the recently unemployed. Although $60 million was spent on PSE, most of it went to assist local governments in meeting their payrolls without having to raise taxes, instead of providing jobs for poor urban residents. Only during its last years did it provide community service jobs in poor minority neighborhoods. This was a far cry from King's vision of a government-guaranteed right to a job.

A Last Attempt to Legislate Full Employment

Beginning in 1974, the Congressional Black Caucus, which had now grown to thirteen members, spearheaded an effort to enact comprehensive full-employment legislation on the scale envisioned by King. Known as the Humphrey-Hawkins Full Employment Act, after its two main sponsors, Senator Hubert Humphrey (D-MN) and Congressman Augustus Hawkins (D-CA), it was not just an anti-recession or a jobs bill. Instead, it contained a two-pronged strategy—to provide jobs for all Americans and to fill unmet social needs. The initial draft would have established a legal right to a job for anyone who wanted to work. Federal economic policies were to be geared toward increasing the overall demand for labor in the economy. The bill also had a strong orientation towards equal employment opportunity.[43]

Although Humphrey-Hawkins had more than eighty congressional sponsors, full employment was not a priority issue among the leadership of the Democratic Party. The AFL-CIO refused to support the bill's first draft, objecting to its guaranteed job provisions. The federation give its endorsement only after a new draft eliminated the right to sue for a job along with the earlier emphasis on workers who faced special obstacles to employment. Jimmy Carter, who emerged as the Democratic candidate in the 1976 elections, gave the bill only lukewarm support. Rather than an across-the-board guarantee of a job, Carter preferred a more selective approach to unemployment that would target projects to pockets of high unemployment and expand the existing PSE program from 300,000 to 600,000 jobs.[44] By the time the bill was finally passed in 1978, its employment goals had been further modified to call for the attainment of a 4 percent unemployment level, without ever defining what constituted "full employment." The final bill emphasized private-sector job creation and paid as much attention to fighting inflation as it did to fighting unemployment. From late 1977 until its passage in October 1978 it came under constant attack by its conservative opponents.[45] Its passage ended all serious congressional debate over guaranteed employment, even though its mandates have never been implemented by subsequent presidents.

Republicans Reject All Public Jobs

Ronald Reagan's election as president signaled a dramatic shift in government attitudes toward the relief of poverty. Throughout the 1970s public support for social programs had declined steadily because many voters regarded them as responsible for a downward redistribution of benefits to blacks and other minorities competing for increasingly limited government resources. Disaffection with the Democratic welfare state was particularly strong among union households and independent voters.[46] The Republicans succeeded in capitalizing on this resentment by challenging the long-standing notion that government had a responsibility to address the needs of the poor. Claiming that his election was a mandate to alter the course of government, Reagan set out to reverse the social policy direction of the previous twenty years. Within the first six months of his presidency, Reagan won approval of two major pieces of legislation: the Economic Recovery Tax Act of 1981, which cut taxes by $747 billion over five years, and the Gramm-Latta budget legislation, which cut domestic spending in a way most damaging to the poor and inner-city residents.[47]

To justify these dramatic reductions in the scope of government, the Reagan administration resurrected old laissez-faire doctrines calling for a return to more limited forms of government so as to allow greater freedom to the self-regulating mechanisms of the private market. Government was supposedly designed not to satisfy specific needs, but to secure the general conditions by which groups and individuals have the most favorable opportunities for providing for their own needs.[48] Government was not responsible for correcting the inequalities of the market, even though its benefits and burdens might in many instances be held as unjust *if* these inequalities were the result of a deliberate allocation to particular people. Efforts to alleviate poverty and inadequate housing and health care risked a disruption of the private market, which when left alone supposedly worked in the best interests of the majority. This line of reasoning found its way directly into the policy initiatives of the Reagan administration. Two of the president's top policy advisors explained their opposition to welfare as follows: "One of the primary tenets of American economic and political relationships is that income earned belongs individually to the people who earn it. It does not belong to the state, nor does it belong by right to any other segment of the population. The income produced belongs, by natural right, to the person who produced it.... Possession of title to the fruits of one's labor is an essential part of American freedoms, for its antithesis is economic servitude."[49]

The elevation of the free market to a sacrosanct principle led to an automatic rejection of any restrictions on the drive for profit-maximization. Government regulations of all kinds, ranging from anti-trust and consumer protection to environmental conservation, were attacked as harmful to the functioning of the free market. The Republican White House strongly opposed any form of government-sponsored jobs, believing that cuts in corporate and capital gains taxes would be a sufficient incentive to create new jobs. In the administration's eyes, people were poor because of individual deviant behavior that locked them into a culture lacking in morals, not because of an inadequate supply of jobs. Government assistance programs had only made the poor less willing to work. Thus, the policy emphasis shifted from efforts to intervene in the economy to efforts to change individual behavior.

The Republican victory left the Democrats in a state of shock, with many accepting the need for a restructuring of social priorities, while others worried that any opposition to a popular president would be labeled as obstructionist. They mounted little opposition to the administration's first round of budget cuts and tax changes. According to one House aide, many of the Democratic committee and subcommittee chairs "just seem to have rolled over."[50] When the Democrats submitted their alternative budget, it contained three-fourths of the Reagan cuts. Leading Democrats actively participated in the process of assembling the "Christmas tree" of tax cuts to special interests.[51]

Some of the biggest cuts occurred in those social mobility programs that most directly improved the labor market position of the poor, especially poor minorities. High on Reagan's hit list were job-creation and training programs. By 1980, eligibility for CETA's training programs had been defined to make them principally programs serving minorities. Minority women were the main beneficiaries of the employment programs, making up roughly 50 percent of all participants. In some large cities, CETA was an overwhelmingly black program. CETA was a favorite target of conservatives pointing to government waste and abuse. Much of the fraud within the program had occurred in the PSE component, which had been the object of considerable political manipulation. After the 1978 amendments, vast administrative resources were devoted to eliminating fraudulent activities, but the image stuck. Reagan proposed to dismantle or diminish the entire system of public service employment programs, public works projects, and training programs for youth and adults. The Democrats were in such a state of confusion that they did little to save CETA.

Reagan sought an immediate end to the $3.1 billion PSE program, public works projects funded by the Economic Development Administration, and employment tax credits. He also wanted a five-year phase-out of the remaining CETA training programs.[52] Congress agreed to eliminate the PSE program, and within a year public employment no longer existed. It appeared briefly as though the country would be without any form of federal jobs policy for the first time since the early days of the Kennedy administration.

Although he succeeded in killing off CETA, Reagan was not able to eliminate all job training permanently from the federal budget. As the country plunged into a deep recession, with unemployment at 10.8 percent by the end of 1981, calls for a jobs programs were heard once again on Capitol Hill. A variety of job-creation proposals came from both parties, ranging from a temporary resurrection of PSE to an ambitious $15 billion package that would guarantee a public-sector job for anyone unable to find work.[53] Reagan remained opposed to all forms of job creation, but faced with the certainty of some sort of legislation passing Congress, he decided to propose a $4.3 billion public works bill. Although politically popular, public works spending is one of the costliest approaches to job creation because it funds high-paying construction jobs. The final bill allotted two-thirds of the funds to public works and the remainder to social services and humanitarian relief. There were no specific eligibility requirements for potential employees of the public works jobs, which meant that most would go to unemployed skilled tradesmen. The people receiving the construction jobs did not even have to be unemployed prior to starting work on one of the new projects. As a result, it was difficult to determine how many jobs had actually been created. "Paradoxically, the coalition-building process in Congress and the need for presidential support produced a law that would barely dent the unemployment problem. The public works approach drove up the cost of each job created."[54]

Business Takes Control of Job Training

In the fall of 1982 Reagan finally endorsed a bipartisan initiative to craft a new job-training program, thus preserving a minimal federal presence in this field. The Job Training Partnership Act (JTPA), as it was called, reflected the Republicans' strong private-sector orientation. All job placements were to be with private companies, necessitating a much more active partnership with the business community. The law assigned a strong oversight role to private industry councils, which were to be composed of at least 51 percent business representatives. Most program administrators saw this as a plus because it would enhance the program in the eyes of private employers, who would then be more willing to hire its participants. Increased private-sector involvement also discouraged the kind of political interference that had plagued the CETA program. In effect, institutional control over federal job training was shifted from elected officials to the private sector. Although this gave it a stronger anchor in the private labor market, it also made it less accountable to public mandates such as the enforcement of equal employment opportunity laws. As training agencies adapted themselves to the needs of private business, their placement patterns began to reflect racial and gender biases in the labor market. Over time, JTPA evolved into a government-sponsored referral system for entry-level, low-wage workers, where potential employees are prescreened by a training agency that is paid for each successful placement.

Instead of handing the funds over to local governments, JTPA allocated resources to the states. As states vied with each other to attract new businesses during the recessionary 1980s, many of them used their discretionary JTPA funds as bait, promising to subsidize a relocating company's employee training costs. For example, Illinois, which had lost over half a million manufacturing jobs between 1969 and 1987, gave $10.9

million in industrial training funds to Diamond Star Motors, a Japanese automaker that had decided to locate in the state. Those dollars were used to train 417 people, amounting to $26,225 per employee.[55] Such uses stretch the purpose of job training from one of retraining laid-off workers to one of providing companies with government resources to train their existing workforce. States justified this by arguing that it was contributing to a reduction of unemployment by creating new jobs. However, true to the Republican philosophy, these were all private-sector jobs with the companies free to hire whomever they wished.

The states disperse the bulk of their federal allotment to local Service Delivery Areas based on a formula that emphasizes unemployment over concentrated poverty. Designed to disperse the funds broadly, it has led to a gross underfunding of urban centers with high levels of poverty in favor of more affluent suburbs and small towns where the percentage of poor people is much lower. Although eleven big cities have the highest poverty rates in the nation, only 12 percent of JTPA funds go to these areas.[56] In fiscal year 1991–92 the City of Chicago received only 1.8 percent of the total federal allotment of JTPA funds, Los Angeles 1.7 percent, and New York 3.7 percent. Since JTPA's main training component can only accept people with incomes below the poverty level, while the funding formula underemphasizes poverty, the big cities end up receiving proportionately less money per each eligible individual. Given the steady drain of jobs from central cities, the funding biases in JTPA mean that proportionately fewer training dollars are allocated in areas of the greatest job scarcity and therefore the most competitive labor markets. Furthermore, inner-city participants generally come with a complicated mix of educational deficiencies and personal problems that have prevented them from working.

The Service Delivery Areas are given considerable discretion in how they use their resources, allowing suburban administrators to create very distinctive programs. Suburban participants tend to be laid-off workers seeking to upgrade their skills, recent divorcees, and homemakers who are seeking to reenter the workforce. While city participants are overwhelmingly black and Latino, suburban participants are mostly white. This has given JTPA a much more favorable image among suburban businesses whose assistance is so crucial in obtaining job placements. Although CETA had been handicapped by the negative perception of being a "black" program, "the dislocated homemaker being served by JTPA is like the girl next door."[57]

Funding for the new program has been much lower than for CETA, which has meant that far fewer people can be served. In 1983 Congress allocated only $3.76 billion, whereas in 1981 CETA received $7.65 billion.[58] Even as joblessness climbed during the 1980s, the amount of money allocated for job training continued its downward trend. Limited funding meant that no more than 5 to 7 percent of the eligible population could be served in any given year. Scarcity forced big city program administrators to emphasize very short-term training so as to maximize enrollments while holding down costs. Much of the training provides a general introduction to the world of work rather than instruction in specific skills, either academic or vocational—even though earlier research found that this type of training does not lead to jobs for many participants.[59] Instead, it functions more as a supplementary educational program, providing some temporary income support to poor teenagers. In more well-to-do suburbs, funds are available for more extensive occupational training in fields such as auto mechanics, desktop publishing, heating and air conditioning repair, clerical, and medical support fields such as respiratory therapy.[60]

In reaction to CETA's stigma as a program fraught with waste and abuse, Congress designed JTPA to be "results" oriented, with a heavy emphasis on attaining job placements at minimal cost. JTPA contractors are often expected to place as high as 75 percent of their participants in jobs. They are only reimbursed the full cost of training once a participant has been placed, creating enormous pressures to enroll only those participants who are certain to get a job. By creaming off the best participants, agencies protect their own survival, but leave those most in need of training outside. While the Chicago public schools produce thousands of new dropouts every year, less than a quarter of the city's JTPA participants are high school dropouts. This is a sharp departure from the CETA days, when more than half of Illinois participants were high school dropouts.[61] Although officials at the Chicago Mayor's Office of Employment and Training deny that any creaming takes place, several Chicago service providers acknowledge that they enroll the most job-ready participants they can find. One agency that places over three hundred young people in jobs each year admits that "in order to place good employees, extensive creaming takes place before training."[62] Another agency specializing in providing pre-apprenticeship training in bricklaying and carpentry only accepts people with high school diplomas because of union membership requirements. The agency's director conceded that the educational requirements are a form of creaming but felt that was acceptable because the agency was still meeting the needs of many young people.[63]

Over time, the program has enrolled increasing numbers of women and youth; adult men are the least likely to gain entrance. The women often receive Aid to Families with Dependent Children (AFDC) and therefore can afford to participate in a program that provides no training stipends, while youth more easily meet the strict income requirements. In Chicago, women make up slightly more than half of all participants. In other large cities such as Atlanta, women comprise nearly 70 percent of the participants. Some states have intentionally made women on AFDC a funding priority, using JTPA dollars to create state versions of workfare. The emphasis on women is also a reflection of the low-wage labor market, which is dominated by traditionally female jobs such as clerical workers, hotel maids, or bank tellers. The authors of a study on Atlanta concluded: "The logic of the JTPA system, along with the continuing strong gender segregation of jobs, produced very strong incentives for training black women for traditional, low-wage jobs with little mobility. Typing and housekeeping could be taught in relatively brief periods with limited budgets. Employers in those occupations were used to hiring black women. It was much less risky to meet JTPA requirements by going with the conventions of the labor market than by trying to change them."[64] Many of these jobs do not enable a woman with children to bring her income above the poverty level.

In 1988, almost half of the JTPA participants in Illinois were under the age of twenty-two.[65] Given the poor quality of urban education, many youth are in dire need of a second chance at gaining a skill. Yet, in the big cities little actual skills training is funded by JTPA. Black youth tend to be channeled into less substantive types of training such as youth competencies or job search assistance, and they consistently receive lower wages upon placement than either Hispanics or whites. Reflecting the reluctance of suburban employers to hire black youth, those few enrolled in suburban training programs are frequently placed into service occupations paying little more than the minimum wage.[66] In response to evaluations showing poor job-retention rates, Congress has amended the program several times, hoping to encourage more long-term occupational skills training. Yet, since the funding has not increased, these requirements have further reduced the number of people who can receive training to the point where the effort is almost insignificant.

Big city agencies committed to providing remedial education or occupational skills training must find those resources through private donations or special literacy grants, using JTPA to provide supplemental instruction in resume writing and interviewing skills. With employment opportunities for poor urban youth so scarce, some agencies use On-the-Job Training (OJT) dollars to subsidize participants' wages at neighborhood fast food restaurants such as Taco Bell and Church's Chicken.[67] By hiring OJT participants, employers not only become eligible for tax credits, but their wage costs for the first eighty hours are reimbursed by JTPA. Given that little training is involved in working at a fast food restaurant, this is really a hidden form of job creation. Rather than performing community service work in a school or daycare center, young people are flipping hamburgers and stuffing tacos. In their zeal to reject "make-work" public-sector jobs, the Republicans have turned much of JTPA into a hand-out to business.

Both the Democrats and Republicans have structured federal jobs policies to benefit their favored constituencies. The Democrats have preferred public-sector job creation, with the bulk of opportunities going to white male union members. The Republicans shifted toward private-sector job creation, where business completely controls who gets hired. The goal of upgrading poor people's skills has largely been marginal to both parties' agendas. Now that JTPA is geared to serving poor people, its funding level and rigid performance standards have rendered it ineffective as an avenue for gaining stable employment. As a nation, we have been willing simply to write off those who face the greatest obstacles in finding a job. In effect, we believe they are not redeemable and certainly not worth the cost required to do so. The consequences of this choice can be seen on the streetcorners of any poor urban neighborhood, where groups of idle men pass their days with absolutely nowhere to go.

Using its position as a key powerbroker within the Democratic Party as leverage, organized labor has fought a protracted battle to protect its traditional white male membership from the potential impact of an Equal Employment Opportunities Commission (EEOC) with real power. The legislative compromise struck at the time of Title VII's enactment sought to forestall the repercussions of granting equal access to minorities and women by exempting current employees from the effects of the law. The unions believed that the resulting law would not cause any significant changes in the American workplace. Some of labor's most blatantly discriminatory practices, such as the maintenance of segregated locals, would probably be eliminated, but earlier AFL-CIO national conventions had already committed themselves to reform on these matters. The lobbyists and legislators who shaped the compromise never anticipated the flood of complaints that came from black workers once equal employment had been established as a legislative right. Normally, heightened protest precedes the enactment of a new law: in this case, however, a far greater number of protests demanding equal employment took place after the passage of the 1964 Civil Rights Act.[1] For blacks, the new law, no matter how inadequate, represented the hope of deliverance from generations of subservience in the workplace.

The pressure to open up union jobs came at a time when the unionized workforce was shrinking dramatically. In 1956, 34 percent of the private nonagricultural workforce was unionized; by 1974, it had fallen to 26 percent. Sixty percent of this decline was the result of the decline in blue-collar industrial jobs, which were the most heavily unionized.[2] With union jobs disappearing, white workers perceived black demands for a complete end to segregated employment as a direct threat to their livelihood. White workers with less skills were particularly intimidated by the possibility of lowering racial employment barriers, since they were the most dependent on such barriers for their own status and income. Those with greater skills or education were insulated from what would now be a more competitive environment.

The unions sought to slow down the pace and scope of change at each step of the way, from the moment the EEOC began its work, through countless court cases, some of which reached the Supreme Court. Some of the literature analyzing the racial backlash among whites suggests that perhaps the pace of racial reform should have been more gradual so as not to alienate the white electorate.[3] Yet, within the labor market, blacks were merely claiming what was rightfully theirs but had been denied them because of racial segregation. Given the lower standards of living that resulted from their exclusion from better-paid employment, blacks could hardly be expected to wait another generation before conditions improved.

Black workers were still locked into a racially segregated labor market where the jobs for which they could compete were markedly inferior to those available to whites with equal skills. This dual labor market operated without any legal mandate. Rather, it was through the decisions of countless individual employers to distribute available jobs in a way that gave whites the first opportunity at employment. Over a long period of time, the nonwhite labor force was effectively confined to the status of a surplus labor pool. Employment opportunities for minority workers expanded only during periods of labor shortages.

White workers, of course, had greatly benefited from these arrangements. A number of the older skilled trades unions still maintained racial barriers to union membership that had been erected during and immediately after World War I in response to increased competition from blacks. The craft unions, such as the plumbers, electricians, and carpenters, had built their power on the basis of exclusion. They maintained strict control over entry into the trades, which was often handed down from one generation to the next, almost like an inheritance. A system of apprenticeships and hiring halls locked major employers into using only union labor. In the 1930s, the construction trades had secured congressional approval of the Davis-Bacon Act, which required that publicly funded construction projects pay the locally prevailing wage. In union strongholds it committed contractors on these projects to hire only union labor. The Congress of Industrial Organizations (CIO), formed to organize the mass production industries during the New Deal, was the first labor federation to acknowledge the importance of interracial solidarity because it knew that black workers, though small in numbers, could prove crucial in close elections. The CIO organizing drives led to some improvements, but the expansion of industrial unionism generally did not lead to qualitative changes in the status of black workers.

Even in the more progressive unions, such as the United Auto Workers (UAW), discriminatory employment patterns remained widespread. Although the UAW was not directly responsible for the auto companies' failure to hire more blacks, it had long allowed a highly unequal employment structure to exist within the plants and within the union itself. In early 1949, Walter White, the national secretary of the National Association for the Advancement of Colored People (NAACP), wrote to UAWs President Walter Reuther complaining of the "almost total failure to break down the color line in some of the St. Louis auto plants which were organized by the UAW-CIO."[4] In 1960, the Chrysler Corporation had only 24 blacks employed among its 7,425 skilled workers and only 1 black apprentice out of a total of 350. A full 80.7 percent of all black autoworkers were concentrated in the three lowest occupations.[5]

In early January 1964, the UAW conducted its own survey to provide its leadership with "some impressions of the degree of progress being made with respect to the 'non-white membership' of the union."[6] The union received responses covering approximately half of its members. The survey confirmed the existence of striking patterns of racial exclusion, many of which were no different than those found in the building trades unions. A total of 12.9 percent of the UAW's production workers surveyed were nonwhite, while only 1.4 percent of the skilled trades members were nonwhite. The survey found that out of twenty-nine states responding, only eight had any nonwhite apprentices in training, and twenty states surveyed did not have a single nonwhite apprentice. It also found that 94.5 percent of all employees enrolled in employee-in-training programs and employee upgrading programs were white. There were only 54 nonwhite apprentices out of a total of 1,958 who participated in the UAW's joint labor-management programs.[7]

Conditions on the union's own staff were not much better. The UAW's 1965 employment records show that the twenty-six member board of directors contained only one black man and one woman. Among its seventeen assistant regional directors, there was one Hispanic man, no blacks, and no women. Among the executive officers, only Walter Reuther had a black man on his staff (see Table 1).[8] There were only nine black men and no women in officer or managerial positions at the UAW's international headquarters.[9] The largest number of black male employees was found among the international representatives who dealt most directly with the union's membership. The majority of black women worked as secretaries.

In the past, the national labor federation had paid lip service to support for equal employment while doing little to change long-standing patterns of discrimination. The AFL-CIO had been very reluctant to discipline member unions that clung to openly racist membership policies. A 1961 NAACP report on the federation's race relations record concluded with a fairly negative assessment: "The national labor organization has failed to eliminate the broad patterns of racial discrimination and segregation in many important affiliated union. . . . Efforts to eliminate discriminatory practices within trade

Table 1 Breakdown of UAW Staff by Occupation, Sex, and Race, 1965

Job Category	Male		Female		Total
	White	Black	White	Black	
Officials/ Managers	119	9	0	0	133
Professional	19	2	1	0	22
Technicians*	630	55	14	4	709
Clerical	7	4	308	78	399
Craftsmen	1	1	0	0	2
Service	32	9	16	6	63
TOTAL	808	80	341	88	1,328

*UAW International representatives
Source: UAW's Employment Equal Opportunities reports based on payrolls of December 18, 1965–December 31, 1966

unions have been piecemeal and inadequate and usually the result of protest by civil rights agencies on behalf of Negro workers. The national AFL-CIO has repeatedly refused to take action on its own initiative."[10]

As late as August 1963, George Meany had refused to give the AFL-CIO's endorsement to the historic March on Washington at which Martin Luther King, Jr., delivered his famous "I Have a Dream" speech.

Unions Undermine the EEOC

Civil rights leaders recognized that after the passage of the 1964 Civil Rights Act the next major battles would involve finding realistic avenues of enforcement.[11] Already in 1964, before the new civil rights laws had even been approved, King wrote prophetically of what lay ahead: "When the legislation becomes law, its vitality and power will depend as much on its implementation as on the strength of its declaration. Legislative enactments, like court decisions, declare rights, but do not automatically deliver them. Ultimately, executive action determines what force and effect legislation will have."[12] King noted the bitter history of how civil rights laws were consistently circumvented while unpopular laws affecting the whole population, such as the military draft or the income tax, managed to work.[13]

The work of the newly formed EEOC was handicapped before it ever heard its first complaint in July 1965. The EEOC had been given an entire year to set up operations, but Lyndon Johnson made no moves even to appoint a chairperson until just two months before it was to start its work. In July, it had only a skeletal organizational structure and no operational procedures in place. From the very beginning it faced acute staffing shortages, including vacancies in major policymaking slots, and an inadequate budget as congressional opponents used the appropriations process as a second chance to restrict its full effectiveness.[14]

Working with limited resources, the EEOC decided to prioritize complaints of racial discrimination against private employers. From the outset it adopted a bias toward handling individual complaints of discrimination, even though it recognized that proceeding on a case-by-case basis would never eliminate job discrimination. As late as 1970, a study done by the U.S. Civil Rights Commission found that even though many complaints involved more than a single instance of discrimination against an individual, the commission's investigations generally were not directed to uncovering instances of class or institutional discrimination.[15]

Like that of its state-level predecessors, much of the EEOC's work was aimed at achieving voluntary compliance. The commission's conciliation procedures were designed to absorb the power of complainants to go to court. If conciliation was successful, complainants were asked to waive their rights to a court hearing. Yet, the EEOC was able to solve relatively few cases through its own mediating efforts. The Department of Justice had the sole power to initiate lawsuits in cases where the EEOC's efforts at conciliation were unsuccessful. The threat of a potential lawsuit was supposed to force defendants to settle complaints against them that were brought to the EEOC. In the first year and a half, however, the U.S. attorney general clearly did not pursue vigorous enforcement. At the end of 1967 the Justice Department had filed only ten suits, of which five had been referred by the EEOC.

Almost from the moment it began operations, the EEOC was deluged with complaints. Within its first year, the EEOC received four times the number of complaints that had been estimated during the congressional hearings.[16] A total of 1,383 such complaints were filed in its first hundred days, of which almost 70 percent came from eleven southern states. Seventy-three percent of these early complaints involved racial discrimination, two-thirds of which came from black workers. Seventy-seven percent (844) of the cases filed were against employers, 20 percent (197) against unions, and 3 percent (33) against state employment offices.[17] In 1967 the commission received a total of 8,512 cases, an average of twenty-three per day.[18] The unanticipated high volume of complaints, coupled with underfunding and staff shortages, quickly led to a severe backlog of EEOC cases. By the end of 1972, only half of the 80,000 cases the EEOC had recommended for action had even been investigated.[19]

The high volume of complaints was testimony to the backlog of long-standing grievances and the systematic efforts of the NAACP and local civil rights organizations in seeking out complainants and assisting them in bringing their cases to the EEOC. The NAACP filed its first complaints the day the EEOC went into operation in July 1965. Two months later, it filed another 214 complaints on behalf of workers from fourteen different states. All of the complaints filed against unions charged them with entering into contract agreements that required discriminatory separate seniority lines.[20]

Even before the EEOC officially began accepting complaints, the AFL-CIO sought to work out an accommodation based on its understanding of the congressional compromise protecting existing seniority rights. Labor leaders sought an agreement that the EEOC would not assert any jurisdiction over seniority issues. In May 1965, representatives of the AFL-CIO met with the EEOC to insist "that the commission refrain from acting affirmatively on complaints filed by Negro workers involving discriminatory job classifications and seniority provisions."[21] In response, the commission initiated an investigation of the seniority problem in order to determine what position, if any, it ought to take on this issue. The investigation concluded "that most seniority arrangements locked blacks into segregated job departments and were therefore unlawful under the statute." Armed with these conclusions, the commission increasingly decided to support the view that black workers were entitled to seniority credits where discrimination had been practiced in the past.[22]

The AFL-CIO also wanted the EEOC to continue the practice of informal complaint processing that had existed under many of the earlier state commissions. The unions were particularly interested in avoiding court cases. The EEOC was not willing to make exceptions of this kind. The commission did offer to submit copies of all complaints that were filed against the unions to the civil rights department of the AFL-CIO, "so that your department may assist in bringing about an early solution."[23]

Even the UAW hoped to continue resolving most complaints through its own grievance procedures, which were designed to handle disputes with management and to enforce existing contracts. In many cases these very contracts would prove to be the main obstacle to a resolution of racially discriminatory practices. Yet, the unions were dedicated to maintaining the integrity of these contracts, which their members had often won through much sacrifice. In rewriting its union bylaws to conform to Title VII, the UAW sought to require its members to "to use the contract grievance machinery before filing a complaint under VII."[24] The union argued that this was required by both its own Constitution and its collective bargaining agreements. This meant that black UAW members were expected to go through a protracted grievance procedure before they could ever approach the EEOC for outside assistance. However, commissioners refused to delay decisions on union cases pending before the EEOC while the identical complaint was processed through the union. The commission contended that it had a legal obligation to proceed posthaste in implementing the law and reaching a resolution of a pending EEOC compliant, notwithstanding the fact that the subject matter of the EEOC complaint was pending in the union's grievance machinery.[25] It was not until 1969, four years after Title VII went into effect, that the UAW formally changed its bylaws to "afford to UAW members the exercise of their public rights under Title VII."[26] Even then, it conceded only that the grievance procedure often took so long that workers missed the ninety-day deadline for filing a complaint with the EEOC.

The UAW also sought an informal arrangement with the NAACP whereby it would be allowed the opportunity to resolve any complaints before formal charges were filed with the EEOC.[27] The NAACP turned down the request based upon earlier experiences in which the UAW failed to respond to complaints of discrimination.[28] When the union's civil rights staff proposed that the UAW work out a relationship with state fair employment commissions to handle complaints under Title VII, the chairman of its civil rights department thought it was unnecessary "to waste time meeting with state agencies to work out agreements in view of the fact that we have so few complaints on fair employment practices in plants under our jurisdiction. I believe we can handle each case on an ad hoc basis without the necessity of formal agreements with anyone."[29] In the year and a half just prior to the start of the EEOC, the UAW's own internal Fair Practices Department had received only fifty complaints of discrimination.[30]

Unprepared for the volume of complaints filed against them, the unions responded by making token efforts. As Herbert Hill expressed it, "At best there has been a minimal, strategic accommodation to the requirements of anti-discrimination laws and federal executive orders but this is often less than tokenism. The racist practices remain intact."[31] The unions refused to accept the majority of the EEOC's compliance recommendations. This was particularly true after the EEOC adopted the principle that remedies had to go beyond providing relief to the individual who had filed the complaint. Remedies now were expected to eliminate the cause of the unlawful conditions. For example, in cases involving craft union exclusion, the EEOC began to require that unions take pro-active steps to seek out potential black members who had heretofore been excluded from joining the union. This stood in sharp contrast to many of the state fair employment commissions, which had often settled a complaint without getting a job for the person who filed it, let alone seeking class-wide solutions.

In a study of union compliance with the EEOC, Benjamin Wolkison found that of the eighty-one cases he examined, the commission was able to reach agreement with the offending union in only nineteen of them. In seven of the eight cases involving union exclusion where the EEOC sought to implement some form of an affirmative action plan, the unions rejected the EEOC's proposed settlement and the racial exclusion continued. The EEOC was unsuccessful in all eight cases where a union had excluded a black worker from an apprenticeship program. They also failed to reach agreements in all five cases where blacks had been excluded from the union hiring hall.[32]

The EEOC met with only limited success in seniority cases where it sought either joint employer–union agreements to restructure the seniority system or direct employer action to promote minority job advancement. It won agreement in only three cases involving segregated lines of progression, and even these were limited victories in that they did not allow black workers to advance into better jobs on the basis of their plantwide seniority. In some cases, new admissions tests to get into craft positions were established after 1964 where none had previously existed. In all five cases involving dual seniority rosters, the commission's efforts were completely defeated.[33] The majority of those cases where agreement was reached did not contain certain measures that the EEOC considered essential to providing adequate relief to the injured party.[34] Wolkison concludes that the "major factor underlying a local union's resistance to the commission's settlement is the high cost it may impose on the union's membership. Discriminatory practices are not just due to prejudice but are rooted in economic considerations. The exclusion of black workers from membership and referral will result in greater numbers of job opportunities for whites. Discriminatory seniority protects young white workers in competition for jobs with minority workers with greater seniority."[35] He goes on to say that the "problem with the commission's remedial process is its powerlessness to impose equal or greater costs upon management and the unions who reject agreements. The threat of litigation was more theoretical than real. . . . In summary, conciliation functioned in an economic and political environment wherein costs to respondents for settling were high, while the probable costs of rejecting were low."[36]

The Courts Push beyond the Congressional Compromise

The inability of the EEOC's conciliation process to resolve many of the more grievous cases of employment discrimination and the unwillingness of the Justice Department to use its legal powers resulted in a flood of private lawsuits. From 1965 to 1971, the number of private discrimination suits outstripped those few filed by the Department of Justice by a ratio of twenty-five to one.[37] The vast majority of these suits were brought to the federal courts with the help of the NAACP Legal Defense Fund and various other civil rights organizations working on behalf of aggrieved workers. These cases led to important breakthroughs in the development of broad group remedies, making the courts the unexpected vehicle for the expansion of Title VII.

As the courts began to rule on cases brought before them, they interpreted the voluminous record of congressional debate on Title VII to mean that Congress had never intended to freeze an entire generation of minority employees into discriminatory employment patterns such as had existed prior to the Act. In their decisions, several judges wrote that a study of the legislative history of Title VII provided no guidance because the lengthy congressional debate confirmed every point of view. The courts' decisions increasingly ran counter to the legislative compromise with the AFL-CIO designed to protect the job status of its current members.

The courts built upon the long history of judicial precedent established in the school desegregation cases. Beginning in the 1940s with the line of cases leading up to *Brown v. Board of Education of Topeka*, the courts had developed an expanded view of the state action concept under the Fourteenth Amendment. Previously the courts had chosen to interpret the amendment's prohibition against discrimination by the states very narrowly to mean only public agencies themselves. Then, in a series of cases brought by the NAACP during the 1940s, the courts began to accept a broader interpretation of state action, recognizing that a state agency can confer its power to a private sovereignty, in which case the private party must adhere to the prohibitions against discrimination as well. For example, in *Steele v. Louisville and Nashville Railroad* the Supreme Court decided that because the railroad unions had been granted exclusive bargaining rights over railway employees by the Railway Labor Act, these unions had the obligation of fairly representing all employees without discrimination.[38]

During the late 1960s and early 1970s the courts began to mandate sweeping remedies. In the 1971 *Griggs v. Duke Power Company* case the Supreme Court went beyond earlier school desegregation cases, which had insisted on a finding of de jure or intentional discrimination. Now the court ruled that any employment practice that operated to exclude blacks and other minorities and could not be shown to be related to job performance was prohibited.[39] The *Griggs* decision placed the burden on employers to prove that their hiring and promotion policies were not discriminatory. The courts' earlier experience with the *Brown* decision had shown that the lack of specificity in their decisions invited an evasion of the law. With this lesson in mind, the federal courts began to move toward a much more precise definition of the types of affirmative action needed to relieve employment discrimination in a much shorter period of time, using the remedial provisions of Title VII as their legal basis.[40]

As more employment discrimination cases were brought to the courts, it became accepted judicial doctrine that Title VII did not require any showing that a person had been intentionally discriminated against. Lawsuits were being won simply by proving that the effect of a practice was adverse to minorities. In exchange, the courts imposed only limited punitive damages in cases where discrimination was proven on more technical grounds. Civil rights lawyers revived old post–Civil War statutes that allowed for awarding larger punitive damages in cases where it was possible to prove intentional discrimination. The legal community began to make widespread use of Section 1981 of the 1866 Civil Rights Act, which guaranteed racial minorities the same contractual rights as whites. The courts accepted employment as a type of contract and agreed that discriminatory employment practices, including the failure to hire, and discriminatory conditions of employment fell within the meaning of Section 1981. Using this provision, the courts began to award plaintiffs punitive damages, which they could not receive under Title VII.[41] The Supreme Court agreed with this application of Section 1981, concluding that "Congress clearly has retained Section 1981 as a remedy against private employment discrimination separate and independent of the more elaborate and time consuming procedures of Title VII."[42]

Between 1966 and 1972 the federal courts firmly established the use of affirmative action as a necessary remedy. The courts embraced the use of hiring quotas because (1) they were seen as an attempt to compensate for past discrimination, (2) they made it less likely that defendants would discriminate in the future, and (3) they were necessary to expunge a company's and a union's discriminatory reputation from the minds of minorities or women who otherwise would be reluctant to seek employment there. In *Quarles v. Philip Morris* the court ruled that the present consequences of past discrimination did fall within the meaning of Title VII. In this case the court decided that a departmental seniority system that prevented blacks who were confined to lower-paid departments from moving into the better-paid jobs could not be considered a "bona fide" seniority system and therefore did not qualify for exemption under Section 703(h) from Title VII's general prohibition against employment discrimination. In its opinion, the district court wrote, "Obviously one characteristic of a bona fide seniority system must be lack of discrimination. Nothing in Section 703(h), or its legislative history, suggests that a racially discriminatory seniority system established before the Act is a bona fide seniority system under the Act."[43] The courts' decisions in these cases were far more concerned with eliminating discriminatory employment practices than with the possibility of "preferential treatment."[44]

From the very beginning the federal courts went to the underlying principles of the Act. The courts repeatedly found that in order to fashion adequate remedies, Section 703(h) notwithstanding, it was necessary to confront the present effects of past discrimination. There was almost a decade of innovative case law in which the courts ordered extensive remedies that required changes in traditional union seniority practices. . . . For the first time, the federal courts began to define the broad social nature of discrimination; they began to understand that racial discrimination in employment was not the result of individual random acts of bigotry, but rather the consequences of systemic institutionalized patterns.[45]

These court decisions had a powerful effect on hiring practices. They moved the scope of corrective action considerably beyond what had been anticipated by the supporters of Title VII during the congressional debates. What had been seen as a bill with limited consequences outside the South was resulting in dramatic changes in employment practices throughout the country. Organized labor adamantly opposed any further restructuring of traditional labor practices, regardless of their discriminatory effects on minority workers. The unions pressed for a return to a narrower interpretation of Title VII to prevent the application of the law to problems of discrimination in seniority and job promotion. As William Gould summarizes,

> The unions, walking lockstep with their employer counterparts, dug in their heels to litigate against any revision of systematic practices which carried forward the effects of past discrimination. . . . Most of the resulting cases involved employment relationships where minorities have been either excluded altogether or consigned to relatively undesirable low-paying work because the effect of the contractual seniority provision or apprenticeship program was to retard or block the integration of the work force. And, in practically every case, hard-earned union dues were wasted in a defendant's defeat.[46]

As the use of affirmative action grew, so did the number of union challenges. According to Nijole Benokratis and Joseph Feagin, when "compared with the generally passive stance of business and industry, unions appear to be more active in discouraging or more sluggish in encouraging the employment of women and minorities."[47] The craft unions remained especially resistant to all efforts at affirmative action, maintaining that the solution was to get minorities "to help themselves."

In some cases, the unions challenged affirmative action plans after they had been agreed to by the company. In 1973 the American Telephone and

Telegraph Company (AT&T) agreed to a consent decree that revised its promotion and job transfer practices, changed its testing procedures, and paid $38 million in back pay and other wage adjustments, a figure that was later increased to $80 million.[48] After the original consent decree was further modified in 1975, it was challenged in court by the three AFL-CIO unions representing AT&T's employees. In August 1976, a federal judge rejected the unions' arguments and held that the consent decree was an acceptable remedy under Title VII, the union contract notwithstanding. The three unions had delayed the implementation of the decree for more than a year.

In another case, *Jersey Central Power and Light Co. v. IBEW Local 327*, the union was able to destroy an affirmative action plan agreed to by the company. The company had accepted an EEOC conciliation agreement in which it would reduce its workforce by 10 percent without causing undue harm to newly hired women and minorities. The union went to court and succeeded in reversing the agreement. The court ruled in favor of maintaining the traditional seniority system in which the last hired were the first fired. This inevitably resulted in large numbers of recently hired women and minorities losing their jobs.[49]

Unions Oppose Strengthening the EEOC

Labor's active opposition to affirmative action led to a deepening rift between organized labor and the black community. On the defensive, the unions accused blacks of being "anti-union." Responding to charges of anti-unionism made by the Jewish Labor Committee, Roy Wilkins, executive director of the NAACP, contended that the whole concept of the black–labor coalition was worthless if such a coalition meant a gentlemen's agreement to refrain from attacking racial discrimination within the labor unions:[50] "We reject the proposition that any segment of the labor movement is sacrosanct in matters of practices and/or policies which restrict employment opportunities. . . .We reject the contention that bringing such charges constitutes a move to destroy 'unity' among civil rights groups unless it be admitted that this unity is a precarious thing, perched upon a unilateral definition of discrimination by each member group."[51]

In 1967, the Leadership Conference on Civil Rights persuaded the Johnson administration to strengthen the EEOC's administrative powers to halt discrimination by including a cease-and-desist provision in its new civil rights bill prohibiting housing discrimination. The bill contained cease-and-desist powers and also strengthened the right of private parties to bring suits. Initially the AFL-CIO endorsed the cease-and-desist amendment, but then "suddenly reversed itself because they didn't feel that the right of the aggrieved individual to bring suit in court against management and labor ought to be continued if the EEOC was to get authority to issue cease and desist orders. Their position was 'either but not both.'"[52] The measures were defeated.

Two years later, during Richard Nixon's first year in office, the Leadership Conference tried again. This time the AFL-CIO was willing to accept both the cease-and-desist provision and the individual right to sue, but in exchange it wanted to consolidate into the EEOC the functions of the Office of Federal Contract Compliance (OFCC), the responsibility for "pattern and practice" suits held by the Justice Department, and jurisdiction over equal employment cases held by the National Labor Relations Board. The AFL-CIO argued that such a merger would free it "from overlapping harassment of different agencies because everything would be in one place, the EEOC."[53] Its goal was to weaken the effectiveness of the OFCC, which recently had issued strict numerical goals and timetables for minority hiring on federally funded construction projects. The AFL-CIO was supported by the National Association of Manufacturers, leading James Mooney, the EEOC's legal counsel, to comment, "The AFL-CIO in its antagonism to federal contract compliance has cooperated with and gotten support from reactionary members of Congress and big defense industrial contractors who are also opposed to contract compliance efforts."[54] This time the Nixon administration opposed granting cease-and-desist powers to the EEOC. The Labor Department and "some of the civil rights people" opposed the transfer of the OFCC because they felt it ought to "be kept where it is so that there are two strings to the civil rights bow."[55] Furthermore, opponents of the transfer noted that the Philadelphia Plan, an innovative affirmative action plan for the building trades, which was "more imaginative than anything that has come out of the EEOC," had been developed by the OFCC officials inside the Department of Labor.[56] Again, nothing was passed.

In 1971 the Leadership Conference made a third attempt to win cease-and-desist powers for the EEOC. Once again, the Nixon administration flatly refused to lend its support, arguing that everything should be handled through EEOC-initiated lawsuits. The AFL-CIO continued to demand the transfer of the OFCC to the EEOC as the price of its support for cease-and-desist powers. The result of this continued stalemate was a legislative compromise in which the EEOC was granted the right to sue in court, but not cease-and-desist powers. Title VII coverage was significantly expanded to include state and local public employees, and a number of other improvements were made in the statute, while the OFCC was left within the Department of Labor.[57]

As a result of the 1972 amendments, the Department of Justice almost completely phased out its participation in litigating private-sector suits. Yet, because of its overwhelming backlog of cases, the EEOC was unable to take the majority of its meritorious cases to court, which meant that the burden of Title VII enforcement continued to fall on private parties. "Ninety-three percent of the litigation under Title VII after 1972 was initiated and conducted by the private bar on behalf of charging parties, and these were the major cases that brought significant relief to large numbers of workers."[58]

The Backlash Triumphs

Organized labor's strident opposition to a broad interpretation of equal employment merged with a larger white reaction to civil rights to transform the American political landscape. The once-solid Democratic South has become a Republican stronghold. Beginning in 1968 white voters increasingly supported Republican candidates in presidential elections. Nixon began the construction of a new political coalition by capitalizing on the breakup of the Democrats' New Deal coalition triggered by the "Negro socioeconomic revolution and the liberal Democrat's ideological inability to cope with it."[59] One-third of white voters switched parties in the 1968 elections. The vote was sharply divided along racial lines, with 97 percent of blacks voting for

Democratic candidate Hubert Humphrey, compared to only 35 percent of whites.[60]

In 1968, the AFL-CIO endorsed the Democratic candidate, as had been its practice since the days of Franklin D. Roosevelt. When reformers took control of the party's organizational apparatus following its 1968 defeat, the AFL-CIO openly rejected the changes in the delegate selection process, arguing that "we don't think that an election machinery that has given the nation a Roosevelt, a Stevenson, a Kennedy, and a Humphrey is so bad that it needs overhauling."[61] Driven out of power in the Democratic Party, alienated by the party's close identification with minorities and women and its growing anti-war stance, organized labor made overtures to the Republicans. When George McGovern became the Democratic presidential candidate in 1972, labor took the unprecedented step of remaining officially neutral in the general election, clearing the way for a number of the skilled trades unions to work openly for Nixon's reelection.

In the face of what appeared to be striking losses in job opportunities for whites, the issue of "reverse discrimination" emerged as the centerpiece of the conservative attack on the Democratic Party's policy agenda. Organized labor found itself aligned with the same conservative southerners who had first raised that banner during the 1964 congressional hearings. The impetus behind vigorous civil rights enforcement was receding. New reverse discrimination cases received widespread attention as whites filed suit, claiming they were now the victims of discrimination. The first round of cases did not result in any major reversals of existing affirmative action programs. The Supreme Court generally upheld the use of affirmative action as a remedy for past discrimination, although it did tighten up the standards of statistical proof. The *DeFunis v. Odegaard*, case, the first of a long string of reverse discrimination cases to come before the Supreme Court, involved a special minority admissions program at a law school. The AFL-CIO joined the National Association of Manufacturers and several major Jewish organizations in filing amicus briefs against affirmative action. The case resulted in an inconclusive decision.[62] In another reverse discrimination challenge, *Weber v. Kaiser Aluminum and Chemical Corn,* the court upheld the company's voluntary affirmative action plan in its apprenticeship training program, which gave preferences to minority applicants. The court ruled that Title VII did not bar efforts to "voluntarily adopt affirmative action plans designed to eliminate conspicuous racial imbalances in traditionally segregated job categories."[63]

Successive Republican victories, culminating in the election of Ronald Reagan, finally brought organized labor the relief it had sought for so long. Support for Reagan's candidacy was most pronounced among middle-income people and blue-collar workers, with union households showing a larger swing than nonunion households. Carter's 4 percent lead over Reagan was the poorest showing among this core Democratic group of any candidate in modern times, except for McGovern in 1972.[64]

Reagan, who was avowedly anti–civil rights, adopted a two-pronged strategy for dismantling civil rights enforcement. He set out to alter the composition of the federal courts, including the Supreme Court, and to dismantle the equal employment and contract compliance regulatory machinery. In the fall of 1981, the Justice Department informed Congress that it would not urge or support in any case "the use of quotas or any other numerical or statistical formulae designed to provide to non-victims of discrimination preferential treatment based on race, sex, national origin or religion" despite their earlier endorsement by the courts.[65] Memos to that effect were sent to the EEOC and the heads of all other federal agencies. As Norman Amaker notes, "The net effect of these statements was verbal repudiation of the legal principles that had evolved over the four decades since President Roosevelt's first executive order. The touchstone of the principles has been affirmative action measures that, whether undertaken by court order or voluntarily, include members of the victimized classes protected by law as well as individuals capable of being identified in particular instances."[66]

Taking its cues from the Justice Department, the EEOC came out in opposition to the use of goals, timetables, and quotas for minorities in the workforce, because of their reliance on "statistical measurement." These statements ran completely counter to the accepted standards for measuring racial disparity as set by the Supreme Court in its *Griggs* decision. In early 1986, the EEOC announced it was abandoning affirmative action hiring goals and timetables in its settlements with private employers. After the Supreme Court upheld their use in July of that same year, Clarence Thomas, then chairperson of the EEOC, reluctantly agreed to drop his opposition because "the Court has ruled. . . . That's the law of the land, whether I like it or not."[67]

Reflecting Reagan's policy of only pursuing the claims of identifiable victims, the EEOC showed a sharp decline in the number of "pattern and practice" lawsuits it initiated. By 1992, systemic cases constituted a mere 8.6 percent of cases filed by the agency.[68] This came at a time when few private attorneys possessed the resources needed to take on a class action suit because of the high costs of preparing such cases. In 1983 the EEOC settled a major lawsuit against General Motors, heralded as the largest of its kind in history, that did not include back pay to members of the injured classes—made up of minorities and women—even though back pay is a remedy specifically mentioned in Title VII whenever a court ordered relief after a finding of discrimination.[69]

The conservative assault on the judiciary bore fruit in 1989 when the appointment of Anthony Kennedy to the Supreme Court finally gave the conservative wing an effective majority. With this ideological shift, the court began to issue a series of rulings that significantly narrowed the scope of future anti-discrimination lawsuits as well as the use of affirmative action as a remedy for past discrimination. Five major cases placed new restrictions on the ability to initiate employment discrimination lawsuits, requiring proof of the existence of actual discriminatory practices while restricting the scope of punitive damages allowed under Section 1981 of the 1866 Civil Rights Act.

In *Wards Cove Packing Co. v. Antonio* the Supreme Court ruled 5–4 that Alaskan natives and Asian-Americans in low-paying jobs at salmon canneries could not prove discrimination with statistical evidence. The decision shifted the burden of proof from the employer (where it had been for eighteen years) to the worker filing the complaint, thereby making discrimination extremely difficult to prove.[70] In *Price Waterhouse v. Hopkins* the court ruled that even if a complainant proves that the employer discriminated, if that employer would have made the same business decision anyway, then a court would not find that the employer had engaged in intentional discrimination. In *Martin v. Wilks* it ruled that white men who think they have been hurt by court-approved affirmative action plans may wage legal challenges years afterward if they were not involved in the original suit, opening the door to the perpetual challenge of consent decrees.[71] In *Lorance v. AT&T Technologies* the court decided that three women had waited too long to file sex discrimination suits against Montgomery Ward. This meant that in many cases, people laid off under an illegal seniority system could not challenge it, even though they had no way of knowing at the time the system was put in place that it would discriminate against them. In *Patterson v. McLean Credit Union,* the court upheld a 1976 law that limited the reach of the law used against discrimination by private individuals and businesses.[72]

These decisions gave aid and comfort to white men who felt they had suffered as a result of government efforts to correct past wrongs against women and minorities, but they had an immediate negative effect on legal challenges of employment discrimination. In the following year and a half, more than fifty cases of employment discrimination were adversely affected in the Chicago area alone. Countless other charges that would have been filed in the past were never pursued because of the new restrictions.[73] The decisions had a chilling effect on the whole labor market, providing employers and unions with the clear signal that affirmative action was no longer necessary.

The most damaging effects of these five cases were later overturned by the 1991 Civil Rights Act, which reaffirmed that employers bear the burden of proof, prohibited future challenges of consent decrees, and extended the statute of limitations on challenges to seniority systems from 180 to 540 days. The Act also provided punitive damages in all cases of unlawful employment practices, including sexual harassment. In a concession to critics of affirmative action, the bill prohibited the use of explicit quotas and outlawed the race-norming of test scores.[74] Although President George Bush vetoed the legislation, it was reintroduced the following year and passed over his veto.

There is no doubt that the countless equal employment lawsuits and affirmative action programs led to noticeable improvements in job opportunities for minorities and women. They have been most successful in expanding job opportunities for middle-class minorities, who have found new opportunities in the expanding white-collar sectors of the economy that are not controlled by the unions. By the end of the 1970s, "minorities and women had greater employment in higher paid jobs, where they had traditionally been underrepresented, than at the beginning."[75] Major increases had occurred in the higher paid white-collar jobs (managers, professionals, technicians, and sales workers) and, for male minorities, in the skilled crafts.[76] The public sector has been the largest employer of professional minorities.

Organized labor's protracted opposition to expanded minority job opportunities restricted access to an important rung of the economic ladder at the very time that increasing numbers of blacks were moving into those occupations. Unionized employment represented an important source of good-paying jobs for non-college-educated workers. The unions' reluctance to alter contract provisions covering seniority and promotions has had a particularly negative effect on young black males. Obviously other factors, such as corporate decisions to leave the urban centers and the poor quality of public education, have also affected the job prospects of young blacks. Had unions been more willing to make changes in seniority structures, however, it would certainly have eased the hardships caused by the loss of manufacturing jobs for blacks, who were the newest entrants into many of these industries and therefore the first to lose their jobs when the lay-offs hit. The continuation of racial barriers in employment has also weakened the potential gains from any improvements in education or job training.

5 | THE STRUGGLE OVER ACCESS TO CHICAGO'S BUILDING TRADES

The construction industry's importance to central city labor markets, its high percentage of good-paying jobs, and the fact that it is heavily financed by public funds have long made it a focal point of national efforts on the part of minorities and women seeking to advance their economic status. Chicago has been one of the national centers of this battle. With the departure of manufacturing employment from the city, construction is one of the last remaining sources of good-paying jobs that does not require a college degree. Yet, despite decades of court-ordered consent decrees and minority outreach programs, the city's building trades remain a predominantly white male domain. In a metropolitan region where African-Americans comprise 20 percent of the population, they hold only 9 percent of the jobs in the largest trades, including carpenters, electricians, plumbers, and painters.[1] The small number of minorities and women currently enrolled in apprenticeship classes suggests that those numbers will improve little in the near future.

The construction industry is a vital sector of the American economy, with new housing starts generally accepted as an indicator of overall economic health. In 1992, new construction was a $400 billion industry in the United States, employing 3.7 million people or about 3 percent of the labor force.[2] It is a highly competitive business, characterized by countless small, family-owned firms with low profit margins and high failure rates. Very few survive beyond one generation. It has a strong ethnic component, with Italian contractors doing business with other Italians, Irish with Irish, and so on. To be successful a contractor must become adept at playing the old-fashioned game of politics, because every project is dependent on obtaining the necessary building permits and many larger ones are financed by public dollars. Both employers and the unions jealously guard entrance into the industry, believing that their own survival is contingent on their ability to exclude all potential competitors. This has made them particularly resistant to any expansion of opportunities for minorities and women.

The unions have responded to pressures to open up their ranks by making the minimal concessions necessary to comply with various government equal employment regulations. At the same time, they have erected a variety of new educational and geographic barriers that, although not overtly discriminatory, make it difficult for all but a trickle of minority and women applicants to gain entrance into their ranks. While the unions continue to admit members' relatives and close friends into apprenticeship training programs through informal referral systems, minorities and women who lack those connections must meet rigid educational requirements to gain admittance. Until recently, the inner-city school systems, including Chicago's, often had minimal math and science requirements, so it is not surprising that many young blacks and Latinos cannot pass the rigorous entrance exams, and those that can have been tracked for college admissions.

Chicago's Building Trades Lock Out Minorities

Well into the 1960s, Chicago's labor market was still completely segregated, the result of long-standing customs rather than legal mandates. Newspapers carried job listings designated "for whites only."[3] Some firms had no black employees, claiming that blacks never applied. Usually, such companies had established a reputation for not hiring blacks, which led others to stay away. Other firms hired primarily through referrals from friends and relatives of current employees, all of whom were white. Consequently, they too had no black employees. Most employers knew that by placing job ads in certain neighborhood newspapers they could determine the racial composition of their applicant pool. By carefully juggling the allocation of advertising to various papers, an employer could develop a fairly precise racial mixture in the applicant flow, since the likelihood of blacks responding to an ad in an all-white neighborhood newspaper was very slim. Neighborhood papers were known to send promotional material to companies stressing the ethnic characteristics of the neighborhoods in which their readership was concentrated: 40 percent German stock, 20 percent Irish stock, and so on.[4]

Racial employment barriers prevented even well-educated blacks from moving into professional jobs open to whites with the same level of training. African-Americans with advanced degrees could be found working as teachers in Chicago's black high schools or as clerks at the post office. Nonwhite income as a percentage of white income actually tended to decline as education increased.[5] Such restrictions in employment opportunities left the city's black communities impoverished. All of its ten poorest neighborhoods in 1966 were black, with a median family income of only $4,810, compared to $8,100 for the city as a whole. Even though the years 1960–66 were characterized by healthy economic growth, the average black family's purchasing power increased only 5 percent, compared with 16 percent for the metropolitan area as a whole.[6]

Chicago's unions, like those elsewhere, generally gave their blessings to this system of racial stratification. A few unions, especially those with historic ties to the Communist Party, had strong records of fighting discriminatory company policies and promoting blacks into leadership positions within their ranks. The Amalgamated Meatcutters Union was one such trailblazer, eradicating racial discrimination within its plants and within the union itself ten years before most other unions took similar steps. Its Chicago director, Charlie Hayes, led the union in becoming the first in the area to support Martin Luther King, Jr., raising $11,000 from its own members on behalf of the Montgomery Bus Boycott.[7] Hayes went on to succeed Harold Washington, Chicago's first black mayor, as congressman from the First Congressional District on the city's Southside. Most other unions, however, resisted any powersharing with their black members. In the summer of 1968 a group of dissatisfied black Chicago Transit Authority employees went on strike, complaining that while blacks made up 81 percent of the drivers, they lacked adequate representation in the union's upper ranks because 3,500 pensioners were allowed to vote in union elections.[8] That summer, black steelworkers were also protesting at their union's national convention, pointing out that while blacks constituted a quarter of the union's 1.2 million members, there was not a single black district director or union vice president.[9]

A hundred years earlier, Chicago had been a hotbed of working-class radicalism. Once the unions won the right to collective bargaining in 1936, however, they were incorporated into the city's power structure. By 1955, the year Richard J. Daley was first elected mayor, the unions had become an integral part of Chicago's political machine, whose control over city, county, state, and even national politics was legendary. For decades, labor routinely pledged its loyalty to the Cook County Democratic Party Central Committee's hand-picked candidates. In exchange for a pledge to avoid all strikes, labor was rewarded with contracts guaranteeing high wages and generous benefits. Although municipal workers, the backbone of the machine's patronage army, were not unionized, a high percentage of the remaining workforce was, including teachers, bus drivers, steelworkers, autoworkers, and packinghouse workers.

Naturally, being in a union town, Chicago's skilled trades were well organized, maintaining monopoly control over the crews on construction projects of any significance throughout the city. Tight control over access to jobs has resulted in very attractive wage rates. In 1994 the average hourly pay for a construction worker in Illinois stood at $19.83, compared to $12.24 for an industrial worker and $8.43 for a bank employee.[10] The city enforced an antiquated building code that increased the complexity of every building project, but also guaranteed the unions additional work while driving up construction costs in the city.

A Structure of Racial Exclusion

The unions' control of the construction market rested on a very clear-cut policy of racial exclusion. This policy was carried out in several distinct but interrelated forms, which together constituted a nearly impervious barrier to entry. For generations, entrance into the skilled trades was handed down through families, much like an inheritance. To this day, the majority of white males enter the skilled trades through referrals made by friends and relatives. The craft unions have long rationalized nepotism as the trade union equivalent of a son inheriting a father's property, being brought along in a business by his father, or entering a law partnership with his father. However, the courts have ruled against these union practices, concluding that "nepotism as a trade union policy is unhealthy, for while the rich may leave an inheritance for their children, the worker may not bequeath job seniority, for that will take a job from another who has no union 'father.'"[11] The Fifth Circuit Court of Appeals ruled that nepotism was more pernicious than a seniority system that reflects past discrimination, since the latter merely slows down the pace of progress while the former makes the status of exclusion permanent. Where the workforce is all or predominantly white, nepotism must be struck down if blacks are to have job access.[12]

The majority of white males who secured a job through family sponsorship received their training on the job, rather than in a formal apprenticeship curriculum. However, most of the mechanical tradesmen, such as electricians, did go through formal training. Apprenticeship programs produce an elite core within the construction industry who will eventually advance to become foremen and supervisors. In Chicago, formal training was available at Washburne Trade School, a postsecondary trade apprenticeship school operated by the Chicago Board of Education, where the unions had complete control over admissions and curriculum. Traditionally, someone gained admission to Washburne only after he had secured a job with a contractor, which, of course, could only be obtained through family connections. Already during the 1940s African-Americans had protested their complete exclusion from Washburne. In response, the Chicago Board of Education established a separate black trade school that offered courses in low-paying trades such as shoemaking, millinery, tailoring, and dressmaking, while omitting all of the high-paying building trades.[13]

Chicago's unions have been unrelenting in their enforcement the Davis-Bacon Act, a law requiring federal contractors to pay the local "prevailing wage." The prevailing wage is almost universally determined to be the same as the union wage of the region. The Act was passed by Congress in 1931, after Congressman Robert Bacon from New York became irate when an Alabama contractor building a hospital on Long Island imported black nonunion labor from the South. The enforcement of Davis-Bacon reduced the number of jobs in the industry, while keeping wages artificially high. Although this appears to be a race-neutral concession to organized labor, it effectively excludes minorities who are not union members from working on any federally funded projects. The law's strict enforcement often forces minority contractors, who are most inclined to hire minority workers, to instead hire white tradesmen through the union hiring hall. One minority contractor was actually driven into bankruptcy after

the Chicago Housing Authority refused to pay him for work he had completed because he had used a nonunion truck driver who lived in the
neighborhood. Davis-Bacon is a clear example of how the federal government's protection of organized labor actually strengthened discrimination in the construction industry. Even though the federal government has
spent millions of dollars enforcing contract compliance and supporting
minority outreach programs, its efforts are counteracted by the insidious
impact of Davis-Bacon.[14]

The discriminatory impact of Davis-Bacon has spawned an unusual
coalition between political conservatives and minority contractors interested in challenging the law. In 1993 a lawsuit was filed by the Institute for Justice (a conservative think tank), eight minority contractors,
and the Resident Management Corporation of the Kenilworth/Park-
side public housing project in Washington, D.C. The plaintiffs contested the legality of Davis-Bacon on the grounds that its implementation is racially discriminatory and unconstitutional.[15] Committees in
both the House and the Senate have approved bills to overturn it, yet
congressional Democrats, protecting their allies in organized labor,
have vowed to oppose any repeal.

In 1969, five years after the enactment of Title VII, African-
Americans and Latinos still made up only 2.7 percent of Chicago's
building trades membership, even though they comprised 34 percent of
the city's adult population. When apprentices were added, the minority
percentage increased to only 3.3 percent. As indicated in Table 2, in
most unions minorities constituted less than 1 percent of the membership, and minority membership was above 10 percent in only two unions.
The glaziers and architectural ironworkers had only one minority member each, while 20 percent of the cement masons and 12.5 percent of the
plasterers were minorities. Not surprisingly, the two unions with the
largest percentage of black members were among the lowest paid and did
some of the dirtiest work.[16] According to the Equal Employment
Opportunities Commission (EEOC), "almost three of every four Negroes in the building trades were members of the Laborers Union," which
handled the backbreaking work of hauling supplies and cleaning up the
site.[17] Of the small number of blacks in Chicago who were union
tradesmen, many were recent immigrants from the South, where entry

Table 2   Union Membership in Chicago by Trade, 1969

	Journeymen	Minorities	%Minority
Architectural ironworkers	907	1	0.1
Asbestos workers	800	3	0.4
Bricklayers	4,400	200	4.5
Carpenters	29,300	200	0.7
Cement masons	2,500	500	20.0
Electricians	7,831	300	3.8
Elevator installers	625	1	0.2
Glaziers	400	1	0.3
Metal lathers	700	0	0.0
Operating engineers	8,00	486	4.6
Ornamental ironworkers	1,000	1	0.1
Structural ironworkers	2,300	12	0.5
Painters	11,000	350	3.2
Pipe fitters	7,800	16	0.2
Plasterers	800	100	12.5
Plumbers	3,440	100	2.9
Roofers	1,070	74	6.9
Sheetmetal workers	4,668	4	0.1
Sprinkler fitters	260	0	0.0
TOTAL	87,801	2,349	

Source: Bureau of Labor Statistics, North Central Regional Office, September 10, 1969

into the trades was easier because the unions did not have the same degree of monopoly control.

Hiring Goals Are Mandated

The first efforts to break down racial barriers in Chicago's construction industry occurred in 1963, when the National Association for the Advancement of Colored People (NAACP) launched a lawsuit objecting to the lack of minority hiring in the construction of a new downtown federal building. Two years later, King made access to the construction trades one of the demands of the Chicago Freedom Movement.[18] Local activities accelerated after President Lyndon Johnson signed a new executive order on contract compliance in 1965 that provided a stronger statutory basis for demanding changes from the recalcitrant building trades. Executive Order 11246 required that federal contractors implement affirmative action at all of their facilities, not just those doing government work.[19] The Office of Federal Contract Compliance (OFCC) was set up as a permanent agency within the U.S. Department of Labor, even though placing it there created a potential conflict of interest, especially in cases involving labor unions, since the department historically sought to protect the interests of organized labor. Like the EEOC, the OFCC was woefully understaffed, with only twenty-eight full-time employees in its Washington headquarters in 1967.[20]

The executive order's far-reaching penalties had the potential to bring about sweeping changes in the American labor force. One-third of all workers were employed by companies covered by the order, including some of the largest and most prestigious firms in the country. Unfortunately, during its first two and a half years, the new agency did little, failing to issue any regulations or to cancel a single contract due to noncompliance.[21] In 1968 it finally issued a set of fairly ambiguous guidelines asking that contractors submit "written affirmative action plans," but still allowing considerable leeway in what was accepted as compliance. Contracts involving the "national interest" were exempted from the requirements, giving the government's largest contracting agency, the Department of Defense, an excuse to ignore compliance. It was not until the spring of 1968 that the OFCC sent out the first notices of disbarment from future contracts to employers. It sued only two noncomplying contractors and held only one investigative hearing against a contractor.[22] When union officials complained about new workforce manning tables designed to implement minority and female hiring goals in the construction industry, the OFCC quickly backed away from the proposals. Its inaction led Herbert Hill to assert that "the failure of federal contract compliance provides a classic example of administrative nullification of civil rights laws."[23]

The OFCC's halfhearted approach to compliance led civil rights organizations once again to turn elsewhere for relief. In 1967 the NAACP won
a major victory when the U.S. District Court in Columbus, Ohio, ruled
that the state of Ohio could not sign agreements with four contractors for
the construction of a $12.8 million building at Ohio State University be-
cause of the contractors' discriminatory hiring practices. The case, known
as *Ethridge v. Rhodes,* affirmed the use of goals and timetables to implement affirmative action in hiring. In the wake of the decision, the NAACP
called on its 1,500 branches to "take advantage of the opportunities for expanded employment opened up by this decision." Chapters were encouraged to engage in negotiations where possible, but if necessary to "initiate
programs that could halt an estimated $76.5 billion in federal and state
construction in the next fiscal year."[24]

The widespread boycotts and pickets of construction sites that followed
became so disruptive that in 1969 the newly elected Richard Nixon decided to impose stronger sanctions on the industry at the very time that
his administration was backing away from civil rights enforcement
throughout the South. Responding to the immediate threat of a shutdown
of several major federal construction projects in Philadelphia, the OFCC
finally issued much stricter guidelines for minority hiring that came to be
known as the Philadelphia Plan. The new guidelines required contractors
to establish manning tables specifying the number of minority workers
who would be hired in each craft at each stage of construction. All contractors bidding on jobs in excess of $500,000 were expected to submit
written plans prior to receiving a contract. Ranges were specified for each
of the six skilled trades that had virtually no black members in 1969, with
the goal that within four years they would have a 20 percent minority
membership.[25]

The Philadelphia Plan was a dramatic departure from the government's
earlier lackadaisical approach to compliance. Never before had specific
numerical goals been mandated in civil rights enforcement. The unions
opposed it immediately, arguing that the small number of minorities in
the trades was due to a lack of interest and inadequate educational skills.
The plan also drew immediate reaction from congressional conservatives.
In August 1969, the U.S. comptroller general declared it to be in violation
of the no-quota provisions of Title VII.[26] Senator Everett Dirksen (R-IL)

agreed, arguing that it violated the prohibitions against preferential treatment contained in Title VII, which he had helped insert into the 1964 Civil Rights Act. Dirksen attached an amendment onto an appropriations bill that would have barred funds for contracts that contained minimum hiring goals. The AFL-CIO lobbied on behalf of the amendment, but the NAACP mobilized its branches and successfully defeated the measure.[27]

The Ineffectiveness of Voluntary Outreach Plans

Once the use of numerical goals and timetables had been approved by Congress, the AFL-CIO shifted its tactics, coming out in support of voluntary outreach programs. Seeing a way out of the confrontation with the building trades, Nixon's Department of Labor supported these outreach efforts, which would give the unions a waiver from the strict standards set by the Philadelphia Plan as long as they made efforts to recruit more minorities. Chicago was chosen as the first site for a federally financed effort to recruit minorities into the building trades. In 1969 a community coalition had picketed and successfully shut down the construction of the University of Illinois's new urban campus. The Coalition for United Community Action (CUCA) was the brainchild of a former member of King's Chicago staff, Reverend C. T. Vivian, who had stayed behind in the city.[28] It was composed of a diverse group of organizations, including Operation Breadbasket (another of King's creations), the Latin American Task Force, representatives of the city's street gangs, and black construction contractors.[29] The majority of CUCA's foot soldiers were unemployed men. CUCA demanded that the unions create ten thousand new apprenticeship positions, waive the pre-apprenticeship tests, admit experienced minority craftsmen into the unions, and abolish the union hall job-referral system, all of which they saw as artificial barriers to minority entry into the trades.

In response to the outcry in Chicago, the Department of Labor decided to hold hearings in the city on discrimination in the construction industry. The first day of testimony had to be canceled when more than four thousand white construction workers blocked the entrances to the hearing site. After moving to a more secure location, the hearings collected extensive evidence on discrimination in the industry. Under pressure from

Mayor Daley as a result of the hearings, the contractors and unions finally agreed to negotiate a settlement with the CUCA.[30] In contrast to the Philadelphia Plan, the voluntary plan that emerged had no mandatory goals or timetables for the individual crafts; moreover, it was entirely dependent on the mayor for enforcement.[31] It contained no contractual duties or obligations and had no legal sanctions. For compliance it relied on the "good faith efforts" of the same employers and unions responsible for the continuing pattern of discrimination, who had repeatedly resisted compliance with the law.[32] The Chicago Plan set a goal of bringing a thousand skilled minority craftsmen into the unions at once, with CUCA responsible for supplying the qualified tradesmen.

Each craft union agreed to accept qualified tradesmen into membership and to accept partial payments of its initiation fee. Less-skilled minority tradesmen who could furnish proof of employment for two or more years in a particular craft would be put to work for a thirty-day probationary period, after which they were to be enrolled as apprentices.[33] An information and recruiting program was designed to reach those with no prior training or skills who were within the age limits required by the particular craft. The whole program was to be paid for by a grant from the U.S. Labor Department.

A year and a half later, after the federal government had spent nearly $1 million, officials acknowledged that the Chicago Plan was a resounding failure. The Department of Labor conceded that its staff could not verify the names of black employees claimed to have been placed under the plan because the participating unions had refused "specific identification data" regarding alleged placements. In one typical case, investigators found that "of the 75 persons who initially started in the program, only 5 of the 46 placed are presently employed." In another case, investigators were able to contact forty-four of the reported seventy-two placements. Only five were employed; twenty-three had been laid off, ten had been discharged, four had quit, and two had joined the Armed Forces.[34] The OFCC concluded: "The Chicago Plan has failed to produce any meaningful jobs at all levels in the construction industry. . . . The Chicago Plan has failed to be the vehicle of providing the preparation necessary to qualify minorities for all crafts. This is particularly clear when attention is given to the higher paying mechanical trades."[35] Hill called the plan "a deliberate hoax."[36]

Making peace with the building trades prior to the 1972 presidential elections, Nixon abandoned any further pretense of enforcing the executive order on contract compliance and decided to rely completely on voluntary outreach plans. Even though the first Chicago Plan had proved to be a disaster, the administration set up the "New Chicago Plan," which once again contained no enforcement powers. The Chicago Urban League, the city's oldest and most established race relations organization, agreed to participate only after the Labor Department made it clear that without the league there would be no plan. The plan was sold to the public as both a cooperative agreement by and for Chicagoans and as a massive federal program that would provide ten thousand jobs, with $1 million in federal money for job training and $750,000 for operating expenses during the first year and additional funds for each of the following years.[37] Ten thousand jobs was a public relations figure, not a real expectation, so the parties entered the New Chicago Plan knowing they could not fulfill the numerical commitment.

By June 1973 the Chicago Urban League's records showed that only 226 minorities had been placed under the New Chicago Plan, a figure which included twenty-five men admitted by the structural ironworkers union as a result of a Justice Department consent decree.[38] The Chicago Urban League threatened to withdraw, hoping that such a move would force the contractors to commit to making the plan work. In the League's own assessment, the new plan "failed because the Government's purpose in creating the plan was not to achieve equal opportunity in the construction industry but to gain political advantage in the 1972 presidential election with the semblance of decisive, effective action that quieted blacks without really pressing organized labor too far. As long as the plan operated, the Government continued to draw political advantage from it, for the plan absolved the Government of responsibility for the enforcement of nondiscrimination and affirmative action laws."[39] The Department of Labor later admitted that after spending $1.7 million over a four-year period, only one in six of the minority workers whom contractors and the unions claimed to have placed were actually working.[40]

Despite the dismal record of voluntary plans, by 1975 the Department of Labor had negotiated such plans in sixty-six different cities, while the OFCC had imposed mandatory plans in only four cities.[41] Between 1967 and 1972, the federal government spent more than $27 million to subsidize minority outreach programs that resulted in virtually no improvement in the percentage of minorities employed in the skilled trades. The voluntary plans were full of loopholes through which contractors and the unions could avoid compliance while claiming to adhere to their requirements. "A good faith effort" was all that was expected. Chicago's first voluntary plan stipulated that contractors "hope to achieve" the hiring of a certain number of minorities "if general business conditions permit."[42] The voluntary plans left control over entry into the trades in the hands of craft unions and the contractors, the same parties responsible for the exclusionary policies to begin with. Department of Labor data revealed that well over half of all participants in the outreach programs were concentrated in those trades, such as carpenters and bricklayers, in which there had always been a higher percentage of minorities.

After his reelection, Nixon rewarded the building trades for their support by appointing one of their own as the new secretary of labor. Following the collapse of Chicago's two voluntary plans, the new secretary, Peter Brennan, who had previously been head of the New York City building trades council, quickly moved to impose a so-called mandatory plan on the city. The government now took on full responsibility for achieving minority entrance into the local construction industry. No minority organizations were involved in its implementation. For the first two plans' voluntary arrangement among unions, employers, and the minority community, the new plan substituted a government-designed, government-implemented program covering only contractors holding federal contracts in excess of $500,000.[43] The Labor Department asserted that equal employment opportunities could be achieved in the Chicago construction industry within five years with no injury to the economic rights of nonminority craftsmen.[44]

This mandatory plan contained countless "good faith effort" escape clauses. Since minority manpower utilization was not calculated by the number of individuals placed on the job, but by the minority manhours worked, contractors could simply move their minority personnel from project to project and thus comply with the plan without hiring any new minority workers. The man-hour requirement could be satisfied by employing minority laborers instead of craftsmen, thereby maintaining the status quo. The government's five-year timetable was completely unrealistic because contractors were only covered by the plan while they held federal contracts.[45]

Access Remains Very Limited

Despite their repeated failures, outreach programs remain the standard response to any serious minority protest against the lack of construction jobs. In 1987, the Chicago Urban League discovered that the state of Illinois had awarded black contractors less than 2 percent of the work on a $210 million reconstruction of the Dan Ryan Expressway, a major thoroughfare running through the heart of the Southside's black neighborhoods. A congressional amendment had recently combined women and minorities into a single "presumptively disadvantaged class" for purposes of allocating the 10 percent of all highway construction funds set aside for affirmative action purposes. Illinois had chosen to implement this single goal by awarding 60 percent of the set-aside contracts to white women.[46] This was a particularly grievous affront because majority contractors commonly undermine the intent of the set-asides by setting up "front" companies in the names of their wives or daughters. Once news of the state's actions became public, a large coalition made up of several major black and Latino community organizations, black state legislators, and minority contractors threatened to bring work on the project to a halt unless the Illinois Department of Transportation (IDOT) undertook immediate remedial action.

By this time, Chicago's most influential minority organizations, the Chicago Urban League and Operation PUSH, had shifted their emphasis from opening up construction jobs for their working-class constituents to creating new economic opportunities for the black middle class. Securing contracts for minority construction companies was now a central goal, and both organizations set up separate divisions just for that purpose. The Urban League's Affirmative Action Division concentrated on obtaining public-sector contracts for African-Americans, while PUSH's International Trade Bureau went after corporate contracts. They justified this by arguing that minority businesses were more likely to hire minority workers and create wealth in minority communities. Unfortunately, in the construction industry the Davis-Bacon Act limits the ability of even the larger minority contractors to hire people from their own communities unless they are union members.

Tagged onto the demands that a larger portion of the Dan Ryan contracts be awarded to minority contractors was a demand that the percentages of minority and female workers on the project be significantly increased. Following a series of negotiations, IDOT agreed that 40 percent of the skilled positions and 60 percent of the unskilled positions would be filled by minorities and women, with half of the set-asides going to women. IDOT also agreed to set aside 190 jobs to be filled through referrals from the ten major community organizations that participated in the coalition. The groups received a $125,000 contract to build such a referral network. The Urban League was designated as the network's fiscal agent, making it the recipient of the majority of the funds.[47] Although this outreach plan targeted a specific project, whereas the earlier ones had been designed to generally increase the number of minorities in the building trades, the formula was essentially the same. The program was loosely constructed so that contractors could easily move minorities from other, less visible projects onto the Dan Ryan project. It had no impact on the hiring practices of other highway construction projects occurring elsewhere in the state, nor was there a guarantee that the unions would accept any new minority applicants. Once again, it created the semblance of change without the substance.

By the following summer, IDOT claimed that 49 percent of the construction work had been done by minorities and 6.7 percent by women.[48] The numbers for women were far below projected percentages, suggesting that the projections had primarily been public relations figures, not reflective of the actual number of women available to work. The Urban League had placed 167 people on the project through the community referral network. However, monitoring of the worksite soon revealed that one contractor who had hired 129 women and minorities had laid off 50 percent of them after a few weeks on the job. Furthermore, the overwhelming number of referrals were for jobs as laborers and carpenters. Minorities were not represented in many of the other trades. The Urban League had received twenty-one requests for specific skilled trades for which it could not find a single minority craftsman. The League concluded that "this was due to the age old problem of the serious minority/female supply-demand imbalance created by discrimination on the part of the building trades unions."[49]

Access to construction jobs will continue to be a highly volatile issue in Chicago as long as large numbers of minority men are without work. In 1994, for the third summer in a row, groups of unemployed African-American men aggressively picketed at various construction sites that scouting teams had identified as employing largely nonblack crews. Many of these sites were in black neighborhoods. The protestors threatened to shut the sites down unless 70 percent of the trades jobs were turned over to them immediately.[50] This time, the city of Chicago announced it would fund an outreach and referral program. Once again, Chicago Urban League was awarded a $500,000 contract by the city for recruiting minority workers to work on the reconstruction of one of Chicago's elevated train lines. The league intended to subcontract with a number of other community groups, including 21st Century Vote, a gang-affiliated political organization.[51] Although the subcontract to 21st Century Vote was later rescinded, the league did receive the contract to play its part in what by now has become a well-rehearsed Chicago ritual. As soon as community protests threaten a possible halt to construction, the federal, state, or local government steps in with a contract to do minority outreach. Minority outreach programs remain a politically expedient, low-cost method of temporarily quieting down periodic protests. They do not break through the structural barriers that prevent more minorities or women from gaining entrance into the craft unions, whose hiring halls are the route through which crews are routinely assigned to work throughout the metropolitan area.

Apprenticeships Form a Permanent Barrier to Entry

The basic fallacy of the outreach programs is that they have never provided minorities and women with equal access to full union membership. They have legitimated the existence of two separate tracks for admissions into the building trades, one through family sponsorship, the other through admissions into apprenticeship training, a route that became increasingly popular as minorities pressed for entrance into the trades.[52] The outreach programs accept the premise that minorities and women have to complete a four- or five-year apprenticeship program in order to gain union status. According to Hill, "The basic fallacy in the Outreach approach is that even if full racial integration of all union controlled apprenticeship programs were achieved, no substantial integration of the craft unions would result because the overwhelming majority of white construction workers do not become journeymen through apprenticeship training. . . . It is only blacks and members of other minority groups who must climb the slow and often futile apprenticeship ladder."[53]

For decades Washburne Trade School was the sole public source of apprenticeship training available to minorities and women in Chicago. Founded in 1919, Washburne held the unique status of being the only publicly funded postsecondary trade training school in the country. Although the board of education budgeted $5 million a year for Washburne and staffed it with board-certified teachers and administrators, strictly speaking, it was not a public institution. The school's founders had turned over control of the apprenticeship programs to the building trades to lessen the unions' fears that it would promote nonunion competition. Operational control over curriculum and admissions to each of the training programs rested with the Joint Apprenticeship Training Committee (JATC), composed of local employers and unions in each particular trade.[54] In effect, the board was supporting a private school run by the JATCs. Even the curriculum was kept a secret from the board. The JATCs reported their efforts to meet the federal goals for minority and female enrollment directly to the U.S. Department of Labor's Bureau of Apprenticeship Training (BAT), completely bypassing the Chicago Board of Education. The BAT in turn certified the apprentices as qualified tradesmen upon completion of the program.

For years Washburne remained the exclusive domain of white men. Since minorities were excluded from membership in the majority of the building trades unions, they could not acquire the sponsorship that was necessary to gain admission into Washburne. In 1961 the Negro American Labor Council and the Congress of Racial Equality (CORE) found that at Washburne "approximately 1 percent of its enrollees were Negro . . . and that out of 12 trades surveyed, only 5 of those had any Negro apprentices."[55] In 1965, 95 percent of the school's apprentices were still white.[56] A year later, Washburne reported that it had enrolled 147 black apprentices. By 1970, minorities made up 14 percent of the 3,467 students enrolled in the school's trade training and apprenticeship programs.[57]

In response to protests against the school's exclusionary admissions policies, a new route was established that essentially placed minority and female candidates on a waiting list from which the unions could choose as openings occurred. The U.S. Department of Labor established new affirmative action goals for each apprenticeship program, requiring that 23 percent of enrollees be minorities and 20 percent women. At the same time, a set of highly selective admissions criteria was put into place, requiring that prospective trainees had completed high school, met certain basic academic and aptitude standards, and successfully passed an oral interview. Even after the waiting lists were set up, sponsored applicants still moved ahead of minorities and women to the top of the waiting lists in some trades.[58] According to Charles Lutzow, Washburne's principal from 1986 until 1992, "If a contractor hired someone as an apprentice that person automatically got into Washburne."[59]

Under the new waiting list system, tests became a device for screening out unwanted applicants. The carpenters administered a test prior to admissions, and all the other trades did so several weeks into training. Those who failed were dropped from the program. Due to the poor preparation blacks and Hispanics received in the city's public schools, they had a much more difficult time meeting Washburne's strict admissions standards than did white applicants. The selection process forced minorities to compete where they are weakest. The written examinations placed a heavy emphasis on mathematical skills, which favor suburbanites who are more likely to have taken some algebra and trigonometry. The oral interview was biased toward those applicants who could demonstrate some prior knowledge of the trade, giving anyone with previous exposure an upper hand.

The creation of a second admissions route did improve the numbers of minorities enrolled in the school. By 1974 minorities comprised more than 30 percent of the apprentices in four of the trades and more than 20 percent in two others, although overall only 10.3 percent of apprentices were African-American or Latino.[60] Several apprentice programs still remained all white. Most of the trades continued to fall below the standards set by the Department of Labor, which based its numbers on the percentage of minorities in the metropolitan region as a whole because the school served both Chicago and suburban residents. Minority enrollments were highest in the lower-paying trades such as carpentry, machinists, plastering, painting, and decorating, while they were much smaller in most of the higher-paying trades. The best-paid trades, such as pipefitting, sheetmetal, and electrical, still had very few minority apprentices.[61]

In 1974, responding to renewed charges by black state legislators of racial exclusion at Washburne, the Illinois Board of Vocational Education and Rehabilitation cut the school's state and federal aid. The funds were partially restored in 1979 after the Illinois board was finally satisfied that genuine efforts had been made to increase minority enrollments in the sheetmetal and carpentry apprenticeship programs, which at the time accounted for approximately half of the school's apprenticeship enrollment.[62] In 1986 the Office of Civil Rights of the U.S. Department of Education concluded that Washburne's apprenticeship programs discriminated against women.

With pressure mounting on the building trades to open up their training programs, the unions began to abandon Washburne, choosing to set up independently operated training programs in the suburbs rather than comply with mandates to open up their ranks. By the early 1980s only eight skilled trades remained at the school—"the other ten left coincidentally with the insistence of state authorities on desegregation in the 1960's and 1970's."[63] Plumbers and ornamental ironworkers had departed years earlier. The pipe fitters left in the spring of 1986.[64] By moving to the suburbs, the unions distanced themselves geographically from Chicago's large minority populations, making it clear once again that they intended to maintain their largely all-white character. By relocating to suburbs that are largely inaccessible on public transportation, the unions successfully erected a modern version of their long-standing racial barriers to entry. In examining the consequences of the unions' departure, Joy Carew and Michael Preston note, "It is logical to assume that black and other minority participation in those craft training programs leaving Washburne ranged from a residual number to none at all. This means that 50 percent of the crafts training has been made inaccessible to blacks and other minorities. Further evidence shows that of the 50 percent still remaining at the school, non-residents continue to make up a significant proportion of the enrollments (42 percent in 1983)."[65]

As trade after trade left the school, Washburne's enrollments dropped dramatically. By 1985 the school's enrollment was only 44 percent of what it had been in 1970. Although African-Americans now comprised 24 percent of the student body and Latinos 10 percent, the sharp enrollment declines meant that the whole struggle for access had produced an increase of only 87 black students and 125 Hispanics.[66] As the unions withdrew, school administrators replaced them with new nonapprenticeship trade training programs.

In 1986, Mayor Harold Washington appointed a new Chicago Board of Education that was determined to take control of the apprenticeship admissions and curriculum at Washburne. The board ordered a radical increase in the number of blacks, Latinos, and women recruited into Washburne, so that for the first time white males would have been in a minority. The school was to produce a student body that was 46 percent black, 14 percent Hispanic, and 40 percent white, approximately reflecting the city's population, but well above the federal standard of 23 percent minority. Women were supposed to make up 20 percent of the apprentices. Although they were intended to expand minority access to the building trades, these unrealistically high numbers were the school's deathblow. Following the board's actions, the pipe fitters announced that they were leaving the school after 62 years. Critical of the board's policy change, Thomas Nayder, president of the Chicago Building Trades Council, expressed the pipe fitters' attitude when he said, "I get the feeling that they think, 'Who needs all this hassle? We've met our court standard, we comply with federal regulations, and now someone else wants to impose another standard.'"[67] The unions further escalated the confrontation with the board by persecuting black staff at the school, telling the apprentices that they should not listen to their black instructors.[68]

In November 1986, the Chicago Board of Education sparked a second major controversy when it threatened to cancel the start of a new class of carpenter apprentices, the largest remaining program at Washburne, after recruitment efforts had yielded a 74 percent white male class.[69] The carpenters had already announced that they were going to start their own training facility in job-rich DuPage County, where the median family income is $55,000 per year and 95 percent of the residents are white. In early December the union, which had been training three hundred to four hundred apprentices a year at Washburne, announced it had made the "irrevocable" decision to leave the school. This meant that carpentry training would no longer be offered to city residents. Union officials said that they would try to recruit their future minority apprentices from areas of the suburbs with substantial minority populations, seeking people better qualified to finish the program.[70] The union did agree to train eighty pre-apprentices each year, who could then enter the apprenticeship program in the suburbs. Following quickly on the heels of the carpenters, the electricians announced that they too were leaving Washburne for the suburbs, having worked out an agreement to operate at a community college southwest of the city. By the summer of 1987 only three construction trades remained at the school.[71] As shown in Table 3, the years of protest had resulted in little improvement. In 1987, white men still comprised 78 percent of all apprentices in metropolitan Chicago, while women constituted a minuscule .05 percent and minority men stood at 22 percent.

Table 3   Metropolitan Chicago Building Trades Apprentices by Race, 1987

Trade	Total	Women	White	Black	Latino	Other
Boilermaker	27	2	26	1	0	0
Bricklayer	167	2	107	41	19	0
Carpenter	1336	72	1022	210	90	14
Cement mason	136	8	107	13	13	3
Construction worker I	40	0	30	5	3	2
Electrician	1,108	62	893	146	60	9
Glazier	28	3	19	9	0	0
Insulation worker	35	2	29	4	2	0
Machinist	94	4	81	4	8	1
Operating engineer	200	41	135	38	19	8
Ornamental ironworker	82	2	65	13	3	1
Painter	390	17	287	54	43	6
Pipe fitter	389	15	311	54	23	1
Plasterer	59	3	27	19	12	1
Plumber	348	13	288	44	14	2
Roofer	818	11	591	151	74	1
Sheetmetal worker	201	14	153	31	17	0
Structural steel	134	8	106	13	6	9
Taper	38	2	13	11	14	0
TOTAL	5,630	281	4,290	861	420	58

Source: Bureau of Apprenticeship Training, U.S. Department of Labor, "Apprenticeship Selective Activity," May 1, 1987

Washburne's final demise came in the summer of 1993, with the announcement that the Chicago Board of Education was handing over administration of the school to the Chicago City Colleges, a city-run system of two-year junior colleges. With three apprenticeship programs and several strong vocational training programs remaining at Washburne, the school had become a mainly minority school. Principal Lutzow is convinced that the decision to transfer the school was made in City Hall: "The Mayor isn't interested in seeing minorities get trained. It was a way of quieting the unions. Daley could close it, but not close it. Giving it to the City Colleges would lessen any negative reaction from African-Americans since the black community is very tied to the City Colleges."[72] In the late 1980s the Chicago Urban League had in fact lobbied for the establishment of a construction trades curriculum at the City Colleges. The board of education claimed the move would save $5 million, although since a portion of those dollars were reimbursed by state and federal sources, the actual savings was much less. The transaction was made without even a contractual agreement outlining what was to be done with the school's expensive shop equipment and internal accounts.[73] The City Colleges began charging tuition for the same training programs that had been available to city residents for free at Washburne. The chefs training was reopened in the old Washburne building, while other programs were transferred to various city colleges. The machine shop, which had a predominantly Asian enrollment, was moved to the Dawson Skills Center. Located a few blocks from Robert Taylor Homes, the world's largest public housing project, the new site will not continue attracting Asians. The auto body and fender shop, which had a mainly Latino enrollment, was moved to Kennedy-King College, located in an all-black neighborhood far from any major Latino community.[74] In essence, the transfer has destroyed the integrity of much of the training that remained at Washburne, without ever officially closing down the school. All this was done without the slightest murmur of protest from the African-American and Latino community. Washburne was never mentioned by either of the two African-Americans who ran for mayor against Richard M. Daley in 1995. The dismantling of Washburne is an even greater travesty when viewed within the context of a growing national emphasis on improving the quality of vocational training offered to those students who are not planning to attend college. While policymakers in the Clinton administration advanced the idea of imitating Germany's successful system of apprenticeship training, one of the premier examples of a successful publicly funded vocational facility has been destroyed.

With the withdrawal of the apprenticeship programs and the transfer of Washburne's remaining programs, the issue of minority and female access to trade apprenticeships has almost vanished from Chicago's political scene. The unions have now hidden their apprenticeship programs from public scrutiny, refusing to release data on the numbers of minorities that are currently enrolled.[75] According to the 1990 census, the only available source of information, three years after leaving Washburne, the carpenters had 50 Latinos, only 10 blacks, and no women among their 172 apprentices in all of Cook County (where Chicago is located). The electricians did not do much better, with 67 Latinos, 28 blacks, and 10 women out of a total of 285 apprentices.[76] Both programs were in compliance with the federal standard of 23 percent minorities even though they are below the percentage of minorities residing in Cook County, which stood at 42.5 percent in 1990. What is most striking is that both unions are achieving their percentages by enrolling a disproportionately whigh number of Latinos. There is absolutely no information on the number of minorities and women who are graduating and going on to become union-certified journeymen.

Today, fewer of Chicago's minorities and women have access to apprenticeship training than they did fifteen years ago. All that remains are several small union-certified pre-apprenticeship training programs funded with JTPA dollars. The unions continue to exercise a virtual lock on the local construction industry, making it difficult for anyone to use the industry as a source of jobs for community residents. In 1993 a community development corporation in one of the city's Mexican neighborhoods had its JTPA contract revoked and was investigated by the U.S. Department of Labor after hiring a neighborhood contractor who used nonunion labor to build a series of moderate-income townhouses. The community organization felt that using a nonunion contractor was the only way to produce jobs for community residents while constructing affordable housing. It sacrificed its long-standing carpentry pre-apprenticeship program to accomplish that goal. With each such loss, one more small crack in the armor of the building trades is sealed, so that soon minorities will find themselves again relegated to laborers' jobs with little chance of ever gaining admission into a skilled trade.

6 | TRICKLE-DOWN ECONOMIC DEVELOPMENT

Flourishing businesses are critical to the health of any community. They provide a local employment base, access to consumer goods and services, and the capital needed to sustain a vibrant cultural, civic, religious, and political life without having to constantly seek funds elsewhere. In the vacuum left by the departure of manufacturing industries from the inner city, minority businesses are a potentially important source of replacement jobs, making their growth a critical part of developing urban structures of opportunity. Nearly all minority-owned firms employ a predominantly minority workforce, while small white-owned businesses, not covered by Equal Employment Opportunities Commission (EEOC) laws, often exclude minorities altogether. Even white-owned firms located in minority communities hire a workforce that is predominantly white, with roughly one-third of such firms employing no minorities at all.[1] Furthermore, minority businesses, despite their smaller size, are more generous in making charitable contributions, especially to religious institutions—demonstrating yet another facet of their significance to minority communities.[2]

In spite of unprecedented public and private support for the expansion of minority businesses, they comprise only a small fraction of all U.S. businesses (less than 11 percent of the total in 1992). The vast majority are individual proprietorships, of which 84 percent have no paid employees and 46 percent report gross receipts under $10,000 annually.[3] Despite being the focus of much of the government assistance provided to minority firms, African-American–owned businesses remain quite small. As of 1992, only 10 percent had any paid employees, and a mere 342 had more

than one hundred employees. Fifty-six percent of all black firms had receipts under $10,000.[4]

The substantial outlay of resources that has gone into building the capacity of minority-owned businesses has created a pattern of uneven development, with a small number of firms reaping most of the benefits,
while the majority remain marginal at best. For the most part, the firms
that have benefited from government assistance are located outside of
predominantly minority neighborhoods and do most of their business
with nonminority customers.[5] The various loan and preference programs
have done little to stem the unrelenting economic decline of poor black
communities, where even the small ma and pa corner stores have suc-
cumbed to competition from larger chain stores located outside of the
neighborhood. All too often, the only remaining retail outlets are liquor
stores, which have the uncanny ability to survive in even the most economically deprived communities.

The billions of dollars in contracts earmarked for minority-owned
firms encouraged many better-educated younger blacks and Latinos to
create and expand firms in new lines of business, including wholesaling,
contracting, and skill-intensive services such as finance. The mean annual
sales of these businesses are much higher than those of traditional minority-
owned businesses. They often have paid employees, serve a racially diverse clientele, and sell to other businesses, including large corporations
and the government.[6] Since much of this new economic elite receives a
substantial portion of its businesses as a result of preference programs, the
conservatives' efforts to eliminate such programs threaten these firms'
very survival.

Minority business programs were created in response to the virtual exclusion of people of color from business opportunities. Today these programs represent one of the most visible signs of the political muscle of the
African-American and Latino middle class. Minority contracting opportunities have evolved into a form of political patronage, skillfully used by
politicians of both parties to command the support of minority businesspeople. In many cases, contracts have been handed out as a reward for political loyalty, rather than for superior business acumen. Recognizing the
value of tapping into this flow of dollars for their own political purposes,
many black and Latino leaders have focused more on the politics of gain-

ing and maintaining contracting opportunities than on improving educational and job opportunities for the less advantaged.

Until the late 1980s, minority business programs enjoyed a high level of bipartisan political support despite their decidedly mixed record in creating successful minority businesses. In sharp contrast to the exhaustive debate that occurred during the enactment of the equal employment mandates of the 1964 Civil Rights Act, there was virtually no congressional debate over the enactment of the first federal minority set-asides. While the enforcement of equal employment opportunities was challenged from the first day the EEOC went into operation, the minority business loan programs and set-asides experienced almost twenty years of uninterrupted growth and development. Prior to the Supreme Court's 1989 decision in *Croson v. City of Richmond,* minority and female set-aside programs existed in more than two hundred state and local jurisdictions.[7] By 1995 there were another 160 such programs scattered throughout the federal government, covering a diversity of activities ranging from agricultural research to Defense Department contracts.[8]

Despite their widespread use, few preference programs have contained clearly defined economic development goals. The politicization of such programs has led many public officials to be overly concerned with achieving certain numerical goals, rather than using them to stabilize and expand minority businesses. Although contracting programs do increase business opportunities, by themselves they cannot address several of the other critical impediments to minority business growth—namely, the lack of access to investment capital and the lower levels of managerial skills possessed by many minority owners. Under some circumstances, preferences have actually been found to be detrimental to a business's longevity. The programs have long been plagued with problems of fraud and abuse, with a sizable share of the contracting work supposedly awarded to minority firms actually being carried out by majority firms with a minority firm acting as a front company or a broker. These widespread practices further limit the programs' potential as a tool to build viable minority-owned firms that could sustain employment opportunities in minority communities.

The Republicans who initiated the first large-scale minority business development programs proclaimed them to be their party's solution to urban decline. Yet, until recently the efforts designed to assist individual entrepreneurs were unconnected to the small-scale efforts to revitalize poor urban communities. Since minority businesses are more likely to hire and promote minority employees and invest in minority communities, efforts to increase their overall market share could have broad social benefits. But the programs are presently structured so that the responsibility for creating a downward trickle of economic benefits is left up to individual minority businesspeople, who are ultimately driven by the same profit-and-loss considerations faced by majority-owned businesses. Since most of the firms that receive special loans and contracting opportunities are located outside of predominantly minority communities, they are at best an indirect stimulus to the economies of poorer neighborhoods.[9]

Segregation Retarded Black Business Growth

Racial segregation severely retarded black business ownership. The long years of slavery and southern sharecropping had conditioned most African-Americans to see themselves only as laborers, not as owners of capital. In the words of a veteran black businessman, "Slavery did a damn good job because it taught us to hate ourselves and each other. It taught us that the white man's ice was colder, his sugar sweeter. We didn't have the stores, so we were taught, 'Somebody else comes in and everything is all right.' They render the necessary service. All we were conditioned to do is supply the labor."[10]

Few blacks had access to the ingredients that go into successful business ownership. With the doors to corporate America closed, few could gain the practical experience of managing a business. Historically, only a handful of African-Americans possessed any formal training in business management. As late as 1969 there were less than 150 blacks with doctorates in business or economics in the entire country.[11] Lower incomes and lower levels of home ownership meant that few possessed the personal equity needed to start up a business, let alone one requiring a large initial investment, such as manufacturing or wholesaling. Lower levels of equity made it much more difficult for minority entrepreneurs to borrow capital because most banks regarded them as poor investment risks. Aside from considerations of personal creditworthiness, the banks had frequently redlined entire black neighborhoods so that no residential or commercial lending occurred within their boundaries. By 1977 there were only four savings-and-loan offices located in the predominantly black residential areas of Chicago. As many of the city's neighborhoods underwent racial transition from white to black, banks had simply closed their offices and moved out.[12]

The majority of black-owned businesses were restricted to selling their products and services to other blacks. Larger corporations generally had established networks of firms with whom they routinely did business. The same was true for government purchasing departments, which were legally required to award their contracts to the lowest bidder but in practice often wrote their bid requests so that only one firm could meet the specifications. All too often these companies had either made substantial campaign contributions or were personal acquaintances of those who controlled the public purse strings. Black companies that lacked the personal relationships with corporate or political decision-makers had difficulty breaking into either of these circles.

Consequently, the total number of black-owned firms remained quite small. Prior to the end of segregation, most black businesses were located in the South.[13] In the burgeoning black urban communities, whites owned most of the sizable retail establishments. In the 1930s, not a single black-owned business occupied a storefront along Forty-seventh Street, one of the central retail strips within Chicago's large black community.[14] In many cities, blacks were not even employed as clerks in the retail shops in their own communities until widespread "Don't Buy Where You Can't Work" campaigns during the 1930s finally forced white storeowners to alter their hiring practices.[15]

Almost half of all black businesses were service-oriented, requiring little start-up capital. The small retail stores, beauty parlors, and funeral homes essentially produced wage income for their owners, resulting in little capital accumulation. As of 1977, 83 percent of all black businesses had no paid employees. Of the 17 percent that did, the average number of employees was four.[16]

The end of legal segregation placed many of these marginal businesses in an even more precarious position. Increasingly, blacks patronized larger chain stores located outside of their own neighborhoods, driving many of the small ma and pa corner stores out of business. The disappearance of these stores in turn threatened the livelihood of the handful of existing black-owned manufacturers, such as Joe Louis Milk and Baldwin Ice Cream, who often could not get shelf space in the larger chain stores. Black manufacturers of commodities marketed exclusively to blacks increasingly found themselves in competition with major corporate producers of similar products, who were discovering the profitability of penetrating this long-neglected consumer market. Black business development took on further urgency in the aftermath of the urban riots, which destroyed many of the established retail businesses in poorer black neighborhoods and accelerated the departure of manufacturing companies that had employed large numbers of unskilled blacks. Even in neighborhoods not immediately affected by the looting and arson, nonblack businesses decided to pull out for fear that they would be the next target. Insurance rates skyrocketed, driving still other businesses into safer communities.

Republicans Adopt Entrepreneurship as Their Urban Strategy

Given the Republicans' current strident opposition to all racial preferences, it is ironic that they were in fact the pioneers of what was at first called "Black Capitalism." As the Republican presidential candidate in 1968, Richard Nixon delivered two campaign speeches calling for the creation of more black businesses, which constituted the full extent of his proposals for the revitalization urban black communities.[17] He also endorsed the Community Self-Determination Act, then pending in Congress. The Act was the brainchild of Roy Innis, who had just become the new national director of the Congress of Racial Equality (CORE), the civil rights organization that had led the southern Freedom Rides. By the late 1960s CORE had rejected its earlier support for racial integration, convinced that minorities first needed to consolidate their power base in their own communities before they could deal with the larger society on the basis of full equality. Innis translated the new call for "Black Power" into the concrete goal of building "a nation within a nation" by developing black community corporations and black ownership of capital to buy factories and businesses that would in turn employ black labor.[18] The Community Self-Determination Act would have provided public resources to achieve those goals. Despite Nixon's endorsement, the bill was defeated in Congress through the combined opposition of organized labor and the more established black business leadership. Organized labor opposed its business orientation, favoring job-training programs over which it had much more influence. The unions still saw industrial labor as the principal avenue into mainstream society for blacks and other excluded minorities. According to Arthur Blaustein and Geoffrey Faux, the AFL-CIO "opposed any program that took away their power to control the pace and direction of the integration of blacks into the mainstream economy."[19]

This new emphasis on the separate and autonomous development of minority communities meshed well with the Republicans' political strategy of courting disaffected white Democrats. At the heart of Nixon's campaign strategy was a rejection of the Democrats' active commitment to furthering racial integration. To win their votes, Nixon had promised angry southern whites that he would halt all federal support of school busing. In that context, support for minority business was quite appealing because it was designed to function within existing racial boundaries. It also fit nicely with the Republicans' strong pro-business, anti-government orientation. In a modern version of the traditional "pull yourself up by your bootstraps" philosophy, it was argued that the new jobs and capital investment resulting from minority business development would lessen the need for government intervention in poor communities. The Democrats' controversial War on Poverty programs could then be rolled back.

Equally as important, this new policy direction offered the Republicans the opportunity to recapture a portion of the black vote by creating a new minority business class that owed its existence to the party's patronage. The Republicans realized that the black middle class was expanding as blacks moved into the many social service jobs created by the War on Poverty and other Johnson-era initiatives. These jobs served as stepping stones into higher-paying professional, managerial, and technical jobs. The Republicans believed these new middle-class blacks could serve as a bulwark against the demands emanating from poorer blacks and would in the long run act as a wedge into the Democrats' stranglehold on the minority vote.

Once elected to office, President Nixon implemented his "Black Capitalism" agenda by signing an executive order establishing the Office of Minority Business Enterprise (OMBE) within the Department of Commerce and expanding certain of the Small Business Administration's existing programs, reorienting them toward minorities. By placing the programs in the Department of Commerce, Nixon intended to take an agency that for years had been hostile to minority businesses and transform it into the vehicle for minority economic development. The OMBE was charged with the responsibility of overseeing and coordinating 116 programs spread over twenty-one departments and agencies that provided assistance to blacks, Indians, Puerto Ricans, Mexican-Americans, and other minority groups.[20] Yet, the OMBE had no direct control over any of the loan funds set up for these businesses. Initially, it did not even have its own administrative budget—money was taken out of the administrative budget of the War on Poverty, which Nixon was scaling back. The Small Business Administration (SBA) retained control over the financial resources available to loan to minority businesspeople.

Following the SBA's reorientation, the dollar value of federal loans flowing to minority businesses increased significantly. Between 1969 and 1971 loans rose from $85.8 million to $197.1 million and the minority share of SBA dollars went from 14 to 19 percent. Yet, the program barely touched the surface of the need, since only 2 percent of minority businesses received loans. Furthermore, only a third of the money ($60 million) was provided in direct dollars. The rest was in the form of federal loan guarantees made to private banks, which in turn were to provide easier access to market rate loans for minority businesspeople.[21]

Nixon also mandated increased minority representation in the SBA's sheltered market program, known as Section 8(a). The sheltered market consisted of a pool of contracts assembled from among the various departments that were deemed suitable to the capabilities of smaller firms lacking the capacity to perform large government contracts. Only small firms were allowed to bid on contracts placed in the sheltered market.[22] Supported by management and technical assistance from the SBA's staff, these contracting opportunities were supposed to enable the companies to grow to the point where they would graduate out of the special set-aside program into the mainstream market, where they could compete for regular government contracts.[23] To make the program more responsive to minority businesses, its eligibility criteria were rewritten to emphasize racial identification rather than low income. New SBA regulations made minority businesspeople automatically eligible for the program. By 1978, Section 8(a) had become almost exclusively a minority business program, with 96 percent of all companies in the SBA's portfolio minority owned.[24]

Refocusing the program made government contracts more accessible, with a total of $66 million awarded to minority-owned firms by mid-1971. It also quickly brought on a suit from a white contractors' association, charging that the new criteria represented an example of "reverse discrimination." The white plaintiffs argued that the use of minority business criteria ran contrary to the original 1954 statute establishing the SBA because it had not included racial or ethnic terms as part of its criterion for small business.[25] In 1978 Congress passed Public Law 95–507, amending the 1954 law and giving the 8(a) program's emphasis on minority businesses the necessary statutory basis and direction.

These programs have had mixed results in creating successful minority businesses. Within a few years of their establishment, evaluations were uncovering serious flaws in the programs. A study done in the early 1970s found that of the 845 minority-owned businesses that had received SBA loans through three district offices between 1969 and 1970, 27 percent had failed and another 25 percent were probable failures. Only 31 percent of the businesses were considered likely to succeed.[26] A lack of managerial capability was the sole reason for failure in almost a third of the businesses and a contributing factor in close to 40 percent. Yet, the SBA had not provided any management assistance to half of the businesses that were in need of such services. The results led the Government Accounting Office to question "whether federal efforts will result in significant increases in the number of successful minority owned businesses in the nation."[27] In 1972 OMBE expanded its management assistance efforts by funding local business development organizations to service area businesses. Even this was of minimal value because assistance was provided in the pre-loan stage, rather than during the ongoing course of doing business once the government-financed loan had been obtained. This reflected the SBA's goals for the program, which emphasized the number and amount of loans made to minority businesses rather than the number of successful minority businesses established.

The 8(a) program has helped create minority firms that otherwise would not have had the resources to go into business, and it has enabled others to increase their sales and income, resolve bonding problems, and improve their credit capabilities. However, almost from its inception 8(a) has been plagued with problems, prompting the oft-cited phrase that the "8(a) program has done too much for too few for too long."[28] Although the government justified taking certain contracts out of competitive bidding and awarding them on a preferential, sole-source–negotiated basis as a means of building and sustaining viable minority businesses, it was later found that in its first twelve years of operation, few firms ever graduated from the program. Rather than weaning themselves off of sheltered market contracts by using the experience to secure work in the private sector, firms remained in the program indefinitely. By 1981, only 166 of the 4,598 participating firms had left the program since its inception.[29] In metropolitan Chicago the 8(a) program consisted of a handful of wealthy and well-connected firms that had become almost as entrenched as the older white firms they had replaced.[30]

Only 2 percent of 8(a) firms had received the lion's share of the contracts, totaling $1.7 billion or a whopping 31 percent of all awards.[31] The majority of these firms had been in the program for at least seven years, and in some cases as long as eleven years. As long as a handful of older firms received the bulk of the contracts, new, up-and-coming firms were denied admission to the program. This suited the interests not only of the fifty minority contractors who received the bulk of 8(a) contracts, but also the SBA staff. Since the 8(a) program also measured success by the total dollar amount of contracts awarded, the understaffed bureaucracy in charge found it expedient simply to award large contracts to the same firms year after year. The SBA collected very little financial information on its participating firms, making it difficult to assess whether firms were making progress toward self-sufficiency.

Fraud has been endemic to the federal sheltered market program as well as the various federal, state, and local set-asides that followed. Eligibility for the race- and gender-based preferences rests on at least 51 percent of a company's ownership being in the hands of a minority or woman. All too often, that ownership is a paper façade, with the actual managerial authority remaining in the hands of a white male.[32] In 1978 the SBA conducted an internal audit of 1,505 firms enrolled in 8(a) and found that 16 percent showed evidence of a nondisadvantaged businessperson exercising managerial control of the firm.[33] This type of fraud has been common among female-owned firms, since is it relatively easy for a man to transfer ownership to his wife or daughters. In response to repeated criticisms of fraud, most federal programs tightened up their certification procedures and now require detailed proof of ownership in order to establish eligibility. However, many state and local jurisdictions still place little emphasis on contract enforcement, requiring only minimal proof of ownership before a company can participate in bidding for preferential contracts. Even in areas with detailed certification procedures in place, the existence of front companies operating as minority or female owned is an open secret.

Even less regulated is the practice of minority- and female-owned firms serving as brokers for a majority firm, wherein they receive a small percentage of the contract for allowing their firm's name to be used in bidding under a set-aside. Brokering is particularly common in subcontracting because governments do little monitoring of these agreements. Since success in these programs is again measured by the volume of contracts awarded, there is little incentive to root out and punish fraudulent contractors. Local minority and women's business associations keep a close watch on how well their jurisdictions are meeting the pre-set contracting goals, further adding to the pressure to produce high numbers. But the prevalence of fronts and brokering lessens the true impact of the large sums of money governments claim to be awarding to minority-owned businesses. Unfortunately, the goal of fostering real business development gets lost in the process of playing the numbers game.

Set-Asides Dominate Minority Business Development

Although the SBA's loan and sheltered market programs expanded the range of business opportunities accessible to minority contractors, they still left the bulk of all federal contracts to the traditional majority-owned contractors. Just as African-Americans had earlier targeted the construction industry in their efforts to open up skilled employment, in the mid-1970s minority contractors began to exert political pressure on their national representatives to earmark a portion of federal construction dollars specifically for minority-owned firms. Minority contractors, many of whom had started their careers as skilled tradesmen, faced a myriad of obstacles to staying in business. Although well versed in their trades, many of them lacked the necessary construction management experience. They usually lacked the large amounts of start-up capital needed to invest in construction equipment. The building trade unions often refused to certify them as legitimate union contractors, so that general contractors locked into agreements with the unions would not hire them on as subcontractors. The minority firms also had difficulties getting special city licenses that were required for more specialized work such as underground sewer construction. They often could not secure lines of credit from banks or suppliers, as well as the necessary bonding from the insurance companies.[34]

Minority contractors believed that more work opportunities would enable them to overcome some of these other obstacles. They focused on construction because it accounted for the majority of local government contracting dollars, yet minorities were being awarded very little of it. The city of Chicago, for example, spent roughly 80 percent of its procurement dollars on construction, but between 1972 and 1974 the six governmental units within the city had awarded less than 2 percent of their $427 million in contracts to minority firms. Only 3 percent of the construction work being done in minority communities had been awarded to minority contractors.[35] Through the National Association of Minority Contractors, a lobbying and advocacy group, contractors began to work for the establishment of a minority set-aside program for federal construction contracts. Beginning in 1973, Congressman Parren Mitchell (D-MD), a member of the Congressional Black Caucus, held four years of nationwide hearings in support of a minority set-aside program for construction in which he collected extensive evidence of the discriminatory barriers that still plagued minority businesses.

In 1977, during the congressional debate on a $4 billion Public Works Employment Act aimed at stimulating the sagging economy, Mitchell introduced an amendment requiring that minority contractors receive 10 percent of all the allocated funds. When introduced on the floor of the House, the proposed set-aside amendment generated little debate. Discussion in the House filled approximately six pages of the *Congressional Record,* while the Senate debate filled two pages. Explaining that minority businesses were receiving only 1 percent of government contracts,

Mitchell argued that the amendment would guarantee that minority businesses got a fair share of the action from the public works legislation.[36] The amendment was passed.

The expansion of minority business programs and the establishment of a specific 10 percent goal triggered a flurry of lawsuits across the country as white contractors charged that it violated their equal protection rights. One of these cases was finally heard by the Supreme Court in 1980. In *Fullilove v. Klutznick* the court found federal minority set-asides to be constitutional. The court deferred to Congress as a coequal branch of government with the constitutional power " 'to enforce by appropriate legislation' the equal protection guarantees of the Fourteenth Amendment."[37] The majority noted that Congress had enacted several other minority business development programs prior to the 1977 set-aside, giving it an abundant historical basis on which to conclude that the traditional procurement practices would continue to discriminate against minority contractors.[38] Yet, no single rationale in favor of the validity of the statute received a majority on the court.[39] In failing to establish a specific formula for evaluating the equal protection issues raised by race-based preferences, the Supreme Court created a "standardless" standard for judicial review of these programs. This amorphous standard of review virtually ensured that reverse discrimination suits against minority business set-asides would continue.[40]

Set-asides flourished in the immediate wake of *Fullilove*. The 1982 Surface Transportation Act required the U.S. Department of Transportation to award 10 percent of all federal transportation dollars to be used for highway and mass transit construction to minority firms and another 5 percent to female-owned firms. (This was transformed into a disadvantaged business program in 1987.) The Department of Defense established a 5 percent set-aside program. The Environment Protection Agency and the State Department have similar programs.

The Department of Transportation mandate created an enormous incentive for local jurisdictions that did not want to risk losing the DOT dollars to begin making serious efforts to award public contracts to minority businesses. In Chicago, the city established an Affirmative Action Office within its Department of Public Works, which for the first time in the city's history began compiling a list of competent minority contractors, sending representatives to meetings of the Chicago Economic Development Corporation, and publishing notification of bids in minority newspapers.[41] Initially, city officials made careful distinctions between those contracts involving federal money where the set-asides applied and their own local dollars that did not require set-asides. The 10 percent set-aside was applied only to federal transportation dollars; nonfederal contracts were still awarded to the same traditional bidders without regard to minority business involvement. As late as 1983, minority firms still received no more than 2 percent of Chicago's nonconstruction contracts.[42]

The federal initiatives created a chain reaction, leading to the establishment of similar programs at the state and local level. As more large cities gained black and Hispanic majorities, the implementation of minority set-asides became a popular policy initiative. Since the majority of black elected officials hold local offices, it is at this level that they can most easily effect policy change.[43] Black mayors have shown a strong commitment to local affirmative action and sheltered market programs for minorities. Being attuned to the multiple barriers faced by minority firms, they have established the most ambitious and innovative programs in the country. For example, after Maynard Jackson was elected as Atlanta's first black mayor in 1974, the city established the nation's first minority set-aside program and within a year the minority share of contracting rose from 1 to 19.9 percent.[44] By 1988 it had risen to 34.6 percent, with more than five hundred minority firms participating in municipal contracting.[45] Discretion over contracts provides a mayor with an opportunity to reward political allies and others who have made financial contributions to the campaign coffers. The proliferation of state and local set-asides has increased the politicization of the minority business community by giving it a strong interest in supporting those politicians willing to maintain the flow of contracting opportunities. Where incumbents have shown a reasonable commitment to minority contracting, they are likely to receive the endorsement of various minority contractors' associations reluctant to risk ongoing business opportunities by supporting a challenger. In this way, set-asides have become part of the calculus for any politician interested in courting the minority vote.

During the 1980s preferential procurement programs became the main form of government assistance targeted to minority businesses. As of 1989, set-asides existed in 236 state and local governments, with many programs reserving a certain percentage of government contracting for bidding by designated minority and female-owned businesses. The goals were generally based on the percentage of the minority population in that particular jurisdiction, so that in cities such as Chicago, Atlanta, and Washington, D.C., with large minority populations, the percentage goals could be set as high as 30 or even 50 percent. Some local set-asides covered only construction, while others included supplies and professional services. Most programs had separate goals for minorities and women. The programs were generally modeled on the original 1977 Public Works set-aside, which had contained a broad definition of "minority" that included blacks, Hispanics, Asians, American Indians, and Aleuts. Generally, no geographic limits applied to the programs, so that a qualified minority business from anywhere in the United States could bid on work under a set-aside.

Frequently the set-aside goals were to be achieved through subcontracting, since few nonwhite firms were large enough to bid as prime contractors. This places the weight of responsibility for enforcing the mandates on the prime contractors, who rather than using subcontractors they were accustomed to working with now had to award as much as 30 to 50 percent of the work to a minority- or female-owned firm.[46] Inevitably, prime contractors sought out minority firms that they could work with consistently and gave them the work on public contracts, while giving their long-standing associates work on private-sector jobs. The result was the establishment of a small circle of politically connected minority firms that received the bulk of newly created public-sector opportunities. The emphasis on subcontracting can keep minority firms from growing to the point where they are able to handle prime contracts on their own.

Many of these programs were established rather arbitrarily, without ever substantiating the existence of past discrimination or the relationship between the set-aside goals and the capacity of local minority businesses to fulfill the required goals. Their numerical goals overestimated the actual extent of the minority contractor community. Under considerable pressure to enforce those goals, jurisdictions were often unwilling to grant waivers from their set-aside requirements even though minority or female firms could not always be found to do the work. Majority contractors had to agree to subcontract a portion of their prime contract to a minority- or female-owned firm or risk losing the contract altogether. This drove many prime contractors to circumvent the system by falsely claiming they had used a minority firm as a subcontractor. It also encouraged brokering, where a minority firm receives a contract but hands the actual work over to a majority firm in exchange for a small brokers' fee.

Set-asides have been a mixed blessing for the minority business community. While many firms have thrived off of them, they have also exacerbated the trend toward a "two tiered economic system where one small tier (of high profile enterprises) is flourishing and the rest all are in distress."[47] For some businesses, receiving a public contract through a set-aside has worsened existing problems. Due to weak capitalization and limited access to capital, minority firms have difficulty financing current operations, much less substantial growth. Receiving a public-sector contract can worsen those liquidity problems if the contract calls for a significant increase in up-front costs with payment only upon completion of the work. Minority contractors consistently report having difficulty securing lines of credit from suppliers. Since governments are notoriously slow in paying their contractors, minority vendors who lack sufficient lines of credit to tide them over often find themselves in severe cash shortages. In the most extensive study done to date of the relationship between set-asides and business longevity, Timothy Bates and Darrell Williams found that businesses that rely on government contracts for more than 25 percent of their business actually have a greater likelihood of failing.[48] On the other hand, in jurisdictions that have shown a commitment to building the economic capacity of their minority contractors by assigning staff to assist them, waiving bonding requirements, and providing working capital assistance, set-asides have been found to contribute to increased longevity of minority businesses.[49] These jurisdictions tend to have presiding black mayors.

Since construction consumes the bulk of public contracting dollars, set-asides have greatly increased the amount of work available to minority- and female-owned construction firms. However, the number of legitimate construction firms that have the capacity to do the work has not kept pace. One majority contractor in Chicago believes that "there are no more minority-owned contractors in the city today than there were twenty-five years ago. Set-asides have not increased the pool of well-trained minority businesses with the capacity to bid on the work that is out here now. They haven't had to really compete in the marketplace."[50]

Taylor Cotton, president of Chicago's Black Contractors United, acknowledges that many of his contractors lack sufficient management skills. "Most of them started out as skilled tradesmen and foremen. That's light years away from being a manager."[51] As a consequence, much of the minority subcontracting is done for "time and materials," which is work paid for on an hourly basis, rather than as a lump-sum contract. This practice meets the set-aside goals while contributing little to building the capacity of firms to bid for work on their own.[52] Among minority construction contractors, who as a group had the highest average sales to government, "selling to government is clearly associated with going out of business, other things equal."[53] With so many minority firms dependent on set-asides, their elimination—which is being threatened by Republicans at the state and national levels—would lead to the demise of many existing firms. A bill introduced in the Illinois legislature in 1995 that would if passed, end all state-sponsored affirmative action could wipe out half of the state's five hundred minority contractors.[54]

A Conservative Court Restricts the Use of Set-Asides

The uninterrupted expansion of set-asides came to an abrupt halt in January 1989 when the Supreme Court invalidated a set-aside program in Richmond, Virginia. Although the justices rejected the Bush administration's position that all affirmative action programs were unconstitutional, *J. A. Croson v. City of Richmond* erected new legal obstacles, making it prohibitive for many state and local governments to maintain their programs. Richmond's majority black city council had established a set-aside requiring nonminority contractors to subcontract at least 30 percent of the value of their contracts to minority-owned firms. Although the council had adopted the plan following public hearings at which testimony was presented indicating widespread racial discrimination in the local construction industry, the court ruled that the evidence was insufficient. The council had failed to adequately document the existence of past discrimination, which the court now ruled was a prerequisite to the enactment of a race-conscious set-aside program.[55]

The *Croson* decision did not overturn *Fullilove*, which still applied to federally mandated set-asides, but it rendered virtually all existing state and local government programs unconstitutional. Together, *Fullilove* and *Croson* established a bifurcated constitutional standard under which federal set-asides were permitted, while state-imposed plans were tolerated only under limited circumstances.[56] The Supreme Court's majority concluded that the Fourteenth Amendment had explicitly limited the power of state and local governments to impose any race-based standards, regardless of whether they were designed to harm or to aid minority group members. The dissenting justices argued that the majority had ignored the profound difference between governmental actions that are themselves racist and governmental actions that seek to remedy prior racism. For the first time, the court applied a "strict scrutiny" standard of measurement, giving legitimacy to the idea of reverse discrimination by stating that "the standard of review under the Equal Protection Clause is not dependent on the race of those burdened or benefited by a particular classification."[57] Therefore, a jurisdiction could enact a race-specific remedy as a last resort only if there was at least some concrete evidence of local or regional discrimination tied to past private or governmental action. Furthermore, any preferential program could apply only to those minority groups present in the local population who were found to have been injured.

The court's majority refused to accept evidence of a disparity between Richmond's minority population and the number of city contracts awarded to minority businesses as proof of past discrimination. The justices argued that the "proper statistical evaluation would compare the percentage of MBEs [minority business enterprises] in the relevant market that are *qualified* to undertake city subcontracting work with the percentage of total city construction dollars that are presently awarded to minority subcontractors."[58] The lack of minority members in the local general contractors' association was also rejected as evidence of past discrimination, since the low numbers might be due to a lack of minority interest in the industry, not discrimination. The court believed that there had to be a clear relationship between the percentage goal of the set-aside and the actual availability of local minority businesses who could do the work. This ignores the fact that availability grows in direct proportion to the number of contracting opportunities. Many minority businesses have only a limited capacity precisely because they have been excluded from so many business opportunities. As long as the opportunities to bid on large contracts remained closed, minorities had few incentives to enter business and those few minority businesses in operation never had the chance to develop the capacity needed to bid on governmental contracts.

The Supreme Court also concluded that Richmond's remedy was overly broad in its scope. The 30 percent contracting goal was not a narrowly tailored remedy because it rested upon the ' "completely unrealistic' assumption that minorities will choose a particular trade in lockstep proportion to their representation in the local population."[59] Furthermore, since the city council had supplied no evidence of past discrimination against any racial groups other than African-Americans, those groups' inclusion in the remedy "strongly impugns the city's claim of remedial motivation."[60] The court also questioned the council's failure to consider the use of race-neutral means to increase minority business participation such as providing city financing for all small businesses.

The ruling has forced the revamping or elimination of state and local set-aside programs across the country. Within a year after the Supreme Court ruling, twenty city, county, and state governments had voluntarily terminated or suspended their programs. Majority contractors, with the aid of the Associated General Contractors of America, vigorously litigated the validity of numerous state and local minority preference plans, while successful bidders found themselves parties to potentially void public contracts. By May 1990, fifty new suits challenging federal and nonfederal set-asides had been filed.[61] Nine jurisdictions were forced to stop enforcing their set-asides after the plans failed to withstand *Croson*-type scrutiny.[62] *Croson* created a whole new consulting industry as jurisdictions that wished to preserve their programs hired high-priced consultants to assemble documentation that would substantiate the historic discrimination needed to justify maintaining their set-aside. By 1994 at least sixty five jurisdictions had completed disparity studies, some costing as much a $1 million.[63]

Although roughly half of all state and local set-aside programs were terminated in the aftermath of *Croson,* they remain universal in big cities despite the expense involved in restructuring them. It appears that especially in cities with large black populations, there has been significant political pressure to maintain set-asides.[64] At the state level, where the political clout of minority communities is not as great, minority business programs have become more diffuse and uncoordinated in the wake of *Croson*. Even in the big cities like Chicago, Atlanta, and Washington, D.C., programs have been modified to link the goals more firmly to minority business availability and to target only those local groups who have experienced discrimination. In Chicago, Native Americans successfully sued the Greater Chicago Water Reclamation District after they were initially omitted from the district's post-*Croson* set-aside program. The district had left them out when they failed to provide documentation of discrimination during hearings held prior to the new ordinance going into effect.[65]

A number of jurisdictions that suspended their programs in the immediate aftermath of the *Croson* decision went through the tedious process of collecting the evidence necessary to reinstate the programs. Some larger cities have used disparity studies to justify maintaining of their pre-existing goals, while others have either moved to a more inclusive disadvantaged business program or broken their goals down for each specific minority group covered by the set-aside. In some cases, the goals are also broken down by industrial category to reflect the different levels of availability in different sectors of the local economy. Many cities have also added race-neutral provisions to their programs, such as altering the bonding requirements to lessen the burden on small subcontractors and instituting direct payments to vendors to relieve contractors of the responsibility of paying their suppliers before they receive payment from the public agency. Frequently, new waiver procedures were initiated, and some of the statutes now have sunset clauses.

With few exceptions, jurisdictions that carefully assembled the necessary documentation of past discrimination have successfully defended their programs against lawsuits from majority contractors, making it clear that state and local set-asides can survive the Supreme Court's strict scrutiny. In several cases, cities accepted hastily done disparity studies only to have their programs struck down in court.[66] However, local program administrators report that if the documentation has been done well, the programs become more stable than they were before *Croson*. Litigation has become much more difficult because there is "no longer an easy way to get a quick win. If you wanted to sue you'd have to hire an expert just to sort through the evidence."[67] *Croson* can be viewed as having strengthened the position of the contracting agencies by giving them more assurance that they can withstand a lawsuit. As one former agency director noted, "It did the agencies a favor by providing a standard."[68] The ruling forced jurisdictions that were committed to set-aside programs to look at the problem of discrimination in a broader perspective. In the post-*Croson* era, more attention has been paid to putting ancillary support systems in place, such as improving access to capital and bonding. Although most of the programs remain focused primarily on subcontracting, more effort is given to awarding prime contracts to minority firms.[69]

For local politicians representing large minority populations, set-asides remain an important patronage tool to be handed out to loyal supporters. Shifting political alliances have turned the preferences into a bitter battleground among various minority groups. As Asians and women have gained in political influence, their share of federally funded construction projects has climbed, while those being awarded to other minority groups have declined. In 1985 the U.S. Department of Transportation awarded roughly half of the $1.6 billion in highway construction dollars set-aside for disadvantaged businesses to blacks and Native Americans. In 1994 those two groups received less than a quarter of the $1.8 billion total.[70] As Latinos have gained political power at the local level, they have received an increasing share of the contracting dollars, largely at the expense of African-Americans, who have seen both their political influence and their proportion of contracts shrink.

In 1995 the Supreme Court handed down a second major set-aside case that overturned the 1980 *Fullilove* decision. In *Adarand Constructors, Inc. v. Peña,* the court extended the same strict scrutiny requirement first imposed in *Croson* to all federal race-based preference programs, with the caveat that in this area "Congress may be entitled to greater deference than state and local governments."[71] Although *Adarand* dealt specifically with minority contracting, it is clear that the present court is applying strict scrutiny to all federal government use of race-based criteria in health, education, hiring and other programs as well. Its standards will apply to any classification that makes race or ethnicity a basis for decision-making.[72] While Justices Antonin Scalia and Clarence Thomas would have banned all forms of affirmative action, the majority stated that it wished "to dispel the notion that strict scrutiny is 'strict in theory, but fatal in fact.' "[73] It went on to affirm that "when race-based action is necessary to further a compelling interest, such action is within constitutional constraints if it satisfies the 'narrow tailoring' test this Court has set in previous cases."[74]

In the immediate aftermath of the *Adarand* decision, the Clinton administration issued a directive calling for the evaluation of all federal affirmative action programs in order to bring existing programs into compliance with the new standards. No programs were to be suspended pending the review. Within weeks of the *Adarand* decision, the Clinton administration issued a long-awaited *Affirmative Action Review* in which the president expressed his continued support for affirmative action as both a remedy for past discrimination and as a tool for promoting inclusion.[75]

Conservatives hailed the decision as a further repudiation of affirmative action. Spokespeople for several 1996 Republican presidential hopefuls vowed to use the decision to introduce legislation at the state and federal levels that would completely dismantle racial preferences. According to the chief pollster for Republican presidential candidate Bob Dole, "It opens the door for our guys to move legislatively. . . . In past years, any issue regarding race was a sensitive issue. . . . This ruling basically gives candidates the ability to talk about this issue under the cover of a Supreme Court ruling."[76] Local administrators in Dade County and West Palm Beach, Florida, although not directly affected by the decision, responded to it by suspending their programs.[77] To prevent other states from doing the same, the federal government threatened to withhold funds from any jurisdiction that did not continue to enforce the federal set-asides. However, minority contractors at the local level are already experiencing *Adarand's* negative repercussions. African-American contractors in Illinois have experienced as much as a 20 to 30 percent drop in jobs from a year ago. "They're being snubbed with fewer phone calls, requests for proposals, and returned phone calls. . . . And some competitors have even told minority contractors that they're looking forward to the demise of affirmative action programs."[78]

Conclusion

From their inception during the Nixon administration, minority business development programs have been seen by, Democratic and Republican political leaders alike as a means of courting the black middle class. Set-asides are the policy expression of a well-mobilized, financially secure minority middle class that seeks support from government for overcoming the remaining obstacles in their struggle to achieve full integration into the mainstream of American society. Minority leaders have been no more concerned than white policymakers with the fact that most of these programs assist larger businesses located in nonghetto areas. These businesses are the direct beneficiaries of preferences with no strings attached. Yet, in their present form they do not realize their full potential as an engine of minority employment and capital accumulation. Their role in the revitalization of poor urban communities has been minimal because trickle-down strategies rarely result in significant resource redistribution to those at the bottom of the economic ladder.

Unless the ideological composition of the Supreme Court changes dramatically, the constitutional questions surrounding set-asides have been settled with the now universal requirement of strict scrutiny. Despite these rulings and the clear evidence that discrimination continues to impede the growth of minority businesses, Republicans have seized on affirmative action as a current issue with the potential to energize the backlash vote. The party that initiated "Black Capitalism" as a means of enticing the black middle class into its ranks has found greater electoral success in a political agenda that is openly hostile to black concerns. Since affirmative action has proven to be such an effective whipping boy for conservative Republicans, the party has shown no interest in examining how these programs can been adjusted to make them more effective instruments of urban revitalization and job creation. In contrast, the Clinton administration, having clearly decided not to alienate its black constituents, has come out in support of affirmative action, committing the resources to the necessary evaluation and restructuring in light of *Adarand.*

The future of set-asides will be settled in the political arena, with the supporters of affirmative action on the defensive in the face of vague and unsubstantiated charges of reverse discrimination. As long as the very existence of these programs hangs in doubt, there will be little political space to examine how they could be transformed into more viable instruments of minority economic development. For the time being, American corporations have voiced their continued commitment to maintaining their own minority contracting programs, although these seldom contain specific numerical goals. Big business has come to recognize that drawing upon minority vendors and distributors makes good business sense in an increasingly multicultural marketplace. Whether these firms maintain their commitment in the face of Republican assaults on affirmative action remains to be seen.

The pace of minority business growth is certain to decline in the wake of continuing restrictions on the scope of set-asides, causing further damage to minority employment opportunities. Governments that remain committed to the expansion of minority businesses will have to experiment with new approaches to encouraging their creation, perhaps through the use of race-neutral mechanisms such as assistance in obtaining operating capital and bonding and insurance as well as the use of incentives for small local businesses, many of which would be minority owned.

7 | CHICAGO'S NEW BLACK POLITICAL ESTABLISHMENT

For decades, Chicago's rigidly segregated housing market forced virtually all blacks to live in highly compact, contiguous neighborhoods, creating favorable conditions for the growth of a small indigenous middle class. Restricted in their access to employment in the mainstream labor market, they made their living catering to the community's needs for a variety of goods and services. With the elimination of segregation and the erection of various forms of affirmative action and minority business set-asides, this middle class has greatly expanded in both size and wealth. Between 1973 and 1982 the number of blacks in professional, technical, managerial, and administrative positions nationally increased at a faster rate than did the number of whites in such positions.[1] Many have now migrated out of older ghetto neighborhoods into upscale areas of the city and suburbs.

At the same time, the departure of industrial jobs from central cities like Chicago, organized labors' stiff resistance to the full implementation of affirmative action in skilled trade occupations, and the virtual disappearance of job training for the least skilled have made job opportunities for poorly educated minorities increasingly scarce. These divergent trends have resulted in a growing economic bifurcation within black communities. By 1992, income inequality among blacks nationwide had become more severe than among whites. The lowest quintile of the black population received only 3 percent of total black income while the highest received 48.8 percent, compared to 4.9 percent for the lowest white quintile and 43.8 for the highest white quintile.[2] Prior to the civil rights revolution, black middle-class income was held down artificially by the weight of segregationist labor market practices. The heavy emphasis since the late

1960s on policies that advance the economic agenda of the black middle class has propelled those incomes upward while leaving those of the poor behind.

These dynamic changes translate into a complex web of new power relationships within black communities across the country, in which an economic elite that has distanced itself from the needs of urban poor expends its political and economic resources furthering its own particularized economic and political goals. Forty years ago, when the majority of African-Americans were relegated to the margins of the nation's economic and political life, a powerful mass movement arose demanding equality of rights and resources. That struggle served as the leading catalyst for social change in America during the latter half of the twentieth century. With the resulting incorporation of the black middle class, the movement was assimilated into mainstream politics, losing much of its earlier militancy. Although the majority of African-Americans still vote Democratic, their policy priorities are increasingly determined by their class position, not their racial identity, even though many of those issues continue to be cast in racial terms. The increasing class polarization has created ever sharper distinctions in policy objectives, with middle-class blacks primarily concerned with maintaining affirmative action and business set-asides while the poor find themselves fighting a rear-guard battle to protect the remnants of meager job training and other economic mobility programs.

Contrary to the predictions made by advocates of Black Power in the late 1960s, the expansion of the middle class has not led to the establishment of an independent black political base. Recognizing the failure of the civil rights movement to empower ordinary African-Americans to take charge of the basic institutions that affected their lives, the nascent Black Power movement called for black control of the instruments of power in areas in which blacks were the majority. Where they lacked a majority, proponents of Black Power called for achieving "proper representation and sharing of control" through the creation of power bases from which black people could "press to change local or nation-wide patterns of oppression."[3] No longer would blacks be forced to rely on various political intermediaries, as had been the case during the debate over the 1964 Civil Rights Act, when the AFL-CIO used its strategic position to protect its own membership from the full impact of the new anti-discrimination laws. It was assumed that once elected to office, blacks would be more sensitive, caring, and concerned about the plight of their poorer brothers and sisters than the white politicians who had once represented them. The same was said to be true for black-owned businesses and black-administered social service agencies.

Conceding that some blacks had always been content to work within the existing political and economic framework, Stokely Carmichael and Charles Hamilton, two of Black Power's most articulate spokesmen, were adamant in insisting that it did not "mean merely putting black faces into office."[4] They criticized the "Negro Establishment," including those politicians who were more responsive to the downtown white machine than to their own community. Such politicians could not be relied upon to make forceful demands on behalf of their black constituents because they placed loyalty to a political party before loyalty to their constituents. Recognizing the stiffening of white resistance to further racial reform, Martin Luther King, Jr, placed increasing emphasis on black political and economic empowerment, but he too acknowledged that "a black face that is mute in party councils is not political representation; the ability to be independent, assertive, and respected when the final decisions are made is indispensable for an authentic expression of power."[5]

In the intervening years, these warnings have become a reality in too many cases. Choosing the path of least resistance, the majority of Chicago's African-American politicians now work within the confines of the city's system of patronage politics. The role of the city's fifty aldermen is primarily to dispense basic city services to the residents of their wards. Since being elected in 1989, Mayor Richard M. Daley has carefully rewarded his allies on the city council while cutting his opponents off from access to city resources. Most of the aldermen have reached an accommodation with the administration in order to obtain any help from City Hall. Only a few have been able to maintain their independence to an extent that allows them to challenge policies that contribute to the growing inequality between the city's rich and poor. Even those who honestly see themselves as vehicles for social change are caught in the predicament of having to solicit donations from well-to-do businesspeople in exchange for special consideration on contracts and other matters. For many others, election to office signals their entrance into the circles of power and influence of the dominant society, allowing them to achieve a measure of self-empowerment. To secure their own positions, they cater to the needs of the businesspeople and political sponsors who provided the resources for their election to office.

The proliferation of minority set-asides has created a business elite that successfully manipulates the rhetoric of racial exclusion while playing the classic political insiders' game of endorsing and supporting candidates in exchange for special consideration on public contracting opportunities. These businesses make their profits by positioning themselves as the minority partner in a wide assortment of deals, ranging from the sale of municipal bonds and health insurance to working as subcontractors on large construction projects. Their dependence on set-asides has made them increasingly conservative, unwilling to risk their continued access to politically driven contracting opportunities by challenging the political status quo.

Local civil rights organizations that once stood at the forefront of the movement for social change have come to see themselves more as power brokers than as advocates and champions of the downtrodden. By the mid-1980s Chicago's two leading civil rights organizations, the Chicago Urban League and Operation PUSH (People United to Save Humanity), although vastly different in their tactics and base of support, had both placed black business development at the center of their work, shifting from an earlier focus on opening up new jobs for blacks to one of securing contracts for black businesses. Both had found it organizationally profitable to function as brokers for minority businesses seeking to enter markets opening up as result of expanding public and private set-asides. Operation PUSH's activities, which preceded those of the Urban League by more than a decade, have mainly focused on securing agreements with large retail corporations, while the Urban League has concentrated its efforts on the construction industry.

King Targeted the Evils of Poverty in Chicago

In 1966, on the heels of two major legislative victories that ended southern racial apartheid, King turned his attention to the much more endemic forms of economic inequality that still plagued his people. He realized that black people's depressed living standards were a structural part of the economic system in the United States.[6] He turned his attention to the vast black ghettos in the North, choosing Chicago as the site of his first northern campaign against racial inequality. The existence of the northern ghetto, with its substandard housing, poor schools, and lack of job opportunities, crystalized the economic exploitation of African-Americans. King had come to believe that "in every city, we now have a dual society . . . , two economies, . . . two housing markets, . . . two school systems. This duality has brought about a great deal of injustice. . . . To deal with this unjust dualism we must constantly work toward the goal of a truly integrated society while at the same time we enrich the ghetto. We must seek to enrich the ghetto immediately in the sense of improving the housing conditions, improving the schools . . . , improving the economic conditions. . . . We must work on two levels."[7]

Prior to King's arrival, Chicago's homegrown civil rights movement had been led by a local coalition of organizations known as the Coordinating Council of Community Organizations (CCCO), which had formed to oppose efforts by the Chicago Board of Education to maintain segregation even though it meant erecting temporary mobile units at overcrowded black schools rather than transferring students to underused schools in white neighborhoods. Grassroots groups representing black workers had begun to fight for access to jobs in the building trades and representation in large unions with increasingly black membership, such as the Transit Workers Union. The city's chapter of the National Association for the Advancement of Colored People (NAACP), once a vocal advocate of racial equality, had fallen silent, coopted by Mayor Richard J. Daley and the Democratic Party machine. The Chicago Urban League, the city's oldest race relations organization, preferred to work quietly behind the scenes, positioning itself as the mediator between the grassroots organizations and the city's political leadership. This left the city without an activist national civil rights organization, a role that King and the Southern Christian Leadership Conference (SCLC) had been invited to play. Once in Chicago, King launched a multifaceted campaign aimed at opening up access to jobs, schools, and housing previously reserved for whites. While he and his local allies chose to make the city's segregated housing market the focal point of what came to be known as the Chicago

Freedom Movement, he also attacked its two-tiered labor market. Speaking before a large rally in July 1966, King called on the city's leadership to make a full commitment to creating structures of economic opportunity for its minority residents by:

1. Publishing the number of whites, blacks, and Latinos employed by the city and in all firms that held contracts with the city.
2. Revoking city contracts held by companies lacking full equal employment plans.
3. Requiring a public head count by businesses and trade unions on racial hiring and membership, broken down by job classification.
4. Creating a program to upgrade and train minority employees with the goal of integrating all levels of public and private employment.
5. Supporting union organizing efforts among minority workers, since they were concentrated in low-paying, unorganized industries.
6. Accepting at least four hundred black and Latino apprentices in the craft unions.
7. Expanding a rapid transit line to O'Hare and the Northwest side of the city to provide access for blacks to the areas of job growth.[8]

King's campaign to integrate Chicago's neighborhoods met with fierce resistance. Open-housing marches into white neighborhoods confronted white mob violence that surpassed the civil rights movement's worst experiences in the South. King was forced to accept a compromise with Daley that led to the signing of an open-housing covenant in exchange for King's withdrawal from the city. King's demands for improvements in job access fell on deaf ears, with even the small procedural reforms that he proposed, such as the provision of a head count of municipal employment by race, having to wait until the election of Chicago's first black mayor.

Operation Breadbasket Inherits King's Economic Agenda

Although King's attempt to expand the scope of racial integration in the North ended in failure, his efforts to build an organization designed to address the second part of his dual strategy—namely, enriching the ghetto—flourished. In 1966, Operation Breadbasket, formed four years earlier as a division of the SCLC, was incorporated into King's Chicago campaign. Jesse Jackson, then a young seminary student at the University of Chicago, was appointed as its director. Breadbasket helped organize supporters during King's marches against segregated housing, but its principal purpose was to organize the buying power of black consumers.[9] Modeled on the successful consumer boycotts led by Reverend Leon Sullivan in Philadelphia, its stated goal was "the economic development and viability of the black community through new job opportunities and the creation of economic benefits through the establishment of black owned and black managed businesses."[10] The organization was premised on the belief that the balance of power in America was shared by Big Government, Big Business, and Big Labor. It was in the interaction of these three that decisions were made. Since African-Americans were not represented in any one of these centers of influence, they lacked power. However, blacks had two forms of power at their disposal—their votes and their consumer dollars. Breadbasket's aim was to leverage black consumer dollars in order to strengthen black economic power. The development of black businesses would enable blacks to control an aspect of the business side of the power structure.[11]

In its early days, Breadbasket sought to make businesses located in black neighborhoods more accountable to their customers through a strategy of pressure marketing. Any white businessperson operating a store in a black neighborhood was expected to put black products on its shelf and to use black scavengers (private garbage disposal companies), insurance companies, banks, or any other services the neighborhood could render. As long as the businessperson was taking dollars out of the community, he or she had to put something back. "Just as in nature, a bee pollinates the flower from which it takes its nectar."[12]

While King confronted Chicago's political machine and its allies among the realtors, Breadbasket launched massive boycotts against supermarkets that were selling poor-quality goods, including rotting meat and stale bread, at exorbitant prices. It won its first victory against Certified Foods, a chain store that had two pay scales, one for its white drivers and a much lower one for its black drivers. The store yielded to the pickets and signed a covenant with Breadbasket.[13] By the end of 1966, Breadbasket's boycotts had forced several other chain stores to sign as well. At first, the covenants focused primarily on increasing minority employment in areas of the company from which blacks had previously been excluded. In the course of repeated negotiations, a broader economic development agenda gradually emerged. Retail stores were asked to stock specific black products such as Grove Fresh Orange Juice or Joe Louis Milk. Additional demands were added that called on the companies to hire black scavenger companies, use black contractors in the construction of new buildings, deposit funds in black-owned banks, and use black insurance companies.[14]

The Chicago Urban League played its customary role as a referral agency for those blacks interested in securing the jobs created through Breadbasket's pickets.[15] Blacks with the skills and education needed to qualify for the newly opened managerial positions were often placed in charge of implementing the company's agreement with Breadbasket. For example, A & P Foods brought two blacks into its top management to implement the employment and contractor goals set forth in its covenant.[16] After Breadbasket boycotted Walgreen's Drug Store, which had opened its very first store in the heart of the black community but had hired almost no black managers, the company promoted some of its own black store clerks.[17] These were breakthrough jobs very similar to those secured through the "Don't Buy Where You Can't Work" campaigns of the 1930s.

Breadbasket also did extensive consumer education to increase awareness and support for black products. As Cecil Troy, the owner of Grove Fresh Orange Juice, explained, "Breadbasket made it so that if you were my neighbor and I came over to your house and you didn't have some Grove Fresh Orange Juice, if you served orange juice, or if you served milk and it wasn't Joe Louis, or if you served ice cream and it wasn't Baldwin ice cream, or sausage if you had breakfast and it wasn't Parkerhouse, you would be ostracized."[18] Grassroots consumers' clubs were set up that visited people in their homes to show them a variety of black products and encourage them to go to local stores and ask for them. The clubs also visited schools and told children about the products.[19] A black business fair, "Black Expo," was launched that interwove information on black businesses together with entertainment by major black performers such as

Roberta Flack and Bill Cosby. Troy, who cochaired six Black Expos, said he witnessed "grown black people stand up and cry because they didn't believe we had all these services and goods to offer."[20] The expos had their desired effect—they increased black awareness, thereby helping black businesses grow. By 1971, Black Expo featured five hundred black business exhibitors from Chicago and forty other cities. It had become the largest and single most important event of its kind within the black or minority communities in the United States.[21]

PUSH Switches from Jobs to Contracts

Over time, Breadbasket's emphasis on securing jobs and educating consumers became secondary to the goal of gaining new business opportunities for black companies. Many black businesspeople became actively involved in Breadbasket, a new phenomenon in the civil rights movement. In some cases, Breadbasket went back to companies with whom they had negotiated for jobs and asked for additional economic development items. One chain store, National Tea, cooperated by awarding a contract to a black scavenger and by contracting with a black construction contractor to build a new store. This was the first new chain store ever to be built by a black contractor, and it was considered such a significant breakthrough that King attended the groundbreaking ceremonies.[22]

After King's assassination in 1968, Breadbasket became the most vibrant part of the national SCLC, with Jesse Jackson becoming the de facto inheritor of the movement. In December 1970, following a protracted battle with the national SCLC leadership, Jackson left King's old organization and established Operation PUSH. Operation PUSH was almost a complete transfer of membership and activities from Breadbasket—all that really changed was the name. Within its first year, Operation PUSH signed national covenants with Schlitz and General Foods that together resulted in more than $105 million in benefits to black businesses. Schlitz agreed to hire 236 blacks. In the agreement with General Foods, valued at $65 million, the company agreed to increase its deposits in black banks, to use black advertising agencies, insurance companies, construction contractors, and auto dealers, and to make donations to black charities. In its second year, PUSH signed major covenants with Avon and Miller Brewing. By 1974 Chicago could boast of eighteen black-owned firms whose sales volume exceeded $1 million each, the second highest number for any city in the country. Breadbasket/PUSH had helped them all, either through covenants or through contracts. Half of the city's millionaire black companies had representatives on PUSH's National Board.[23] PUSH went on to sign covenants with Coca-Cola, Anheuser-Busch, Coors, Burger King, Ford Motor Company, and others. In most of these cases, the result was the provision of company franchises to black businesspeople.

Since PUSH's strategy focused on securing concessions from the private sector, its momentum was unaffected by the government's declining commitment to civil rights reforms under the Nixon administration. As securing contracts for black businesses increasingly dominated the organization's work, its earlier efforts to open up jobs and promote consumer awareness waned. By 1976, the annual Black Expos were discontinued and the consumer clubs had been abandoned. Rhetorically, the organization continued to claim that its efforts on behalf of black businesses were part of the movement for black equality. Exactly how the benefits of PUSH's support of individual black entrepreneurs accrued to its broader black constituency was hazy at best.

The growing disconnection between work on behalf of particular black businesses and service to its broader constituency is highlighted by PUSH's role in fostering the development of two of Chicago's black-owned banks. Started in the early 1960s, both Seaway Bank and Independence Bank were struggling to stay open until Breadbasket's covenants began requiring that white-owned companies place deposits in black-owned banks. These deposits were the banks' first large "white accounts." Independence Bank had been on the verge of going under when it received a major infusion of new money through Breadbasket's covenant with A & P Food Stores. Breadbasket also worked out an agreement with Adlai Stevenson, then treasurer of the state of Illinois, to put state funds into both banks. Breadbasket protected the banks and their investors from community pressure to adopt more aggressive lending policies. Alvin Boutte, the former president of Independence Bank, explained how PUSH acted as an intermediary by telling community residents, "'Look you can't go up in there and ask for these stupid loans and if you do that, you've got to come and see me.' They gave me time to stay in harmony with the community because we had to start off very conservatively."[24] By 1974, Chicago's black community had the largest and strongest financial base of any black community in the nation. Both Seaway and Independence now rank among the top ten black banks in the nation.

With PUSH's help, the banks' stockholders have become quite wealthy, but the communities in which they are located have reaped few benefits from these banks' success. The majority of stock in Independence Bank is owned by ten investors, including Boutte and George Johnson, founder of Johnson Products, Inc.[25] One of the bank's executives admits that the growth of Independence Bank has not benefited poor blacks. "There is an underclass, no question. And they're not being affected by this bank. But, I can't wait for them. What I'm doing, I can't wait. We've got to start this now. And when you start it now you got to deal with people who first have the intelligence and the expertise to at least have a chance to succeed. And, secondly, have a certain pool of capital that they are willing to put at risk."[26]

By the early 1990s both Seaway and Independence ranked among the top one-third of Chicago area banks based on return on average assets, but neither was an aggressive community lender. Much of the banks' success has come from providing services, investing in securities, and making commercial loans to Fortune 500 companies looking to do business with minority-owned banks. Independence chose to specialize in financing black-owned franchises nationwide because in Boutte's opinion these were safer deals than lending to small black businesses located in the neighborhoods surrounding the bank or to businesses that held city contracts. As a result, the majority of the bank's assets were in investment securities, with loans making up only 40 percent of its portfolio.[27] Independence Bank's poor record of community lending came to light in 1988, when the bank's holding company, Indecorp, attempted to buy Drexel Bank, another small neighborhood bank. At the time, community groups pressed Indecorp and its owners, including Boutte, for an agreement to increase its neighborhood lending. In 1993, Seaway Bank, which by then had become Chicago's largest black-owned bank, received a "needs to improve" rating in its first examination for compliance with the sixteen-year-old federal Community Reinvestment Act (CRA), effectively barring it from buying other banks until it improved its ratings. Seaway, with assets of $202 million, had provided only twenty-four loans for mortgages and home improvements in 1991, totaling a mere $1.9 million, while Independence made twenty-eight, totaling $1.4 million.[28] For many years these black-owned banks held a virtual monopoly on bank lending in black neighborhoods because the larger financial institutions had withdrawn when the communities' white residents pulled out. However, during the 1990s larger downtown banks, faced with growing pressure from CRA requirements that they lend a portion of their funds in undercapitalized communities, have returned to set up branches in black neighborhoods, effectively competing with the black banks already located there.

When PUSH launched its national boycott against Nike in 1990, its demands were narrowly focused on securing contracts for black businesses. The types of employment-related demands that would create economic opportunities for ordinary blacks, who were being asked to give up Nike products were completely absent. As it had done with other companies in the past, PUSH called for a boycott against Nike products, charging the company with exploiting the poor black youth who were paying exorbitant prices for Nike shoes. In Chicago, small groups of PUSH supporters held picket lines outside of a few sporting goods stores. PUSH's main demands were that Nike start using black law firms, advertising agencies, and banks, hire more black executives, and put more blacks on their board of directors, all of which would have benefited a small group of black businesspeople. Conservative columnist William Raspberry accused PUSH of hocus-pocus in using the plight of poor blacks to promote the interests of a small number of already advantaged blacks.[29] Traditionally, consumer boycotts have been used to force companies to do more for their customers, as was the case with Breadbasket's early boycotts against neighborhood grocery stores, or for their own employees, as was the case with the United Farmworkers' grape boycotts. However, in the Nike case, PUSH called for a national boycott to gain benefits for a small number of businesspeople who could easily afford the price of a pair of Nike shoes for themselves and a couple of poor kids as well.

The Nike boycott proved to be a disastrous failure. Local sporting goods outlets, even in black neighborhoods, reported steady and, in some cases, even increased sales of Nike products, while nationally the company reported that orders for its products were up 42 percent.[30] Embarrassed by the boycott's failure and now $250,000 in debt, the PUSH board fired its young executive director, Tyrone Crider, and Jackson quickly called upon his old friends in the black business community to bail out the organization.

Although Jackson blamed the organization's indebtedness on a faltering economy that had led to increased business failures and joblessness, it was clearly a sign of PUSH's dwindling base of support. Attendance at its Saturday morning community forums, traditionally an activist gathering point in Chicago, had dropped off sharply. Many former supporters had become alienated by the organization's silence on a growing number of community issues coupled with its leaders' growing ties to the Democratic Party leadership, including the endorsement of Mayor Daley by several ministers closely associated with PUSH. Following Jackson's 1988 presidential campaign, both Jesse Jackson, Jr., and Reverend Willie Barrow, the senior Jackson's longtime second-in-command at PUSH, had been given seats on the Democratic National Committee, placing them in the inner circle of the party. For many old PUSH supporters who were staunchly anti-Daley and viewed themselves as reform Democrats, this was seen as an unacceptable compromise with the establishment.

PUSH has never demanded that the minority firms it assisted be held accountable to the broader community that their growth is theoretically supposed to benefit. Instead, the exchange has been on a much more personal level. Jackson has frequently tapped into the financial resources of these firms for contributions to both of his presidential campaigns as well as the expenses incurred in the operation of the National Rainbow Coalition and Operation PUSH. To pay off PUSH's 1991 debts, Jackson turned to Elzie Higginbottom, the owner of a successful realty company, who spearheaded an aggressive fundraising campaign among black businesspeople, ministers, and politicians. Higginbottom was also a major black fundraiser for Mayor Daley's 1995 reelection campaign, choosing to support the incumbent with whom he was negotiating a lucrative public works contract rather than the black challenger, Commissioner Joseph Gardner.[31] In January 1996, when a fatal fire broke out in a high-rise building managed by Higginbottom's company that had previously been cited for numerous building code violations, including nonfunctioning smoke detectors, neither Daley nor Jackson were willing to publicly criticize Higginbottom's poor maintenance of the building. His contributions to both had bought him immunity from criticism for his company's role in a blaze that cost four tenants their lives.

The Urban League Brokers Deals for Black Contractors

Following the lead of its national parent organization, the Chicago Urban League has long positioned itself as the moderate voice of black civil rights. Beginning in the midst of the 1960s marches and boycotts over the desegregation of Chicago's public schools, the Urban League took on the role of negotiator and conciliator, working behind the scenes while quietly providing funds for the efforts of the Coordinating Council of Community Organizations. With an operating budget of $7.2 million, mostly in the form of grants from federal, state and local government, the League is by far the wealthiest civil rights organization in the city.[32] Its president and CEO, James Compton, is far more comfortable in quiet corporate boardrooms than in crowded community meetings or on the picket line. The League pays Compton a six-figure salary and provides him with a car and driver. In addition, he sits on the board of Commonwealth Edison, Chicago's electric utility, and is past president of the Chicago Board of Education, the Chicago Library Board, and the Chicago World's Fair Committee.

Since the organization's founding in 1910, the National Urban League's chapters across the country had emphasized job placement and training. Traditionally, the League had not tried to train blacks in business skills, focusing instead on gaining entrance onto the lowest rungs of the industrial ladder.[33] In the 1960s the Chicago Urban League became party to a series of minority recruitment plans for the construction industry (described in Chapter 5) that for the first time led the organization into the field of minority business development. As a few black tradesmen gained a foothold in the building trades, the League began to provide them with training in construction management aimed at setting them up as independent construction contractors.

By the time Congress enacted the first 10 percent set-aside as part of the 1977 Public Works Employment Act, the Urban League had created a pool of black tradesmen who were poised to take advantage of the new set-asides. In 1983 it set up the Affirmative Action Division as a distinct subdivision of the organization. While its name implies that the division was involved in securing jobs, its primary purpose was to act as a broker between minority contractors and majority firms that were seeking minority subcontractors to comply with the growing number of set-aside requirements on public and private construction projects. Beginning with Mayor Harold Washington's 1985 executive order requiring that 25 percent of city contracts be awarded to minority firms and continuing through the late 1980s, Compton took advantage of his numerous corporate contacts to position the League as the leading broker on major construction projects, including the construction of the United Terminal at O'Hare Airport, Ameritech's corporate headquarters, and the new AT&T Center in downtown Chicago. The establishment of the Affirmative Action Division coincided with a major construction boom in downtown Chicago that rapidly transformed the organization's newest division into a major source of income for the League as a whole. At its height, the Division had between twenty-five and thirty consultant agreements, contributing $5 million to the League's coffers during a three-year period in the late 1980s.[34] At times, funds from the Affirmative Action Division provided the dollars needed to cover expenses in other League programs whose own funding sources were slow in paying.

The Urban League also sponsored Black Contractors United, the city's largest black contractors' association. Many younger contractors who were not part of the Urban League's inner circle accused the League of favoritism in steering subcontracting opportunities to the old guard that controlled Black Contractors United. With the end of the downtown construction craze, the reduction in set-asides following the 1989 *Croson* decision, and the election of Richard M. Daley as mayor, the Affirmative Action Division's fortunes began to decline. Much of its professional staff took jobs with competitors that were now sprouting up to pursue a share of this newly created market. By the early 1990s contracts that had once flowed to the Urban League were being awarded to the Target Group, a privately owned firm that started as a subsidiary of one of the mayor's favorite construction management companies, Richard Stein and Company. The Target Group's owner, Joe Williams, has been one of Mayor Daley's staunchest black supporters.

Minority Contracting as a New Form of Political Patronage

With the exodus of whites to the suburbs, many central cities now have predominantly minority populations, creating unprecedented opportunities for minority political empowerment. During the fierce debates over the 1964 Civil Rights Act, there were only six black members in the U.S. House of Representatives and not a single black U.S. Senator. By 1994 there were forty African-Americans and Hispanics in Congress. In 1965 there were fewer than 500 African-Americans holding elective office throughout the United States; by 1990 those numbers had climbed to 7,370.[35] With the exception of those jurisdictions that maintain at-large elections, most legislative districts with more than 65 percent minority populations now have minority representation. Even though the majority of urban poor are now represented by minority politicians in city councils, state legislatures, and in the U.S. House of Representatives, they often lack effective political representation at any level of government.

Much of the literature on African-American politics notes that black politicians have made important symbolic improvements in the empowerment of their constituents, but have not been able to substantively improve conditions of the black working class and the poor. Generally the argument is made that due to economic contraction and, in particular, the deterioration of urban economies, black politicians are limited in their ability to make improvements in the conditions of the communities they represent. Although this is no doubt true, it assumes that the majority of black politicians still regard themselves as advocates for their poor constituents. This is not necessarily true. It also assumes that black politicians are motivated primarily by a sense of racial solidarity rather than by the same considerations about winning reelection and personal status that motivate their white counterparts.

From 1983 to 1987, Chicago stood as the nation's premier example of progressive black political empowerment. Harold Washington, the city's charismatic black mayor, had been elected by a grassroots movement that sought an end to racial injustice and traditional machine politics. Having come out of the Democratic machine himself, Harold, as he was affectionately known, was able to bind together an extremely diverse coalition of supporters ranging from militant community activists to old-time ward politicians. As a maverick, Washington was committed to opening up access to City Hall for groups that had long been locked out of any meaning-ful participation in the city's affairs. He recruited a group of young re-formers into his administration who envisioned Chicago as a city of revi-talized urban communities, relying on small and minority businesses to generate jobs in the neighborhoods. Even those black businesspeople and politicians who felt more comfortable under the old regime were forced to conform, for fear that their constituents would turn on them if they did not publicly support the extremely popular mayor. With Washington's sud-den death in November 1987, the coalition he had put together collapsed overnight. First, there was a major rift within the black community as it broke into two warring camps, each supporting the claims of a different al-derman seeking council appointment to fill Washington's unfinished term in office. Then, with Daley's election as mayor in 1989, the black machine politicians quickly returned to the fold. By his second election in 1991, Da-ley was able to secure the endorsement of a number of prominent black ministers, businesspeople, and politicians. Daley has cultivated a circle of wealthy black supporters who are routinely awarded a variety of city busi-ness, ranging from legal work to road construction.

Under the old machine, most of the city's business had gone to a small group of politically connected firms, who often received contracts after a perfunctory bidding process. Needless to say, very few minority firms had the political connections needed to secure lucrative city contracts. Court-ing the support of the minority business community following his narrow election, Washington implemented the city's first set-aside program as an executive order in 1985. Previously, the city's Purchasing Department had carefully applied federal set-asides only to those projects involving federal dollars. Modeled on the 1977 Public Works Employment Act set-aside, the executive order required that 25 percent of all city contracts be awarded to minority-owned firms and 5 percent to female-owned firms. Like most other local set-sides, the Washington administration's numerical goals were set to reflect the percentages of minorities in the city's total popula-tion, which a 1985 consultant's report admitted were "far in excess of the current representation of minority and women owned firms (M/WBEs) in the business community."[36] The high goals were justified as a means of en-abling minority firms to catch up to where they ought to be, were it not for the effects of past discrimination, as well as providing an assurance to minority entrepreneurs that a sufficient demand was being established to warrant their entry into the market.[37]

Following the Supreme Court's 1989 Croson decision requiring that cities not only prove the existence of historic discrimination, but also set the level of their set-aside in accordance with actual minority business availability, the city urgently needed to produce a predicate study that would support the continuation of its set-aside. Started in the final months of Eugene Sawyer's administration (Sawyer was the black alderman picked by city council to succeed Washington), the task of producing the study was inherited by the Daley administration following his election in April 1989. Daley was faced with a highly volatile political situation, caught between minority and women contractors who wanted to preserve the set-aside and majority contractors who were eager to see it discontinued.

The administration responded by publicly committing itself to the maintenance of the set-asides, while doing the minimum amount of research and documentation work necessary to withstand a court challenge of its program. The researchers hired to assemble the evidence of historic discrimination were instructed not to include data on events prior to 1979, thereby protecting the elder Daley from being implicated in the city's history of discrimination against minority contractors.[38] Both Sawyer and the younger Daley had committed to maintaining the existing 25 percent set-aside for minority contractors, even though the earlier consultant's report acknowledged that minority firms did not represent 25 percent of available businesses in the Chicago metropolitan region. Researchers were faced with the challenge of finding a statistical justification for the 25 percent goal as required by Croson even though the Census Bureau's 1987 survey of businesses showed that female- and minority-owned firms constituted only 12 percent of all businesses in metropolitan Chicago.[39] Officials in the Daley administration decided to use the number of minority- and female-owned firms on the city's own vendors list as its measure of availability. However, the vendors list greatly inflated the percentage of available minority firms because the Purchasing Department had aggressively recruited more minority firms onto the list during the Washington administration, while purging older firms that had not bid on city work in a long time. This weak statistical underpinning leaves Chicago's entire set-aside program vulnerable to suit by white contractors, who can easily argue that it does not meet the standards of evidence set by *Croson*.

Despite the weaknesses in the research, Daley secured the support of the prominent minority contractors' associations for his post-*Croson* set-aside program by establishing a new Sheltered Market Program into which 10 percent of city contracts would be placed. Representatives of the various minority contractors' associations were given seats on an oversight committee that decided which contracts were to be placed into this pool to be set aside exclusively for bidding by minority firms. Having been given what appeared to be a direct hand in the selection of contracts, the minority contractors signed on to the overhaul of the program and gave public testimony in support of the Daley administration's new ordinance. Except for the set-aside goals, Chicago's program contains no business development provisions designed to assist smaller firms who may lack adequate bonding or financing capabilities. The city's program went unchallenged until 1996, when Chicago's General Contractors Association filed suit against it. Once again the minority contractors' associations mobilized, seeking to use their political clout to bring pressure on the general contractors to withdraw their suit.

Although black contractors have repeatedly complained that Daley has not given them their "fair" share of contracts, favoring Latino and Asian contractors instead, they have nonetheless given him their almost unanimous political support. Those black businesspeople who are dependent on government contracting now tend to support whichever candidate is most likely to maintain the flow of contracts, regardless of race. Prominent black businesspeople have actively raised funds for Mayor Daley's last two reelection campaigns, while Joe Gardner and Roland Burris, his two black challengers in the 1995 election, were starving for resources. Several prominent black businessmen, including Al Johnson, founder of one of the nation's first black car dealerships, and Ed Gardner, founder of Soft Sheen Products, gave Gardner their support. Yet, his single largest campaign contribution came from a majority contractor who does considerable business with the Water Reclamation District, where Gardner served as one of nine commissioners.[40] When interviewed at a $250-a-ticket fund-raiser for Daley sponsored by Elzie Higginbottom, Larry Huggins, the vice president of Black Contractors United (BCU), remarked that Chicagoans must remember "that businessmen have business interests." At the time, Huggins's company had contracts to provide concrete work at O'Hare Airport and at the McCormick Place expansion project, an addition to the city's convention center.[41] In 1996, Huggins's company received one of the largest minority contracts to be awarded for the Democratic Party's 1996 Chicago convention.

The same exchange of endorsements for contracts has occurred at the state level, where during Illinois's last two gubernatorial campaigns, BCU gave an early endorsement to the Republican candidate, Jim Edgar. In the last three months of his 1991 campaign Edgar gave BCU $20,000 in cash and advertising, along with a promise to maintain set-asides on state-funded construction projects such as the McCormick Place expansion project.[42] Edgar was able to parlay BCU's support and that of several prominent black community leaders into an unprecedented number of black votes in the general election. The Republican won 20 percent of the vote in Chicago's nineteen black wards, beating his Democratic opponent by only 83,909 votes statewide, of which half were black votes.[43] Had they gone the other way, Edgar might well have lost the election. BCU endorsed Edgar a second time in 1995, even though as governor he refused to increase state funding for Chicago Public Schools and oversaw the dismantling of Illinois's General Assistance program, leaving 82,000 poor, mostly black men in Chicago without any income.

Chicago's Silent Black Aldermen

The depopulation of the nation's big cities has left its urban cores with less and less political muscle in both state and national legislatures, which in many cases are now controlled by Republicans openly hostile to the needs of central cities and their poor residents. With much of the middle class having retreated to the suburbs, cities are composed of two sharply contrasting worlds—attractive, upscale communities that are home to highly paid professionals, and decaying, largely abandoned neighborhoods made up only of poor people. In their struggle to remain viable in the postindustrial era, big city mayors have sought to transform their central business districts into attractive centers for commerce and tourism while minimizing their expenditures on those blighted communities that primarily house poor people—unless, of course, those neighborhoods have significant redevelopment potential.

In Chicago, the city government has gradually carried out a plan to completely redevelop the neighborhoods surrounding its central business district by replacing housing for the poor with expensive new townhouse and loft development. Public housing located in the redevelopment zones on the near Northside and near Westside is being torn down and replaced with market-rate townhouses. The majority of these communities' poor residents are being pushed to the city's periphery and into suburban ghettos. Except for the five years during which Washington served as mayor, there has been little opposition to this transformation.

In June 1996, the city and the Chicago Housing Authority announced plans to demolish eight public housing high-rises in Cabrini-Green on the city's near Northside and replace them with 2,300 new units of housing, of which only 650 would be reserved for current residents. Cabrini-Green borders one of the hottest real estate markets in the city and has therefore become a prime target for private redevelopment. One thousand new units of housing, much of it consisting of townhouses, would be sold at market rates. The majority of the current residents, most of whom are on public aid, would be relocated to other black neighborhoods on the city's periphery.[44] One of only two local elected officials to speak out against the demolition was Congressman Bobby Rush, whose own congressional district does not even include Cabrini-Green. The congresswoman, state representative, and alderman who represent the residents did not make any public comments.

At present, even though the majority of the city's fifty aldermen are either black or Latino, they have largely failed to speak out against the increasing marginalization of their constituents, much less initiate any proactive steps to address the crises of education, violence, and joblessness that plague their communities. Following in the footsteps of the old ward bosses, the majority of black and Latino aldermen representing Chicago's poor wards have given Mayor Daley their complete allegiance in exchange for assistance on their reelection campaigns, special consideration on zoning in their wards, infrastructure repairs, and contracts or jobs for friends and relatives. On paper, Chicago has a strong city council—weak mayor system of government; in reality, however, Mayor Daley now runs

City Hall with no opposition. Even certain aldermen who consider themselves to be progressive Democrats have learned to choose their battles carefully, knowing that to remain in the opposition will make it difficult for them to deliver services to their wards.

The few instances in which minority aldermen have publicly opposed the mayor during the last several years have all involved issues of affirmative action. In early 1993 black aldermen joined forces with a number of their white ethnic colleagues to block a proposed tax increase.[45] The African-American aldermen objected to the administration's failure to insist on the inclusion of an affirmative action clause in the newest police officers' contract. A second case involved the tiny number of African-Americans and Latinos who passed the city-administered test for police sergeant. When only forty blacks and twenty-two Latinos scored among the top five hundred test-takers, black aldermen held public hearings at which they raged against the Daley administration.[46] The hearings provided a convenient forum at which these politicians could evoke the traditional symbols of racial injustice, but once they were over nothing was done to change the outcome of the test, nor did the public display of anger translate into decisions not to endorse Daley in his 1995 reelection campaign.

Political independence is also compromised by the overwhelming financial demands of running for reelection. Generally lacking their own personal wealth and having more limited access to corporate and political action committee (PAC) contributions, black politicians easily become dependent on financial support from party leaders, who in turn expect close adherence to the leadership's legislative agenda. It is a standard practice for politicians to raise campaign contributions from businesspeople who are either seeking contracts from government or are hoping to gain support for certain pieces of legislation. Minority politicians representing poor communities have fewer such opportunities because there are fewer legitimate businesses located in their districts.

In early 1996, the federal government revealed that it had carried out a four-and-half-year corruption probe targeting several dozen Chicago politicians. The FBI had recruited a construction contractor who had handed out roughly $150,000 in bribes to numerous black and Latino aldermen in exchange for their permission to dump construction debris on vacant lots in their wards. The mole had given one now-deceased alderman monthly payoffs of $5,000 in exchange for permission to create a dumpsite the size of two full city blocks in the middle of a poor residential neighborhood. The jagged mound of concrete, dirt, and other garbage made the struggling neighborhood look like East Beirut—the street was torn up, buildings were abandoned, and at one point the kids attending a neighboring school could not go outside at recess because of the dust.[47] Another alderman, whose complicity was uncovered in the midst of his bid for one of Chicago's three black congressional seats, justified his support of the dump site in his ward as a form of "economic development." He had apparently received $31,000 in illegal bribes from the government's mole. Other politicians caught in the sting argued that the money was taken as campaign contributions and that they never did any of the favors requested by the contractor. Local civil rights organizations such as Operation PUSH charged that the probe was racially motivated because such a disproportionate number of the suspects were minority. It was apparent that these politicians had been particularly susceptible to under-the-table deals because they had fewer legitimate sources of making money from their aldermanic positions than did the white aldermen, most of whom are lawyers. The large number of politicians caught in the sting and the length of the operation, however, suggests a serious lack of accountability to the constituents they were elected to represent.

Shortly before the 1996 Democratic Party convention arrived in Chicago, two separate news articles, one in the *Chicago Tribune* and one in the *Wall Street Journal,* heralded the city's rebirth. The *Tribune* reported the results of an opinion survey showing a marked improvement in residents' perceptions of the quality of life in the city.[1] The *Wall Street Journal* focused on the city's economic vitality as "the commercial center of the region that is leading the U.S. economic expansion." The *Journal* went on to say that "increasingly, people with the job skills or affluence to live anywhere choose Chicago."[2] After years of steady decline, other cities, including Detroit, are experiencing a similar renaissance.

While urban revitalization reaffirms the centrality of cities to their regions' economies, it may actually lead to a deeper isolation of the city's poor population. The return of the affluent city dweller reverses a long-term trend of middle-class out-migration that began with the invention of the streetcar.[3] As trendy coffee shops and condominiums replace run-down apartments in the neighborhoods surrounding the central business districts, these areas' poor residents are being pushed out. This transformation is clearly visible on Chicago's near Westside, a dilapidated warehouse district that for many years served as the city's skid row. Anchored by the expansion of the University of Illinois and Oprah Winfrey's production studio, the area began to undergo a wholesale condo conversion in the early 1990s. City Hall has encouraged this transformation by using its extensive zoning powers to force almost all of the single-room occupancy hotels and homeless shelters that once served the transient population into leaving, thereby "cleansing" the neighborhood of its undesirable population.

Such uneven patterns of economic growth increasingly create two separate realities within the same city, with some communities alive with around-the-clock activity while others remain vast empty spaces littered with abandoned buildings, empty lots, and rusting cars. In *The Closing Door*, Gary Orfield and Carole Ashkinaze examine the effects of such uneven growth patterns in the job-rich labor market of Atlanta, Georgia. There, phenomenal suburban growth rates have done little to lift the economic fortunes of poor blacks living in neighborhoods cut off from access to the suburban labor market. Orfield and Ashkinaze document how cuts in federal social service spending made by conservatives during the 1980s exacerbated the isolation of poor blacks.[4]

Much of this new economic activity is driven by private investors, spurred on by generous incentives from state and local governments. The steady drain of manufacturing jobs and the resultant loss of municipal revenues led cities across the country to adopt real estate–driven economic development ventures in the hope that new business activity would offset the deep tax concessions they had granted to attract new investment. Local governments sought to leverage the small amounts of federal aid they were still receiving in the 1980s by creating much-touted "public–private partnerships" to finance large-scale redevelopment projects such as festival marketplaces and downtown sports arenas.[5] Chicago's city government, which was committed to a strategy of balancing neighborhood and downtown growth during the Washington administration, has since reverted back to a capital-intensive downtown development strategy aimed at creating big ticket tourist attractions along the lakefront. The renovation of Navy Pier created an urban amusement park along the lake complete with a giant Ferris wheel, while the construction of a major addition to McCormick Place has greatly enlarged the city's convention capacity. The Reagan administration loosened restrictions on federal housing dollars, allowing their use in the construction of upscale housing developments in depressed areas immediately surrounding the downtown business district. In the early 1980s, Chicago mayor Jane Byrne used Community Development Block Grant (CDBG) money to subsidize the construction of Presidential Towers, four luxury apartment high-rises just west of downtown. The boom in downtown real estate construction meshed well with a policy emphasis on minority business development, since local governments could easily build set-aside requirements into projects partially funded with public dollars, thereby satisfying powerful interests among their minority constituents.

Chicago's racial geography is an unspoken but ever-present factor in determining which areas are targeted for residential conversion. Since much of the real estate speculation is aimed at high-income professionals, most of whom are white, the areas of development tend to be either on the predominantly white Northside or in areas immediately surrounding the Loop, the city's commercial center. Residential and retail development, which carries a higher market value, has displaced existing manufacturing in the Clybourne Avenue corridor on the near Northside, bordering the upscale Lincoln Park neighborhood. Large sections of the nearby Cabrini-Green housing project, whose occupants are overwhelmingly black, are slated for demolition for the same reasons. Most of Cabrini-Green's residents will be resettled into rental apartments located in other predominantly black communities on the city's fringes.

While City Hall has poured resources into megaprojects such as Navy Pier, the new convention center, along with proposals for casino gambling and a third airport, it has done little to stem the flow of high-paying manufacturing jobs from the city. During the 1980s the city continued to lose twelve thousand factory jobs a year. As of 1993, the city had ten thousand acres of vacant industrial property and a string of moribund or near-empty industrial parks.[6] During the past decade, eighty thousand Chicago jobs shifted from manufacturing to services, with another thirty-five thousand shifting from traditional warehousing and distribution businesses to communications and transportation industries.[7] Under enormous pressure from small industries and community development groups, Mayor Richard M. Daley created three Planned Manufacturing Districts (PMDs) on the near Northside to protect the remaining manufacturers from the encroachment of commercial and residential development. Although the PMDs slowed down the artificial hyperdevelopment occurring on the gentrifying Northside, the city failed to develop a coherent industrial policy for the rest of Chicago aimed at retaining the remaining industrial employment base. It has been slow to respond to the day-to-day needs of neighborhood-based industries such as street repair and fly-dumping (illegal garbage dumping) or to develop low-cost industrial parks that would provide industries with much-needed expansion opportunities.

The city's principal industrial retention strategy has been to offer generous tax subsidies to businesses that agree to remain. With the federal government unwilling to fund the direct creation of jobs in areas of continued high unemployment, state and local governments have turned to subsidizing businesses in exchange for commitments to increase the size of the firms' workforces. The tax subsidies do not appear on state or local budgets as direct expenditures, but they result either in decreasing the jurisdiction's revenues or shifting the tax burden onto other businesses and residents. Since businesses frequently use the tax subsidies to modernize their facilities, including installing newer labor-saving equipment, at best they are able to slow the loss of jobs, not halt it.

The most popular tax subsidies are tax increment financing (TIF) districts, property tax abatements, and enterprise zones. TIFs are most commonly used by municipalities to finance certain types of real estate development costs. Rather than placing the additional revenues generated by property taxes on the site's increased value into the jurisdiction's general operating budget, in TIF districts the additional funds are used to pay for certain development costs such as land acquisition or site clearance. Theoretically, TIFs are to be used for the development of blighted areas that require public subsidies to spur investment; in reality, however, they are given to businesses under almost any circumstances. Since the revenues collected in TIF districts are used to pay off development costs that otherwise would have been absorbed by the company, municipalities risk the possibility of creating a net revenue loss.

In 1983 the city of Chicago had no TIF districts; by 1996 it had thirty, with more in the proposed stage.[8] They have been used both for industrial retention and for residential construction. The second largest TIF in Illinois consists of one thousand acres of mixed commercial and industrial park located on the long-abandoned site of the city's old Union stockyards in the Back-of-the-Yards neighborhood of Chicago. This has been the city's only successful industrial park constructed in the last decade—it has brought three thousand jobs into the neighborhood since the TIF was first created in 1989.[9] In other cases, businesses that threatened to leave the city were given TIFs as an inducement to stay. In 1993 $10 million in TIF-related expenditures were given to two firms, Luster Products and Culinary Foods, Inc., to prevent the exodus of eight hundred jobs to the suburbs.[10] In 1994, despite opposition from several vocal community groups and advocates for the homeless, Mayor Daley pushed a TIF designation through city council for a new 325-acre residential development on the near Southside. The tax losses from this Central Station TIF are expected to exceed all previous combined losses by 30 percent.[11]

The use of TIFs has slowed the departure of jobs from the city, but at a significant cost to local government. As of 1992, $306.9 million of Chicago's property tax base was committed to TIFs. Although this loss does not significantly affect the city, since it only receives fifteen cents of every property tax dollar collected, it does decrease the resources available to other independent taxing bodies in the city and in surrounding Cook County, including the Chicago Board of Education.[12] The continual loss of revenues by the Board of Education threatens to undermine ongoing attempts to improve the quality of education in the city's schools.

Cook County has offered similar tax abatements on commercial and industrial property taxes since 1979. The abatements reduce the tax rates on certain businesses to the same lower rate paid by residential property owners for a period of thirteen years. Again, the tax breaks supposedly target economically depressed areas of the county, yet the requirements were written in such a way that most of the county can qualify. A 1988 study found that by 1985, ninety-five industrial plants in Chicago had been granted reduced assessments. These plants alone will have shifted $68 million in property taxes to the county's residential taxpayers by the time these properties are fully restored to the tax rolls. Forty percent of these dollars were lost by the Chicago Board of Education and almost a fourth by the city of Chicago.[13] The abatements were concentrated among a few firms, with nearly half of the reduced assessments benefiting only 6 percent of the plants receiving subsidies. Despite the claim that they would create jobs, the subsidies had little effect on increasing employment at the plants.[14]

All of these types of subsidies provide public assistance to a select group of firms, giving them a competitive advantage over other manufacturers of similar products. While the tax break helps one plant, it may be damaging the financial health of a competing company. The subsidies do nothing to add to the overall demand for their own or their competitors' products, simply redistributing the economic pie without increasing its size.

Grassroots Organizations Work to Revive Poor Communities

Government's heavy reliance on tax-driven policies fits well with the current preferences for market-driven approaches to economic development. It has helped reduce job losses in select industries while quickening the pace of upscale housing development in once marginal communities. It has also resulted in some very clear losers, including funding for public education, neighborhood infrastructure repair, and community-based economic development. Free market development strategies alone have a negligible impact on poor minority communities that have virtually no remaining market activity. The lost jobs and commercial activity have been replaced by an illegal drug trade, supplemented by federal, state, and local social service dollars. Residents of Chicago's Grand Boulevard neighborhood, site of the longest stretch of public housing in the nation, received an estimated $152 million in public social service, housing, and education funds in 1994.[15] Currency exchanges replaced departed banks, while liquor stores often became the most common retail outlet. Although the housing market in some parts of the city was booming, these communities had virtually no activity in the private housing market. In Grand Boulevard only eighty-eight home mortgage transactions were completed in 1990, which brought a total of $4 million into the community. In contrast, in the trendy Northside neighborhood of Lincoln Park there were 1,396 home loans that same year, for a total investment of $241 million.[16]

In the absence of a private job or housing market, responsibility for the well-being of these communities has fallen into the hands of an uncoordinated array of community-based social service and economic development agencies. Together with local churches, these nonprofit agencies have sought to maintain a minimal infrastructure of support for those people in our resource-rich society who are in the greatest need. Social service agencies, each with a different set of funding sources, provide a patchwork of services such as job training, alcohol and drug abuse counseling, teen pregnancy counseling, HIV/AIDS awareness, and peer mentoring, to name a few. With deep cuts in government social service spending, many of the agencies are facing severe financial crises. To cope with the reduction in available funds, states are revamping their provision of social services to more closely resemble private-sector practices by placing agencies on fee-for-service contracts, requiring the use of outcome-based performance measures, and raising their accreditation requirements. Many smaller agencies that lack the capacity to adjust to these new requirements are going out of business, leaving behind a handful of very large, politically connected providers operating out of multiple facilities. Too often, the older social service agencies, some of which have been in existence for well over twenty-five years, have become comfortable sinecures for highly paid top administrators, giving them a virtual investment in the continuation of urban poverty.

Social service agencies in poor communities tend to reflect the communities they serve. The grants they receive from governments and private foundations are for the delivery of specific services, not to strengthen their organizational capacity. The larger service providers, such as Catholic Charities or the Boys and Girls Clubs, have multiple cash-flow sources, while the smaller organizations have to survive on a single source.[17] This leaves them at the mercy of changing funding priorities, forcing them to add and subtract services based on what they are able to receive money to do, not based on the needs of the people they serve. Until recently, there was little coordination among agencies operating in the same neighborhood, since their funding came from different government agencies that also supplied them with a flow of clients. There is a high turnover among their line staff, which is often young and inexperienced. Salaries are so low that staff members are often not much better off than the people they are serving. With limited resources and small staffs in the face of overwhelming needs, these agencies operate in an almost constant crisis mode, making it difficult to develop any long-range goals for addressing the community's needs.

Responsibility for the economic revitalization of Chicago's poor communities now rests in the hands of an array of community-based development corporations (CDCs). Under the Daley administration the city has almost entirely abandoned efforts to do community economic development. Although community-based job creation proved difficult during the Washington administration, the Department of Economic Development (DED) was continuously experimenting with new programs for small businesses, aimed at increasing employment in the neighborhoods. Washington's most explicit job-creation program was a loan program for small businesses unable to secure conventional loans. To get the loan, the businesses had to commit to hiring a certain number of community residents. When Daley came into office, "his people were disturbed by the program's high default rates and decided to turn it over to the banks to run."[18] Shortly thereafter, DED was consolidated into the Department of Planning, and further pro-active attempts to build the capacity of small neighborhood businesses came to a halt.

While lacking their own capital, the CDCs have been able to make deals in places where the private market had decided they could not be made. In the process, they have gained a wealth of knowledge of the world of business and finance. In these communities, the presence of a CDC is often the main engine of economic activity, defying the conventional market choices by steering resources into activities deemed as lacking a sufficient rate of return for private investors. CDCs represent a geographically focused anti-poverty strategy, in contrast to social service efforts that seek to help poor people as individuals or as families. Although they suffer from many of the same weaknesses found among social service providers, these agencies are often the visionaries within poor communities, seeing assets where outsiders see only obstacles. Many of these organizations have successfully carried out extensive housing construction and rehabilitation with the limited resources at their disposal. According to the National Congress for Community Economic Development, the nation's two thousand CDCs had produced a total of 320,000 units of housing by 1991.[19] This is three times the production of public housing. On average, CDCs produce twenty-one units of housing per year, although the amount varies greatly depending on the organization's capacity.[20] Unfortunately, CDCs have been much less successful in generating neighborhood economic revitalization. Until very recently, community-based economic development efforts lacked the financial tools and expertise needed to direct increased capital toward inner-city business development.

Unlike social service agencies, which are often connected to specific government agencies that fund their activities, CDCs generally are not funded specifically by any agency within the federal or most state government. Only about half of CDC operating funds come from government sources; the rest comes from private foundation grants.[21] The funds they receive are activity related, making it difficult for many of them to build an organizational infrastructure. Most CDCs are undercapitalized, which restricts their ability to do multiple projects. In Chicago, only twenty CDCs have budgets of more than $2 million, the threshold for what is considered to be a successful CDC able to engage in multiple projects simultaneously. Among those CDCs, two-thirds of their budgets are program specific.[22]

The Origins of Community Development

Community development corporations were created in the aftermath of widespread rioting following Martin Luther King, Jr.'s death in the spring of 1968. Senators Robert Kennedy and Jacob Javits sponsored a further amendment to the War on Poverty legislation creating CDCs, which were designed to increase the tools available to poor communities seeking more control over local business opportunities. Kennedy and Javits were influenced by the recommendations of the Kerner Commission, which had been charged with determining the causes of the urban riots. The commission advised the government to encourage minority business ownership as a means of giving poor residents a greater stake in their own communities. In introducing the measure, Kennedy spoke of his vision: "Through the CDCs, residents of the ghettos could at once contribute to the betterment of their immediate conditions, and build a base for full participation in the economy—in the ownership and the savings and self-sufficiency which the more fortunate in our Nation already take for granted."[23]

Gradually the community action organizations established with earlier War on Poverty money incorporated community economic development as one form of the community empowerment they were seeking to achieve. Rather than simply assisting individual businesspeople who may or may not have been located within poor communities, these nonprofits sought to give residents control over the economic resources within their communities. The CDCs' emphasis on community participation in economic planning made them significantly different from the subsequent

minority business loan programs and set-asides. Although well inten-
tioned, most early CDC staffers were community organizers with little
knowledge about what actually went into successful business development. Furthermore, the CDCs had no power over private sector investment decisions, especially the banks' continued unwillingness to lend in
poor minority communities.

The Office of Economic Opportunity (OEO), the agency created to
oversee the anti-poverty programs, was given responsibility for the new
economic development efforts just as it was coming under increasing criticism from big city mayors and urban congressmen for its challenges to
the local political establishment. By the end of the Johnson administration, the big city mayors, led by Mayor Richard J. Daley, had taken control of the anti-poverty programs and moved to shut down the OEO. Congress passed the Green Amendment, requiring that local elected officials
sign off on any federal funding to community organizations, thereby giving them veto power over dollars flowing into poor communities. From
then on, federal dollars would have to pass through the hands of local
politicians, who could dole them out to their favored organizations while
punishing their opponents by withholding the federal funds.

After Richard Nixon took office, funding for the OEO-sponsored community organizations was cut even further. In the North, the Republicans'
electoral strategy rested on building support among their emerging white
suburban and ethnic blue-collar constituents. The community action
agencies threatened those plans because the inner city residents they organized clearly voted Democratic. The Nixon administration was determined to eliminate all grassroots planning mechanisms such as project
area committees, environmental impact reviews, and model cities, which
it felt gave ordinary citizens too much say over private-sector economic
development.[24] Before long, Nixon dismantled the OEO itself, placing its
most successful programs such as Headstart and the Job Corps into mainline agencies, where they could be brought under stricter bureaucratic
control. Nixon replaced these Democratic initiatives with his own urban
strategy centered on assisting individual minority entrepreneurs regardless of where they were located.

As the federal government withdrew funding from the roughly one
hundred CDCs then in existence, the Ford Foundation, where many for-

mer members of the Kennedy and Johnson administrations had formed a sort of government-in-exile, picked up the initiative. In this way, some limited funds continued to flow to the old OEO-funded community organizations, which maintained scaled-back versions of their earlier economic development efforts. Originally, the CDCs had sought to correct three market failures that were seen as key obstacles to business development in poor communities: (1) the inability of potential investors to see opportunities in the neighborhood; (2) corporate profit-maximizing that prevented socially conscious investing; and (3) social and legal restrictions on investment, such as zoning laws. However, as government support disappeared, CDCs had to give up these broader goals, accommodating themselves to the financial priorities set by the private market, on which they were now more dependent for raising the capital they needed to be effective developers.[25]

Lacking significant funding or capital of their own, the CDCs' efforts remained small in scale. Even the most active organizations could do little to stop the ongoing drain of businesses from poor communities. Increasingly, their greatest successes came in rehabbing deteriorated housing and building new low-income housing.[26] In the early years, the tenants who lived in housing built or rehabbed by the CDCs served as a natural constituency for voter registration drives and other political campaigns the organizations were still involved in.[27] Over time, the emphasis on organizing waned, though it has never disappeared entirely. Many of these organizations also incorporated various social service functions into their portfolios, since funding was more readily available for those activities than for community organizing or economic development.[28]

In a critique of these first-generation CDCs published in 1977, Harry Edward Berndt, who had worked for one as the director of development, assailed community development as a doomed strategy rooted in the long American tradition of prescribing self-help for poor communities rather than undertaking structural solutions dealing with root causes of poverty. Berndt argued that CDCs were no more able to make money in poor communities than private enterprise because these neighborhoods are inherently inhospitable to profitable businesses.[29] In retrospect, Berndt was wrong, having failed to foresee the possibilities for low-income housing development, though he was not entirely mistaken in his predictions of the difficulties of establishing businesses. Arguments similar to Berndt's have been made by other authors, including a well-known 1994 critique by Nicholas Lemann published in the *New York Times Magazine,* which argued that despite three decades of effort, there is no evidence that poor communities can be economically revitalized.[30]

CDCs Create Housing, Not Jobs

By working in undercapitalized communities, CDCs are attempting to create economic activity in neighborhoods that have largely been abandoned by the private market. To criticize them for their inability to turn these communities around fails to address the fact that to be successful they must secure resources from mainstream financial institutions that have been reluctant to invest in poor communities. In the profit-maximizing private market, capital follows capital, so that over time it concentrates in areas of high growth, making them grow even faster, while draining out of areas of slower growth, thereby hastening their demise. Having redlined these neighborhoods as they became majority black and Latino in the 1960s and 1970s, conventional lenders have only recently begun to return as a result of government using a combination of pressure and special incentives.

Most potential deals in poor communities, whether for multifamily housing or small businesses, are not bankable using the industry's conventional underwriting criteria of assessing risk. The expense of clearing the land of existing structures and removing environmental contamination drives up construction costs, while higher vacancy rates, more frequent repairs, and greater security requirements drive up the operating costs of apartment complexes and small businesses.[31] As a result, in order to package housing or business deals CDCs must assemble an assortment of traditional loans, below-market-rate loans, and subsidies. The larger, more successful CDCs have become quite adept at accessing a wide range of financial tools. Many have gained a certain credibility with private sector institutions; others have developed partnerships with a variety of government agencies.

Over the past twenty years, the financial tools needed to create affordable single-family housing have been far more developed than those needed to do small business loans. Banks and other lenders are better able to assess the risks involved in housing, even though CDCs in very poor communities are now discovering that their multifamily rental properties were frequently undercapitalized because bankers did not take into account the higher long-term operating costs in those locations.[32] Ultimately, lenders know that if a housing loan defaults, they will at least have ownership of the property to cover their losses, whereas with a business, a default can leave a bank with far fewer tangible assets. By the end of the 1980s a rudimentary national nonprofit housing development sector had emerged consisting of CDCs at the local level, linked to national financial intermediaries that could mobilize capital and provide technical assistance. After the Nixon administration withdrew its support for community development, the Ford Foundation set out to construct a new, privately supported, freestanding source of capital that would replace the lost public dollars. This intermediary would be able to seek out successful CDCs and enlist project dollars from private and public sources to help them achieve higher levels of effectiveness and self-sufficiency. By 1979 Ford had created the Local Initiatives Support Corporation (LISC), the first of a number of national intermediaries designed to provide financing for community development efforts. Initially capitalized at $10 million, LISC has since raised another $880 million from 1,100 separate private-sector sources to support the activities of 875 CDCs in thirty different cities and regions.[33]

Fair housing policies created in response to the redlining of poor minority neighborhoods have given community groups added leverage in forcing banks to be accountable for an equitable distribution of their loan dollars. Since Congress enacted the Community Reinvestment Act (CRA) in 1977, the nation's banks have been under an obligation to provide credit to all segments of their service market, including low- to moderate-income neighborhoods. The Act requires the Federal Reserve System, along with other federal regulators, "to encourage such institutions to help meet the credit needs of the local communities in which they are chartered." The legislation mandated that the Federal Reserve take a bank's CRA performance into account in ruling on its request to merge or acquire another bank and allowed for a period of public comment from community groups on their assessment of the bank's compliance with

CRA. The public's role in CRA compliance was enhanced in 1989 with the passage of the Financial Institutions Reform, Recovery, and Enforcement Act (FIRREA), which requires the Federal Reserve to publish its CRA ratings as well as certain portions of its examination reports.[34] President Bill Clinton, who articulated a renewed federal commitment to community reinvestment upon coming into office, further strengthened CRA by refocusing compliance on bank loan performance and neighborhood service, rather than on process measures. However, the Federal Reserve Board rejected a proposal that would have required banks to collect race and gender data on applicants for small business loans similar to the data already collected on home mortgage applicants.[35] The existence of the home mortgage data has been critical to documenting racial discrimination in mortgage lending by banks and savings and loans.

The banking industry was initially slow to respond. The expansion of bank mergers and acquisitions following deregulation in the 1980s, however, fueled a greater concern with CRA compliance within the industry. According to Bank of America CEO Dick Rosenberg, "When the Federal Reserve denied a major banking acquisition in 1989 based on CRA grounds, a great many people in our industry sat up and took notice."[36] Furthermore, new competitive pressures in the industry drove banks and savings and loans to develop new markets aggressively. As some banks began to study the low-income housing market and develop products to meet its needs, they discovered an untapped market where the risk was no greater than in the conventional mortgage market. Anecdotal evidence indicated that low-income borrowers, especially single women with children, were often better at repaying their home loans than conventional borrowers. This was confirmed by a 1992 study of more than two thousand loans made nationwide by seven lenders with solid track records in CRA lending. The study found that delinquency rates on all single-family loans were seven or eight times higher than those on community reinvestment single-family loans. The success of the CRA borrowers was thought to be related to the screening, counseling, and preparation for home ownership that accompany many CRA loans.[37] Similarly, the Bank of America has reported that loans in its low-income mortgage portfolio, which have had some time to reflect long-term performance, show delinquency rates that are 25 percent below their conventional counterparts.[38]

The threat of negative CRA ratings has driven banks back into neighborhoods they had abandoned more than twenty years earlier. Within the last three years, at least four major downtown banks have built new branch offices in black neighborhoods on the Southside of Chicago. With the branches comes an influx of loans and banking services for residents, many of whom have never before even had a checking account. The result has been a dramatic increase in home mortgage lending, as high as 50 percent in some Chicago neighborhoods, much of it to low- and moderate-income first-time home buyers.[39] With CRA making home loans more easily obtainable in predominantly minority communities, the demand for housing in these communities is increasing for the first time in years. With that has come rising property values, soaring by as much as 43 percent in some predominantly minority areas of New York City.[40] In the long run, those increases will raise the amount of equity capital available for business ventures in minority communities.

As part of their opposition to the "excesses" of affirmative action, the new Republican Congress elected in 1994 attempted to gut CRA by shortening and in some cases eliminating the public comment period, which has proved to be a powerful weapon for community groups seeking to leverage more investment dollars from reluctant banks. In the guise of streamlining government regulations, the Republicans also proposed an expedited review process for bank mergers and acquisitions in which a bank's CRA record would play much less of a role in the approval process.[41] However, the most detrimental proposals would have exempted 84 percent of U.S. banks—those with less than $250 million in assets—from having to report their loan data.[42] Fortunately, the Republicans' deregulation agenda stalled before they were able to finalize these changes.

The 1986 creation of affordable housing tax credits opened the door for previously untapped corporate investors to enter the affordable housing market at a time when federal budget cuts had brought publicly funded multifamily housing construction to a halt. The tax credit, enacted under the sponsorship of Congressman Dan Rostenkowski (D-IL), then chairman of the House Ways and Means Committee, created a financial mechanism by which corporations could invest in the construction of affordable housing in exchange for credit on their federal tax liabilities. Each state receives an allocation of tax credits based on population, which can then be used to finance housing construction with a certain number of units set aside for low-income residents. The value of the tax credit amounts to roughly 35 percent of the project and can serve as the equity portion needed to secure other forms of commercial credit from banks and mortgage lenders, who in turn can count their share of the deal toward their CRA compliance. Its widespread use has spawned the creation of a secondary financial market in which the notes held by individual corporations are bundled together and securitized.[43] "At this point tax credits are structured in such a way that its pretty much a no-brainer for the corporations. They do that and nothing else."[44]

Even the nation's community development banks, of which there are now four, including the nationally recognized South Shore Bank, have had their greatest successes in housing rehabilitation, not small business development. South Shore has drawn customers from all over the country to invest in its development deposits, which have conventional competitive yields and liquidity but are used specifically to renovate deteriorated apartment buildings in the bank's lakefront service area on Chicago's Southside. Drawing on the wide variety of public and private financing tools now available for housing rehabilitation, the bank's development corporation has renovated large sections of the South Shore community that contained deteriorating apartment buildings, some with as many as twenty-four units. It has made dozens of loans to smaller neighborhood entrepreneurs who have renovated two- and three-unit buildings.[45] Yet, the bank admits having great difficulty in doing small business lending, in part because its initial efforts at commercial development along the shopping strip in its South Shore neighborhood were not accompanied by a strong commercial redevelopment program and management assistance to the minority entrepreneurs located on the strip. Only by taking on the task of coordinating an overall redevelopment strategy for the strip has the bank gradually had some success outside its area of expertise in multifamily housing rehab.[46]

Unfortunately, without an accompanying effort to provide employment, all of this housing activity does not have a significant multiplier effect on the overall well-being of a community. Housing construction and rehabilitation does not necessarily result in employment for community people. As discussed in Chapter 5, much of the urban construction market is still controlled by unions that exclude minority workers except for those very few who have gone through union-approved apprenticeship programs. The building materials are manufactured and purchased outside the community as well, so the actual construction work has a negligible economic impact on the neighborhood. One of the great paradoxes of the CDC movement is that "the vast majority of CDCs give out the best jobs and contracts to outsiders who come in and work right under the noses of the residents who would do anything for a job, yet are called lazy because they don't work."[47]

Furthermore, an emphasis on housing in poor communities, in isolation from other economic development initiatives, does not necessarily lead to improvements in the overall quality of life. In the absence of solutions to the drugs and gang violence that plague many of these communities, new affordable housing will not be able to attract and retain the stable families these neighborhoods so desperately need. The creation of these various financial tools has not been sufficient in jump-starting the housing market in all communities. They work best in transitional neighborhoods, where there is a base of middle-class homeowners mixed with low- and moderate-income rental property. The absence of a functional market in very poor communities means that a new housing development is losing value from the moment it is completed, making it difficult for any developers, whether commercial or nonprofit, to break even without access to deep public subsidies. On the other hand, in communities located close to downtown business districts, housing alone can quickly lead to gentrification as the area becomes an avant-garde location for young professionals.[48]

The Unfulfilled Promise of Empowerment Zones

President Clinton presented Congress with the Empowerment Zones and Enterprise Communities Act of 1993, touted as a new solution to urban disinvestment. In reality it is the Democratic version of enterprise zones, first championed by conservative politicians in the early 1980s as the favored policy remedy for urban disinvestment. Believing that burdensome taxes and overregulation stifled business growth, conservatives advocated the establishment of geographic areas in which companies would enjoy relief on both scores. First developed in England, the concept found one of its earliest American proponents in Ronald Reagan, who made it his urban policy during the 1980 presidential campaign. Although various versions were introduced in Congress during the 1980s, some with bipartisan support, the legislation was never enacted at the federal level. George Bush introduced the last version in 1992 in the aftermath of the Los Angeles riots, but he later vetoed the bill because it was part of a larger tax-relief package that he did not support.[49]

While the legislation was stalled in Congress, the states moved ahead, and by the early 1990s thirty-seven states had passed some type of enterprise zone laws. States designated certain areas as enterprise zones based on an assortment of broadly defined criteria—some related to community distress such as unemployment, low incomes, business decline, and disinvestment, others tied to evidence of economic potential as demonstrated by community commitment and availability of public and private resources for zone activities. Too often, the criteria were so general that vast regions within the state could be designated as eligible. Illinois, for example, has no poverty or unemployment standards for its zones, enabling even economically vibrant suburbs to become enterprise zones. Consequently, most of the businesses that have benefited from the state's enterprise zones are huge industrial firms with more than two hundred employees that are usually not located in inner-city neighborhoods.[50] States generally offered companies that located within the zone a tax credit for hiring additional employees, an investment tax credit, reductions in property and sales taxes, and preferential access to other sources of state and federal funding.

Their popularity notwithstanding, enterprise zones showed quite mixed results. Although businesses report some interest in taking advantage of the property tax and sales tax reductions as well as the investment credit, very few report taking advantage of the job-creation tax credit.[51] Generally, businesses value those incentives that can be taken immediately, such as sales tax reductions. A study of a Chicago enterprise zone done by the Chicago Urban League concluded that "while some businesses might be inclined to make use of incentives, there is little evidence that the incentives help generate jobs or new investment. Therefore, while a select number of businesses respond favorably to the availability of enterprise zone incentives, the program may not serve public policy ends."[52] While a number of businesses had relocated their facilities into the zone, almost all of them (83 percent) had moved from another part of Chicago. Rather than stimulating new business and investment, the existence of the zone had encouraged the redistribution of businesses and jobs already in the local economy.

There is little evidence that tax breaks have a significant impact on companies' locational decisions. A survey of 150 businesses done by the Deloitte and Touche Consulting Group found that tax incentives ranked fourteenth out of seventeen factors contributing to a firm's locational decisions. Companies were most concerned about real estate costs, quality of the labor force, and transportation. Even utility costs, community image, and quality of life ranked above the tax incentives.[53] A study of Illinois enterprise zones supports these conclusions—a large number (62 percent) of businesses rated labor force characteristics as the critical factor in making locational decisions, followed by overall community characteristics, and location of customers.[54] The repeated emphasis placed on the quality of the local labor force in making locational decisions highlights the misplaced priorities of countless municipal governments that shortchange their public school systems while granting tax breaks to attract and retain local businesses. The ineffectiveness of direct business subsidies was pointed out in a groundbreaking 1995 article by Michael Porter in the *Harvard Business Review,* in which he argued that inner-city communities have competitive advantages that could enable certain types of businesses to flourish, despite the higher costs of site development and security. However, in order to take advantage of those assets, government ought to use its funds for site assembly, extra security, environmental clean-up, and other investments designed to improve the business climate.[55]

Having positioned himself as a "new Democrat" who favored market-driven solutions to social problems, Clinton appropriated the centerpiece of the Republicans' urban strategy and made it his own. The proposed Empowerment Zone and Enterprise Communities (EZ/EC) legislation consisted of various federal tax incentives for businesses who locate in the designated zones along with substantial direct federal expenditures on social service and economic development activities in the zones. In a significant departure from previous versions of enterprise zones, the legislation created a strong planning role for community organizations working in neighborhoods seeking zone designation. Although it bore a striking resemblance to the old OEO community-participation model of the 1960s, the Clinton administration's emphasis on community-based planning was a component of its vision for "reinventing government." Championed by Vice President Al Gore, one of the cardinal premises of reinventing government was to empower citizens who best understand their own needs by pushing control over decision-making out of the bureaucracy into the community.[56]

As passed, the legislation called for the creation of nine empowerment zones, of which three would be rural, and ninety-five enterprise communities. In sharp contrast to the state-enacted enterprise zones, Clinton's empowerment zones had to be areas suffering from high levels of poverty and unemployment. Each zone was to receive a 20 percent employer wage credit for the first $15,000 of wages paid to a zone resident employed in the zone, increased allowances from $10,000 to $20,000 for expensing of depreciable property in the first year of business, and expanded use of tax-exempt state and local bond financing when applied to certain zone properties. The ninety-five enterprise communities are only eligible for tax-exempt financing. Judging by the legislation's heavy emphasis on wage tax credits, it would appear that the administration did not learn from the states' experiences the ineffectiveness of offering tax credits for new employees to businesses located in an enterprise zone. In addition to the tax incentives, each empowerment zone also received $100 million over two years under the Health and Human Services Title XX block grant for social service and economic development programs, and each enterprise community received $2.8 million.[57]

The U.S. Department of Housing and Urban Development (HUD) was given the task of selecting the nine empowerment zones and overseeing the program's implementation. In order to be eligible, communities had to meet specific socioeconomic distress criteria, submit a strategic plan, and be nominated by their state and local governments. To guide the community planning process, HUD issued a strategic planning book that emphasized the creation of a process starting at the grassroots community level with residents, store owners, and others, and working up the political ladder. In Chicago, community groups that had previously never worked together came together to prepare proposals. Much of the detailed work that went into preparing the initial proposals was carried out by a new group of community leaders who were not a part of the city's traditional poverty elite. Through their involvement, many of them gained a new sense of vision and excitement about the possibilities for improvements in their communities. As one participant describes it, "On the Westside it was wonderful. Before we had all operated in our own little bubbles, but the empowerment zone planning process created a new collaboration. Suddenly we were looking at what we wanted to have happen on the whole Westside. It was an honest bottoms up process to get the proposal in."[58]

Chicago was one of the six cities to receive an empowerment zone designation. HUD selected three separate areas, two predominantly black communities encompassing the near Southside and a large stretch of the Westside and a primarily Mexican community known as Pilsen/Little Village. As soon as the city received its designation, all the traditional powerbrokers became interested in how the $100 million would be distributed. As one foundation program officer put it, "All the older organizations came out of the woodwork."[59] The aldermen demanded to have a say over the dollars going into their wards. They expected the Governance Council (GC) designated to oversee the distribution of the funds to conduct "business as usual," meaning that the decisions would rest on political favoritism and relationships. The community groups that had led the planning process had a different vision of how the GC would function. In the description of the GC written into the original proposal submitted to HUD, the community was to pick its representatives, who would hold a majority on the decision-making body. Instead, the mayor, with the backing of city council, decided that he would appoint all the members of the GC based on nominations from community people. Once again, the inherent conflict over who would control dollars earmarked for poor communities—the community groups working in those neighborhoods or the local elected officials—had come to the surface. As one of the leaders of Chicago's EZ/EC movement explained, "By funneling all the dollars through local governments, the legislation showed no recognition of the natural conflict between local governments and poor communities."[60] HUD removed itself from the resultant conflict, realizing "that none of the big city mayors who are crucial to Clinton's reelection are going to suffer any sanctions for using their clout to shape the EZ/EC the way they want."[61]

It took Mayor Daley over a year to select the GC. In the meantime, an interim council, heavily weighted toward downtown interests, developed the Requests for Proposals (RFPs) that would govern to selection of the first round of programs to be funded by the $100 million. Of the permanent GC's thirty-nine members, twenty are from community groups, nine from business, and ten from government, so community forces hold a majority on the decision-making body. Nonetheless, maintaining community input and participation is an ongoing struggle, made more difficult by the lack of funding that would allow communities to continue to strengthen their participation.[62] In early March 1996 the city announced the winners of the first round of $8 million to be disbursed. The selections showed little innovation, with most of the awards being for the delivery of standard social services such as community health care centers, Chicago Public School Learning Centers, and housing rehab. Few had either a job-creation or an economic-development focus. Some community activists protested that the final selection favored well-funded, established organizations that had experience writing proposals or had the funding to hire professionals to do the work.[63] Since most of the grants are only for one year, the long-term benefits of spending on a myriad of little programs will be negligible.

Unless the next round of grants shows a greater emphasis on collaborative projects that target employment skills and economic development in the empowerment zones, it is unlikely that the $100 million will lead to a turn-around in the poor communities receiving the dollars. After battling with the city for over a year and watching the outcome of the first round of proposals with dismay, community leaders have scaled back their expectations of what the EZ/ECs will achieve. Wanda White, executive director of the Community Workshop on Economic Development (CWED), which coordinated the intense planning process leading to the submission of the city's proposal, hopes the EZ/ECs will foster "enough local innovative development projects that it will justify the use of community economic development approaches in the future. It has also identified new and emerging community leadership and helped to foster some community partnerships that were not possible before."[64] Congressman Bobby Rush, whose district includes the Southside's empowerment zone, laments that with City Hall controlling the disbursement of the funds and community groups fighting with each other over who is going to get the dollars, the Chicago EZ/EC is "going to accomplish a lot less than its potential."[65]

Often forgotten in the midst of the great tug of war over the $100 million has been the central goal of the Empowerment Zone legislation, namely, increased business activity within the zones with the jobs going to area residents. Direct business participation in the EZ/ECs has been slow to come forward. Throughout the planning process, only a representative from the Bank of America participated.[66] Although nine of the seats on the present GC are designated for business, participation has actually come from associations that broker relationships between local businesses and the community. Most importantly, the primary incentives for businesses to locate within the zones are employee tax credits that kick in as a company makes money and expands its workforce. The larger firms that would benefit most from a tax credit are not the ones most likely to move into these communities. According to Alton Bathrick, a Milwaukee investment banker who has championed the development of financial tools to bring institutional investors into undercapitalized communities, "These tax credits don't mean anything to small minority-owned businesses because they usually are not profitable within three years."[67] Unlike the affordable housing tax credits, these are nontransferable, making it difficult for a secondary market to develop as has been the case for the housing tax credits.

There have been a few exceptions to the general lack of business response to the EZ/ECs. Burger King has announced that it intends to open up 125 new restaurants in EZ/EC communities to take advantage of the employment tax credits. Burger King is following the lead of other franchisers, including MacDonalds and 7-Eleven, who are discovering that they can reap more sales dollars per square foot in the city than from their same-sized suburban locations. Marketing studies have shown that African-Americans and Latinos are more likely than whites to frequent certain fast food and convenience stores. The lack of retail stores enables a business that is attuned to the needs and preferences of inner-city shoppers to establish a loyal customer base quickly. These franchisers are also discovering the advantages of tapping into poor neighborhoods' underemployed residents, who are still willing to work at little more than minimum wage and are less likely to quit their jobs.[68] Establishing a reputation of hiring from the community can also lessen the security concerns that are often seen as one of the greatest obstacles to cost-effective business activities in inner-city neighborhoods.

Some Positive Steps Forward

The expansion of franchisers in inner-city communities represents a new recognition that profitable businesses can exist in poor minority neighborhoods. Rather than viewing poor neighborhoods as inhospitable to profitable businesses, firms are increasingly aware that locating in these communities may provide distinct advantages. According to Porter, these include strategic location in proximity to downtown and entertainment and tourist centers, local market demand because poor neighborhoods lack adequate retail outlets, integration with general business clusters also located in the vicinity, and a workforce eager to work.[69] Thus, private and public efforts that build on these advantages while seeking solutions to the countless obstacles that do exist can lead to successful inner-city business development.

The tools cannot be driven by theoretical assumptions about the role of the private market. Instead, they must meet real needs and be built in conjunction with the CDCs that for years have been the main vehicle of grassroots change in these communities. Recognizing that housing alone does not generate sufficient economic activity to sustain poor communities, CDCs have begun to prioritize business development. Bethel New Life, a larger CDC located on Chicago's Westside, changed to a jobs emphasis four or five years ago and is only now beginning to see some results. Bethel developed a paper recycling plant in a local industrial park, which it has since sold to a minority entrepreneur. It also brought a paper deinking plant to the same park and has actively pursued commercial development at an elevated train superstation in the neighborhood. Had Bethel not taken the initiative and done the planning, the Chicago Transit Authority would likely have located the station in another neighborhood further to the west.[70]

The Local Initiatives Support Corporation has begun to transfer the expertise it gained in providing equity capital for affordable housing construction into direct business development. Having created a $24 million pool of capital, LISC is now working with ten large banks, insurers, and other institutions to provide equity financing for the creation of inner-city grocery stores in fourteen cities. Big chain supermarkets had abandoned inner-city locations nationwide in favor of much larger, more profitable suburban locations. Bringing chain stores back into the city can greatly enhance the quality of life in older communities. Yet, it requires the same type of creative financial packaging that has spurred the affordable housing market. It also necessitates a committed retailer, active involvement from local government prepared to use its powers of eminent domain to assemble a large enough site, and active involvement from a CDC that can provide local input and attract low-cost financing that is available to nonprofit developers.[71]

Building on the success of South Shore Bank and other development financing institutions, President Clinton introduced the Community Development Banking and Financial Institutions Act of 1994, designed to create a publicly funded loan fund that would further increase the flow of capital to the various community development financial institutions, including development banks, credit unions, and private community development intermediaries. At $382 million in capitalization over four years, the proposed Act was rather modest; nonetheless, such an infusion would have increased the capacity of the community development financing industry by 40 percent. Equally as important, the fund was empowered to provide "technical assistance including training, and grants for technical assistance" to community development financial institutions.[72] Unfortunately, the Republicans who gained control of the House and the Senate in 1994 did not approve of this type of support to community self-help efforts and slashed the loan fund's first-year allocations in half, to $45 million in fiscal year 1995.[73] Although it is still a positive step in the creation of greater pools of capital, at its present size the loan fund will be far less effective. The Clinton administration's newly implemented CRA regulations are also designed to encourage more small business lending by banks. To accomplish that, banks are experimenting with various nontraditional lending practices, some of which have successfully been used to make micro-loans in third world countries. In addition, banks can now receive CRA credit for providing financial resources to clean up brownfields (former industrial or commerical sites that may be polluted and therefore stand idle), another major impediment to increased inner-city business activity.

These grassroots efforts at job creation, although small, take on an ever-greater importance as the federal government steps away from even a minimal commitment to addressing the needs of the urban poor. While increased corporate recognition of the profit potential to be found in minority communities is long overdue and much needed, a continued role for CDCs that advocate on behalf of the communities' residents is equally important. CDCs have proven to be the only organizations in many of these communities committed to real participation and empowerment of the residents. Government has to play a greater role in providing new tools for use by for-profit and not-for-profit investors and community organizations interested in business development in poor communities. Accomplishing that will require holding many of the politicians who represent these communities to a higher sense of purpose than they display at present.

NOTES

Notes to Chapter 1

1. Douglas Massey and Nancy Denton, *American Apartheid: Segregation and the Making of the Underclass* (Cambridge, Mass.: Harvard University Press, 1993), 128.

2. Ibid., 135.

3. Shelby Steele, *The Content of Our Character* (New York: St. Martin's Press, 1988), 15.

4. Nina Wallerstein, "Powerlessness, Empowerment, and Health: Implications for Health Promotion Programs," *American Journal of Health Promotion,* 6, no. 3 (January–February 1992): 198.

5. Paulo Freire, *Pedagogy of the Oppressed* (New York: Continuum Press, 1994), 29.

6. Martin Luther King, Jr., *Why We Can't Wait* (New York: Harper & Row, 1964), 27–40.

7. Lawrence Mead, *The New Politics of Poverty* (New York: Basic Books, 1992), 212.

8. Ibid., 157.

9. Nathan Glazer, *Ethnic Dilemmas, 1864–1982* (Cambridge, Mass.: Harvard University Press, 1983), 85.

10. Thomas Sowell, *The Economics and Politics of Race: An International Perspective* (New York: William Morrow, 1983), 141–42.

11. Ibid., 251.

12. Charles Murray, *Losing Ground: American Social Policy, 1950–1980* (New York: Basic Books, 1984), 73.

13. Ibid., 188.

14. Nathan Glazer, *Affirmative Discrimination: Ethnic Inequality and Public Policy* (New York: Basic Books, 1978), 43.

15. Murray, *Losing Ground.* 1984.

16. David Swinton, "Labor Market Trends from the Early 1970's to the Early 1980's: A Decade of Declining Utilization of Black Workers," paper presented at the Chicago Urban League conference "Civil Rights in the Eighties: A Thirty Year Perspective," June 15, 1984, 68.

17. Arthur Ross and Herbert Hill, eds., *Employment, Race, and Poverty* (New York: Harcourt, Brace & World, 1967), 18.

18. Hobart Rowen, *The Free Enterprisers: Kennedy, Johnson, and the Business Establishment* (New York: G. P. Putnam's Sons, 1964), 267.

19. Tom Kahn, "The Economics of Equality," in Louis Ferman, Joyce Kornbluh, and Alan Haber, eds., *Poverty in America* (Ann Arbor: University of Michigan Press, 1966), 162.

20. Rowen, *The Free Enterprisers,* 268.

21. Margery Austin Turner, Michael Fix, and Raymond J. Struyk, *Opportunities Denied, Opportunities Diminished* (Washington, D.C.: Urban Institute Press, 1991), 9.

22. "Labor Market Reality: Few Entry Level Jobs Available in Illinois," *Illinois Welfare News* 1, no. 5 (Chicago: Welfare Reform Information Center and the Legal Assistance Foundation, January 1996): 3.

23. John Kasarda, "Cities as Places Where People Live and Work: Urban Change and Neighborhood Distress," in Henry Cisneros, ed., *Interwoven Destinies: Cities and the Nation* (New York: W. W. Norton, 1993), 84.

24. Mead, *The New Politics of Poverty,* 12.

25. Ibid.

26. Thomas Lee Philpott, *The Slum and the Ghetto: Immigrants, Blacks, and Reforms in Chicago, 1880–1930* (Belmont, Calif.: Wadsworth Publishing Co., 1991).

27. Charles Flint Kellogg, "The Negro in the American Economy," in Ross and Hill eds., *Employment, Race, and Poverty,* 25.

28. Stanley Lieberson, *A Piece of the Pie: Blacks and White Immigrants since 1880* (Berkeley: University of California Press, 1980), 250.

29. Arthur Altmeyer, *The Formative Years of Social Security* (Madison: University of Wisconsin Press, 1966), 34–35; Paul Douglas, *Social Security in the United States* (New York: McGraw-Hill, 1936).

30. Jerry Cates, *Insuring Inequality: Administrative Leadership in Social Security, 1935–54* (Ann Arbor: University of Michigan Press, 1983), 73.

31. Dennis Dickerson, *Out of the Crucible: Black Steelworkers in Western Pennsylvania, 1875–1980* (Albany: State University of New York Press, 1986), 149.

32. Herbert Hill, "The Equal Employment Opportunity Acts of 1964 and 1972: A Critical Analysis of the Legislative History and Administration of the Law," *Industrial Relations Law Journal* 2, no. 1 (spring 1977): 19.

33. E. E. Schattschneider, *Semisovereign People* (Hinsdale, Ill.: Dryden Press, 1975), 97.

34. Garth Mangum, *The Emergence of Manpower Policy* (New York: Holt, Rinehart & Winston, 1969), 49.

35. Sar Levitan and Richard Taggart, *The Promise of Greatness* (Cambridge, Mass.: Harvard University Press, 1976).

36. Martin Luther King, Jr., *Where Do We Go from Here?* (New York: Harper & Row, 1967), 19.

37. Author interview with James Farmer, former executive director of CORE, March 23, 1988.

38. King, *Where Do We Go From Here?* 3.

39. Gary Orfield, "Race and the Liberal Agenda," in Margaret Weir, Ann Orloff, and Theda Skocpol, eds., *The Politics of Social Policy in the United States* (Princeton, N.J.: Princeton University Press, 1988), 336.

40. Ibid., 328.

41. Polling data taken from Michael Brown, "The Segmented Welfare System: Distributive Conflict and Retrenchment in the United States, 1968–84," paper presented at the American Political Science Association Annual Meeting, Washington, D.C., August 28–31, 1986.

42. Ibid., 36.

43. Thomas Byrne Edsall and Mary Edsall, *Chain Reaction: The Impact of Race, Rights, and Taxes on American Politics* (New York: W. W. Norton, 1991), 158.

44. Schattschneider, *Semirsovereign People,* 69.

45. Peter Bachrach and Morton Baratz, "Two Faces of Power," *American Political Science Review* 56 (December 1962): 947–52.

46. Ibid., 950.

47. Wallerstein, "Powerlessness, Empowerment, and Health," 198.

48. Henry Aaron, *Politics and the Professors: The Great Society in Perspective* (Washington, D.C.: Brookings Institution, 1978), 7.

49. "Taxpayers Are Angry; They're Expensive Too," *New York Times,* November 20, 1994, sec. 4, p. 7.

50. Michael Dawson, *Behind the Mule: Race and Class in American Politics* (Princeton, N.J.: Princeton University Press, 1994), 35.

51. Cornel West, *Race Matters* (New York: Vintage Books, 1994), 58.

52. William Julius Wilson, *The Truly Disadvantaged: The Inner City, the Underclass, and Public Policy* (Chicago: University of Chicago Press, 1978), 49.

Notes to Chapter 2

1. Hobart Rowen, *The Free Enterprisers: Kennedy, Johnson, and the Business Establishment* (New York: G. P. Putnam's, 1964), 16.

2. Ibid., 50.

3. Ibid., 260.

4. Allen Matusow, *The Unraveling of America: A History of Liberalism in the 1960's* (New York: Harper & Row, 1984), 61.

5. James Harvey, *Black Civil Rights during the Kennedy Administration* (Jackson: University and College Press of Mississippi, 1971), 19.

6. They were Adam Clayton Powell (D-NY), William Dawson (D-IL), Charles Diggs (D-MI), Robert Nix (D-PA), Augustus Hawkins (D-CA), and John Conyers (D-MI). Marguerite Ross Barnett, "The Congressional Black Caucus: Illusions and Realities of Power," in Michael Preston, Lenneal Henderson, and Paul Puryear, eds., *The New Black Politics: The Search for Political Power* (New York: Longman, 1982), 31.

7. Mark Stern, "Black Interest Group Pressure on the Executive: John F. Kennedy as Politician," paper presented at the American Political Science Association Annual Meeting, Chicago, September 3–6, 1987, 35.

8. James Sundquist, *Politics and Policies: The Eisenhower, Kennedy, and Johnson Years* (Washington, D.C.: Brookings Institution, 1970), 256–57.

9. Michael Sovern, *The Legal Restraints on Racial Discrimination* (New York: Twentieth Century Fund, 1966), 104.

10. Sundquist, *Politics and Policies,* 63.

11. Ibid., 115–16.

12. Kenneth B. Clark and Jeanetta Hopkins, *A Relevant War against Poverty* (New York: Harper & Row, 1969), 4.

13. Sundquist, *Politics and Policies,* 260.

14. Charles Whalen and Barbara Whalen, *The Longest Debate: A Legislative History of the 1964 Civil Rights Act* (Cabin John, Md.: Seven Locks Press, 1985), 19.

15. Doug McAdams, *Political Process and the Development of Black Insurgency* (Chicago: University of Chicago Press, 1982), 159.

16. Sundquist, *Politics and Policies,* 261.

17. Leadership Conference on Civil Rights, "Proposed Statement on President's Message," April 15, 1963, from the UAW President's Office files, box 90, folder 11, Archives on Labor History and Urban Affairs, Wayne State University.

18. Elliott Rudwick, *W. E. B. Du Bois: The Voice of the Black Protest Movement* (Urbana: University of Illinois Press, 1982), 285.

19. Harvey, *Black Civil Rights during the Kennedy Administration,* 56–57.

20. Author interview with Joseph Rauh, July 25, 1987.

21. Harvey, *Black Civil Rights during the Kennedy Administration,* 58.

22. Sovern, *The Legal Restraints on Racial Discrimination,* 26.

23. Ibid., 34.

24. Ibid., 51.

25. Herbert Hill, *Black Labor and the American Legal System* (Madison: University of Wisconsin Press, 1985), 42.

26. Garth Mangum, *The Emergence of Manpower Policy* (New York: Holt, Rinehart & Winston, 1969), 47.

27. Henry Aaron, *Politics and the Professors: The Great Society in Perspective,* (Washington, D.C.: Brookings Institution, 1978), 66.

28. Ann R. Horowitz, "The Patterns and Causes of Changes in White-Nonwhite Income Differences: 1947–1972," in George von Furstenberg, Ann Horowitz, and Bennett Harrison, eds., *Patterns of Racial Discrimination,* vol. 2 (Lexington, Mass.: D.C. Heath and Co., 1974), 161.

29. Author interview with Joseph Rauh, July 25, 1987.

30. Testimony of George Meany, in *Civil Rights: Hearings before Subcommittee No. 5 of the House Committee on the Judiciary,* 88th Congress, 1st Session, 1963, 1791.

31. Philip Foner, *Organized Labor and the Black Worker, 1619–1973* (New York: International Publishers, 1978), 319.

32. Author interview with Norman Hill, executive director of the A. Philip Randolph Institute, July 22, 1986.

33. Phil Meyer and James Robinson, "Labor Aids Bias Fight," *Detroit Free Press,* April 14, 1965, from the UAW President's Office files, box 578, folder 2, Archives on Labor History and Urban Affairs, Wayne State University.

34. Ibid.

35. Author interview with Herbert Hill, August 25, 1986; Sundquist, *Politics and Policies,* 264–65.

36. Leadership Conference on Civil Rights, memo by Arnold Aronson, "How Good Is the Civil Rights Compromise?" November 4, 1963, from the UAW President's Office files, Archives on Labor History and Urban Affairs, Wayne State University.

37. Mangum, *The Emergence of Manpower Policy,* 49.

38. Nicholas Lemann, *The Promised Land: The Great Black Migration and How It Changed America* (New York: Vintage Books, 1991), 192–93.

39. Bernard J. Frieden and Marshall Kaplan, *The Politics of Neglect* (Cambridge Mass.: MIT Press, 1979), 32–33.

40. Sundquist, *Politics and Policies,* 142–45; August Bolino, *Manpower in the City* (Cambridge, Mass.: Schenckman Publishing Co., 1969), 104–8.

41. Letter from Jack Howard, NYC administrator, to Roy Wilkins, July 28, 1966, from the NAACP files (DOL 66–67) in the Manuscript Division of the Library of Congress.

42. Lemann, *The Promised Land,* 154.

43. Margaret Weir, "The Political Limits of American Economic Policy: The Federal Government and Employment Policy, 1960–1980" (Ph.D. dissertation, University of Chicago, 1986), 120.

44. Mangum, *The Emergence of Manpower Policy,* 47.

45. Weir, "The Political Limits of American Economic Policy," 112.

46. Mangum, *The Emergence of Manpower Policy,* 48.

47. Sundquist, *Politics and Policies,* 144; Lyndon Baines Johnson, *The Vantage Point* (New York: Popular Press, 1971), 74.

48. Letter from Jack Howard to Roy Wilkins, July 28, 1966.

49. Lemann, *The Promised Land,* 156.

50. Clark and Hopkins, *A Relevant War against Poverty,* 69.

51. Gary Orfield and Helene Slessarev, *Job Training under the New Federalism: JTPA in the Industrial Heartland* (Chicago: Illinois Unemployment and Job Training Research Project, 1986), chapter 2.

52. Sovern, *The Legal Restraints on Racial Discrimination,* 73–89.

53. Editorial, *New York Times,* May 15, 1964, from the UAW President's Office files, box 578, Archives on Labor History and Urban Affairs, Wayne State University.

54. "An Analysis of Senator Dirksen's Proposed Amendment No. 511 to Title VII of H.R. 7152 reported in the *Congressional Record,* 4/21/64, 8330–31," from the Leadership Conference on Civil Rights Legislative files, box 6, Manuscript Division, Library of Congress.

55. *Congressional Record,* Senate, March 30, 1964, 6550.

56. Charles Kothe, ed, *A Tale of 22 Cities: Report on Title VII of the Civil Rights Act of 1964 Compiled from NAM Seminars* (New York: National Association of Manufacturers, 1965), 7–8.

57. Herbert Hill, "The Equal Employment Opportunity Acts of 1964 and 1972: A Critical Analysis of the Legislative History and Administration of the Law," *Industrial Relations Law Journal* 2, no. 1 (spring 1977): 31.

58. Author interview with Herbert Hill, August 25, 1986.

59. *Congressional Record,* Senate, March 20, 1964, 5820.

60. "AFL-CIO Comments on Lister Hill's Criticisms," January 31, 1964, 1, from the AFL-CIO Department of Legislation files, box 009, folder 13, George Meany Memorial Archives, Washington, D.C.

61. "AFL-CIO Press Release," January 31, 1964, 1, from the AFL-CIO Department of Legislation files, box 009, folder 13, George Meany Memorial Archives, Washington, D.C.

62. "AFL-CIO Comments on Lister Hill's Criticisms," 2.

63. Ibid., 3.

64. "AFL-CIO Press Release," 2.

65. Industrial Union Department, "Legislative Alert," May 1964, from the UAW President's Office files, Archives on Labor History and Urban Affairs, Wayne State University.

66. Walter Reuther reply to Lister Hill, February 11, 1964, from the UAW President's Office files, box 275, folder 17, Archives on Labor History and Urban Affairs, Wayne State University.

67. Hubert Humphrey, *Congressional Record*, Senate, March 30, 1965, 6549.

68. Ibid., 6548.

69. "Help on Civil Rights Starting at the Top," *Businessweek*, August 22, 1964, from the UAW President's Office files, box 578, Archives on Labor History and Urban Affairs, Wayne State University.

Notes to Chapter 3

1. Joseph Mooney, "Housing Segregation, Negro Employment and Metropolitan Decentralization: An Alternative Perspective," *Quarterly Journal of Economics* 83, no. 2 (1969): 301.

2. Richard B. Freeman, John T. Dunlop, R. F. Schubert, "The Evolution of the American Labor Market," in Martin Feldstein, ed., *The American Economy in Transition* (Chicago: University of Chicago Press, 1980), 359.

3. Ibid., 309.

4. Richard Kluger, *Simple Justice: The History of "Brown v. Board of Education" and Black America's Struggle for Equality* (New York: Vintage Books, 1977), 256–57.

5. Charles Silberman, *Crisis in Black and White* (New York: Vintage Books, 1964), 40.

6. Tom Kahn, "The Economics of Equality," in Louis Ferman, Joyce Kornblum, and Alan Haber, eds., *Poverty in America* (Ann Arbor: University of Michigan Press, 1966), 165.

7. Bayard Rustin, "From Protest to Politics: The Future of the Civil Rights Movement," *Commentary* 39 (February 1965): 25–31.

8. *Contact Magazine* 2, no. 12 (July 1971): 21, from the Chicago Urban League files, box 158, folder 21, University of Illinois, Chicago Archives.

9. Martin Luther King, Jr., *Where Do We Go from Here?* (New York: Harper & Row, 1967), 7.

10. "Dr. King Asserts Rights Movement Close to Split," *New York Times,* July 9, 1966, from the Chicago Urban League files, box 116, folder 12, University of Illinois, Chicago Archives.

11. "Press Release on Poor People's Campaign," from the Chicago Urban League files, box 169, folder 6, University of Illinois, Chicago Archives.

12. Charles Fager, *Uncertain Resurrection: The Poor People's Campaign* (Grand Rapids, Mich.: William B. Eerdmans, 1969), 15.

13. Ibid., 141.

14. Letter from Leon Keyserling to Bayard Rustin, September 28, 1966, from the files of the A. Philip Randolph Institute, New York.

15. A. Philip Randolph's Statement at the White House Conference "To Fulfill These Rights," November 18, 1965, from the UAW President's Office files, box 487, folder 6, Archives on Labor History and Urban Affairs Wayne State University.

16. Letter from Leon Keyserling to Bayard Rustin, September 28, 1966.

17. "Memo from Bayard Rustin," from the files of the A. Philip Randolph Institute, New York.

18. Letter from Leon Keyserling to Rev. Shirley Greene, February 24, 1967, from the files of the A. Philip Randolph Institute, New York.

19. Author interview with Joseph Rauh, July 25, 1987.

20. Letter from Floyd McKissick, national director of CORE, to A. Philip Randolph, October 10, 1966, from the files of the A. Philip Randolph Institute, New York.

21. Letter from John Morsell, assistant executive director of the NAACP, to Bayard Rustin, June 17, 1966, from the files of the A. Philip Randolph Institute, New York.

22. Author interview with Norman Hill, July 22, 1986.

23. Lee Rainwater and William Yancey, *The Moynihan Report and the Politics of Controversy* (Cambridge, Mass.: MIT Press, 1967), 273.

24. Ibid., 50.

25. Ibid., 130.

26. Ibid., 274.

27. John C. Donovan, *The Politics of Poverty* (New York: Pegasus, 1973), 119.

28. "Remarks by Senator Clifford P. Case," prepared for delivery on the Senate floor, Monday, September 25, 1967, from the UAW President's Office files, box 532, folder 5, Archives on Labor History and Urban Affairs, Wayne State University.

29. Garth Mangum, *The Emergence of Manpower Policy* (New York: Holt, Rinehart & Winston, 1969), 62.

30. "Urban Coalition Report," September 1968, from the Chicago Urban League files, box 168, folder 13, University of Illinois, Chicago Archives.

31. John Gardner, Chairman, "Opening Statement at the Nov. 13, 1968 Steering Committee of the Urban Coalition," from the UAW President's Office files, box 533, Archives of Labor History and Urban Affairs, Wayne State University.

32. Margaret Weir, "The Political Limits of American Economic Policy: The Federal Government and Employment Policy, 1960–1980" (Ph.D. dissertation, University of Chicago, 1986).

33. Grace Franklin and Randall Ripley, *CETA: Politics and Policy, 1973–1982* (Knoxville: University of Tennessee Press, 1984); Gary Orfield, *Congressional Power: Congress and Social Change* (New York: Harcourt Brace Jovanovich, 1975), 241.

34. Joseph Loewenberg, Richard Leone, Karen Koziara, and Edward Koziara, *The Impact of Public Employee Unions on the Public Employment Program* (Philadelphia: Temple University Center for Labor and Manpower Studies under contract with the Manpower Administration of the Department of Labor, Contract # 92–42–72–17, 1973).

35. Orfield, *Congressional Power,* 236–38.

36. Gary Orfield and Helene Slessarev, *Job Training under the New Federalism* (Chicago: Unemployment and Job Training Research Project, 1986), 40.

37. Franklin and Ripley, *CETA: Politics and Policy,* 15–17.

38. Congressional Quarterly, "Jobs Programs: How Well Do They Work?" *Weekly Report* 35, no. 8 (February 19, 1977): 303.

39. U.S. National Commission for Manpower Policy, *Job Creation through Public Sector Employment: An Interim Report to Congress* (Washington, D.C.: National Commission for Manpower Policy, 1978), 53–56.

40. Franklin and Ripley, *CETA: Politics and Policy*, 19–44.

41. William Mirengoff and Lester Rindler, *CETA: Manpower Programs under Local Control* (Washington, D.C.: National Academy of Sciences, 1978), 76.

42. U.S. National Commission for Manpower Policy, *Job Creation through Public Service Employment*, 49.

43. Helen Ginsberg, *Full Employment and Public Policy: The United States and Sweden* (New York: D.C. Heath, 1983), 65.

44. Congressional Quarterly, "Candidates Far Apart on Jobs and Inflation," *Weekly Report* 34, no. 38 (September 18, 1976): 2525.

45. Ginsberg, *Full Employment and Public Policy*, 73.

46. Polling data taken from Michael Brown, "The Segmented Welfare System: Distributive Conflict and Retrenchment in the United States, 1968–84," paper presented at the American Political Science Association Annual Meeting, Washington, D.C., August 28–31, 1986.

47. Thomas Edsall, "The Reagan Legacy," in Sidney Blumenthal and Thomas Edsall, eds., *The Reagan Legacy* (New York: Pantheon Books, 1988), 9.

48. Friedrich Hayek, *Law, Legislation, and Liberty*, vol. 2 (Chicago: University of Chicago Press, 1976), 2.

49. Robert Carleson and Kevin Hopkins, "The Reagan Rationale," *Public Welfare* 39, no. 4 (Fall 1981): 9.

50. "Hill Barons Sidetracked," *Washington Post*, February 2, 1981.

51. Elizabeth Drew, "Politics and Money, Part I," *New Yorker*, December 6, 1982.

52. Donald Baumer and Carl Van Horn, *The Politics of Unemployment*, (Washington, D.C.: Congressional Quarterly Press, 1985), 157–58.

53. Ibid., 169.

54. Ibid., 172.

55. Merrill Goozner, "A Relocation of Opinion on State Subsidies to Firms," *Chicago Tribune*, July 6, 1989, Business Section, p. 1.

56. Memo to Mayor Richard Daley from Jack Connelly at Jobs for Youth, Chicago, July 1, 1992.

57. Author interview with Stanley Dale, chairman of the DuPage County PIC, April 23, 1992.

58. Orfield and Slessarev, *Job Training under the New Federalism*, 53.

59. Ibid., 215.

60. Author interview with Loraine Volz, administrator of the DuPage County, Illinois, Service Delivery Area, April 2, 1992.

61. Fifty-three percent as of 1980; see Orfield and Slessarev, *Job Training under the New Federalism*, 100.

62. Author interview with Marvin Coklow, Demico Youth Services, Chicago, April 15, 1992.

63. Author interview with Arturo Vasquez, executive director, 18th Street Development Corporation, Chicago, April 29, 1992.

64. Gary Orfield and Carole Ashkinaze, *The Closing Door: Conservative Policy and Black Opportunity* (Chicago: University of Chicago Press, 1991), 195.

65. Helene Slessarev, "Racial Inequalities in Metropolitan Chicago Job Programs" (Chicago: Chicago Urban League, 1988), 3.

66. Ibid., 28–31.

67. Author interview with Hector Gamboa from Latino Youth, Chicago, April 15, 1992.

Notes to Chapter 4

1. Paul Burstein, *Discrimination, Jobs, and Politics: The Struggle for Equal Employment Opportunity in the United States since the New Deal* (Chicago: University of Chicago Press, 1985), 74.

2. Richard B. Freeman, John T. Dunlop, and R. F. Schubert, "The Evolution of the American Labor Market," in Martin Feldstein, ed., *The American Economy in Transition* (Chicago: University of Chicago Press, 1980), 368.

3. An example of this is Thomas Byrne Edsall and Mary Edsall, *Chain Reaction: The Impact of Race, Rights, and Taxes on American Politics* (New York: W. W. Norton, 1991).

4. Letter to Walter Reuther from Walter White, February 2, 1949, from the UAW President's Office files, box 85, Archives of Labor History and Urban Affairs, Wayne State University.

5. James A. Gershwender, *Class, Race, and Worker Insurgency: The League of Revolutionary Black Workers* (Cambridge: Cambridge University Press, 1977), 43.

6. Memo to Walter Reuther from William Oliver, "Resume of *UAW Survey* and Local Union Questionnaire," January 16, 1964, from the UAW President's Office files, box 90, folder 12, Archives of Labor History and Urban Affairs, Wayne State University.

7. Ibid.

8. UAW EEO-1 Report, October 6, 1967, from the UAW President's Office files, box 76, folder 11, Archives of Labor History and Urban Affairs, Wayne State University.

9. Ibid.

10. Philip Foner, *Organized Labor and the Black Worker, 1619–1973* (New York: International Publishers, 1978), 331.

11. Herbert Hill, "The Equal Employment Opportunity Acts of 1964 and 1972: A Critical Analysis of the Legislative History and Administration of the Law," *Industrial Relations Law Journal* 2, no. 1 (spring 1977): 1–96, 31.

12. Martin Luther King, Jr., "The Hammer of Civil Rights," *The Nation*, March 9, 1964, 232.

13. Martin Luther King, Jr., *Where Do We Go from Here?*. (New York: Harper & Row, 1967), 82.

14. U.S. Civil Rights Commission, *Federal Civil Rights Enforcement Efforts* (Washington, D.C.: Government Printing Office, 1970), 271.

15. Ibid., 309, 333.

16. Richard Nathan, *Jobs and Civil Rights* (Washington, D.C.: United States Civil Rights Commission, 1969), 22.

17. Leadership Conference on Civil Rights, "Internal Memo," 1966, from the Chicago Urban League files, box 169, folder 21, University of Illinois, Chicago Archives.

18. Nijole Benokratis and Joseph Feagin, *Affirmative Action and Employment Opportunities: Action, Inaction, and Reaction* (Boulder, Colo.: Westview Press, 1978), 103.

19. Charles S. Bullock III and Charles M. Lamb, *The Implementation of Civil Rights Policy* (Monterey, Calif.: Brooks/Cole Publishing Co., 1984).

20. NAACP press release, "214 Job Bias Complaints Filed by NAACP and Fund," September 17, 1965, from the NAACP files, Manuscript Division, Library of Congress.

21. Herbert Hill, "Racial Practices of Organized Labor: The Contemporary Record," in Julius Jacobson, ed., *The Negro in the American Labor Movement* (Garden City, N.J.: Anchor Books, 1968), 319.

22. William Gould, *Black Workers in White Unions: Job Discrimination in the United States* (Ithaca, N.Y.: Cornell University Press, 1977), 74.

23. Letter from Franklin D. Roosevelt, Jr., to Don Slaiman, director of the AFL-CIO Civil Rights Department, September 30, 1965, from the files of the George Meany Archives, Washington, D.C.

24. Memo from Irving Bluestone to Emil Mazey, "Draft Letter to FDR," October 28, 1965, from the UAW President's Office files, box 85, folder 3, Archives of Labor History and Urban Affairs, Wayne State University.

25. Memo from William Oliver to Walter Reuther, "Proposed Procedures for Handling of Title VII Cases," April 11, 1969, from the President's Office files, box 91, folder 12, Archives on Labor History and Urban Affairs, Wayne State University.

26. Ibid.

27. Letter from William Oliver to Herbert Hill, February 7, 1966, from the UAW President's Office files, box 90, folder 14, Archives on Labor History and Urban Affairs, Wayne State University.

28. Author interview with Herbert Hill, August 25, 1986.

29. Memo from Emil Mazey to William Oliver, March 9, 1966, from the UAW President's Office files, box 90, folder 14, Archives on Labor History and Urban Affairs, Wayne State University.

30. Memo from William Oliver to Emil Mazey, March 15, 1966, from the UAW President's Office files, box 90, folder 14, Archives on Labor History and Urban Affairs, Wayne State University.

31. Memo from Herbert Hill to Mr. Henry Lee Moon, NAACP director of public relations, "NAACP Labor Director to Address Auto Workers National Anti-Discrimination Conference," June 26, 1967, from the NAACP files, Manuscript Division, Library of Congress.

32. Benjamin Wolkison, *Blacks, Unions, and the EEOC* (Lexington, Mass.: D.C. Heath, 1975), 61–62.

33. Ibid., 81–84.

34. Ibid., 95.

35. Ibid., 99.

36. Ibid., 102.

37. Hill, "The Equal Employment Opportunity Acts," 29.

38. Gould, *Black Workers in White Unions*, 35.

39. Ibid., 92.

40. Ibid., 101.

41. Author interview with Judson Miner, civil rights lawyer and City of Chicago corporation counsel under Mayor Harold Washington, July 13, 1989.

42. Gould, *Black Workers in White Unions*, 50.

43. Ibid., 75.

44. Benokratis and Feagin, *Affirmative Action and Employment Opportunities*, 20–22.

45. Author interview with Herbert Hill, August 25, 1986.

46. Gould, *Black Workers in White Unions*, 424.

47. Benokratis and Feagin, *Affirmative Action and Employment Opportunities,* 93.

48. Herbert Hill, "The AFL-CIO and the Black Worker: Twenty-Five Years After the Merger," *Journal of Intergroup Relations* 10, no. 1 (spring 1982): 41–42.

49. Ibid., 42–43.

50. Hill, "Racial Practices of Organized Labor," 350.

51. Ibid., 349.

52. Letter from Joseph Rauh to Walter Reuther, January 7, 1970, from the UAW President's Office files, box 375, folder 17, Archives of Labor History and Urban Affairs, Wayne State University.

53. Ibid.

54. Hill, "The Equal Employment Opportunity Acts," 43.

55. Letter from Joseph Rauh to Walter Reuther, January 7, 1970.

56. Ibid.

57. Hill, "The Equal Employment Opportunity Acts," 50.

58. Herbert Hill, "The Equal Employment Opportunity Commission: 20 Years Later," *Journal of Intergroup Relations* 9, no. 4 (winter 1983): 52.

59. Kevin Philips, *The Emerging Republican Majority* (New York: Arlington House, 1969), 37.

60. Philip Converse et al., "Continuity and Change in American Politics: Parties and Issues in the 1968 Election," *American Political Science Review* 63, no. 4 (1969): 1083–1105.

61. "Labor Shuns Democrats Reform Drive," *Washington Post,* September 21, 1969, from the UAW President's Office files, box 347, folder 8, Archives of Labor History and Urban Affairs, Wayne State University.

62. Herbert Hill, "Black Labor and Affirmative Action: A Historical Perspective," in Steven Shulman and William Darity, Jr., eds., *The Question of Discrimination* (Middletown, Conn.: Wesleyan University Press, 1989), 257.

63. Norman Amaker, *Civil Rights and the Reagan Administration.* (Washington, D.C.: Urban Institute Press, 1988), 123.

64. Walter Dean Burnham, "The 1980 Earthquake: Realignment, Reaction or What?" in Thomas Ferguson and Joel Rogers, eds., *The Hidden Election: Politics and Economics in the 1980 Presidential Campaign* (New York: Pantheon Books, 1981), 105.

65. Amaker, *Civil Rights and the Reagan Administration,* 124.

66. Ibid.

67. Ibid., 114.

68. Testimony of Nancy B. Kreiter, research director of the Women Employed Institute. *Oversight on Activities of the Equal Employment Opportunities Commission,* Hearings before the Subcommittee on Employment and Productivity of the Committee on Labor and Human Resources, Senate (Washington, D.C.: Government Printing Office, 1992) 233.

69. Amaker, *Civil Rights and the Reagan Administration,* 112.

70. *Wards Cove Packing Co. v. Antonio,* 57 U.S.L.W. 4583 (1989).

71. *Martin v. Wilks,* 57 U.S.L.W. 4616 (1989).

72. *Patterson v. McLean Credit Union,* 57 U.S.L.W. 4705 (1989).

73. Chicago Urban League and Chicago Lawyers' Committee for Civil Rights Under Law, *The 1991 Civil Rights Act: Restoring Our Basic Protections* (Chicago: n.p., 1991), 3.

74. Ibid., 4–9.

75. Potomac Institute, *A Decade of New Opportunity: Affirmative Action in the 1970's* (Washington, D.C.: Potomac Institute, 1984), 5.

76. Ibid.

Notes to Chapter 5

1. J. Linn Allen and Jerry Thomas, "Hammering Away at Prejudice," *Chicago Tribune,* September 4, 1994, sec. C., p. 1.

2. Toni Henle, *Construction Training Report for the South Suburban Communities of Harvey, Dixmoor, Ford Heights, Phoenix, and Robbins* (Chicago: University of Illinois, Chicago, Center for Urban Economic Development, 1994), 3.

3. Chicago Urban League, memo to CUL Executive Director, "1960 Basic Fact Sheet on Race Relations in Chicago Area," from the Chicago Urban League files, box 158, folder 21, University of Illinois, Chicago Archives.

4. David Taylor, *The Unskilled Negro in the Chicago Labor Market* (Chicago: Chicago Urban League, 1965), from the Chicago Urban League files, University of Illinois, Chicago Archives.

5. Ann R. Horowitz, "The Patterns and Causes of Changes in White-Nonwhite Income Differences: 1947–1972," in George von Furstenberg, Ann Horowitz, and Bennett Harrison, eds., *Patterns of Racial Discrimination,* vol. 2 (Lexington, Mass.: D. C. Heath, 1974), 161.

6. Taylor, *The Unskilled Negro in the Chicago Labor Market,* 7.

7. Author interview with Congressman Charles Hayes, June 9, 1986.

8. "CTA Boycott Called by Breadbasket Leader," *Chicago Defender,* September 5, 1968, from the Chicago Urban League files, box 116, folder 11, University of Illinois, Chicago Archives.

9. Dennis Dickerson, *Out of the Crucible: Black Steelworkers in Western Pennsylvania, 1875–1980* (Albany: State University of New York Press, 1986), 234. For a detailed discussion of black caucus activity in the steelworkers union and in other unions, see Herbert Hill, "Black Dissent in Organized Labor," in Joseph Baskin and Robert Rosenstone, eds. *Seasons of Rebellion* (New York: Holt, Rinehart & Winston, 1972), 55–80. See also Charles Denby, "Black Caucuses in the Unions," in Burton H. Hall, ed., *Autocracy and Insurgency in Organized Labor* (New Brunswick, N.J.: Transaction Books, 1972), 137–46.

10. Toni Henle, *Construction Training Report for the South Suburban Communities,* 5.

11. William Gould, *Black Workers in White Unions: Job Discrimination in the United States* (Ithaca, N.Y.: Cornell University Press, 1977), 288.

12. Ibid., 288–89

13. David Green, "Vocational Education from a Black Perspective: The Case of Chicago and the Building Trades, 1919–1970," paper presented at the Annual Meeting of the American Educational Research Association, New Orleans, April 1988, 21.

14. *Removing Barriers to Opportunity: A Constitutional Challenge to the Davis-Bacon Act* (Washington, D.C.: Institute for Justice, 1993); "Sop for Labor: Saving Davis-Bacon" (editorial), *Chicago Tribune,* April 17, 1995.

15. "How Davis-Bacon Discriminates," *Washington Times,* November 22, 1993.

16. Bennett Hymer, *The Negro Labor Market in Chicago, 1966: Conditions in Employment and Manpower Training* (Chicago: Chicago Urban League, 1966), from the Chicago Urban League files, University of Illinois, Chicago Archives.

17. Herbert Hill, *Labor Union Control of Job Training: A Critical Analysis of Apprenticeship Outreach Programs and the Hometown Plans,* Occasional Papers, vol. 2, no. 1 (Washington, D.C.: Institute for Urban Affairs and Research, Howard University, 1974), 16.

18. "Dr. King Plans Sweeping Demand for an Open City," *Chicago Daily News,* June 8, 1966; "Dr. King's Big Gamble," *Chicago Daily News,* July 9, 1966, both from the Chicago Urban League files, box 116, folder 12, University of Illinois, Chicago Archives.

19. Majority Staff of the Committee on Education and Labor, U.S. House of Representatives, "Investigation of the Civil Rights Enforcement Activities of the Office of Federal Contract Compliance Programs, U.S. Department of Labor," 100th Congress, 1st session, October 1987, 33.

20. U.S. Civil Rights Commission, *Federal Civil Rights Enforcement Efforts* (Washington, D.C.: Government Printing Office, 1970), 156.

21. Richard Nathan, *Jobs and Civil Rights* (Washington, D.C.: U.S. Civil Rights Commission, 1969), 92.

22. U.S. Civil Rights Commission, *Federal Civil Rights Enforcement Efforts,* 163.

23. James Harvey, *Black Civil Rights during the Johnson Administration* (Jackson: University and College Press of Mississippi, 1973), 119.

24. "NAACP Launches Program to Open Building Jobs for Negro Journeymen," NAACP press release, July 1, 1967, from the NAACP files, Manuscript Division, Library of Congress.

25. Arthur Fletcher, *The Silent Sellout: Government Betrayal of Blacks to the Craft Unions* (New York: Third Press, 1974), 64–65.

26. Ibid., 65–66.

27. See statement by Herbert Hill, national labor director of the NAACP, testimony before the Senate Subcommittee on the Judiciary, Washington D.C., *Congressional Record,* October 28, 1969.

28. Author interview with Timuel Black, December 11, 1989.

29. Author interview with Rev. Calvin Morris, founding member of Operation Breadbasket, December 9, 1989.

30. Fletcher, *The Silent Sellout,* 73.

31. Gould, *Black Workers in White Unions,* 304.

32. Hill, *Labor Union Control of Job Training,* 68–69.

33. Sanford Kanter, *Blacks and the Chicago Construction Industry: Which Way Now* (Chicago: Chicago Urban League, n.d.), from the Chicago Urban League files, University of Illinois, Chicago Archives.

34. Hill, *Labor Union Control of Job Training,* 72–73.

35. Ibid., 73.

36. Kanter, *Blacks and the Chicago Construction Industry,* 11.

37. Ibid., 15.

38. Ibid.

39. Ibid., 28.

40. "Most 'Plan' Recruits Not on Job," *Chicago Daily News,* August 21, 1973, from the Chicago Urban League files, box 158, folder 21, University of Illinois, Chicago Archives.

41. Nijole Benokratis and Joseph Feagin, *Affirmative Action and Employment Opportunities: Action, Inaction, and Reaction.* (Boulder, Colo.: Westview Press, 1978), 102.

42. Kanter, *Blacks and the Chicago Construction Industry.*

43. Ibid., 30.

44. Ibid., 34.

45. Ibid.

46. "The Chronology of a Major Urban League Advocacy Campaign," December 22, 1988, from author's files. Internal briefing paper prepared by the Chicago Urban League's Advocacy Department.

47. Ibid., 6.

48. James Warren, "Minorities Getting Ryan Share," *Chicago Tribune,* June 12, 1988.

49. "The Chronology of a Major Urban League Advocacy Campaign," 7.

50. J. Linn Allen and Jerry Thomas, "Hammering Away at Prejudice: For Blacks Trades Jobs Not on Level," *Chicago Tribune,* September 4, 1994, sec. C, p. 1.

51. John Kass and George Papajohn, "Group's Rapid Success a Real Inside Story," *Chicago Tribune,* July 24, 1994.

52. Gould, *Black Workers in White Unions,* 282.

53. Herbert Hill, "Address to the Sixty-First Annual Convention of the NAACP," Cincinnati, Ohio, June 30, 1970, 9. From the files of the George Meany Archives, Washington, D.C.

54. Author interview with Dr. Charles Lutzow, principal of Washburne Trade School, December 13, 1989.

55. U.S. House of Representatives Committee on Labor and Education, *Equal Employment Opportunity,1965* (Washington, D.C.: Government Printing Office, 1965), 197.

56. Green, "Vocational Education from a Black Perspective," 26.

57. Edward Marciniak, *Washburne Trade School* (Chicago: Center for Urban Policy, Loyola University, 1986), 25.

58. Office of Civil Rights, U.S. Department of Education, "Statement of Findings," March 28, 1986, 10.

59. Author interview with Charles Lutzow, April 28, 1995.

60. Beverly Hurst, *Barometers of Black Economic Achievement: The Reality and the Myth* (Chicago: Chicago Urban League, 1974), from the Chicago Urban League files, University of Illinois, Chicago Archives.

61. Joy Carew and Michael Preston, *The Washburne Report: The Exclusion of Blacks and Other Minorities from the Construction Trades in Chicago, 1977–84* (Chicago: Chicago City Colleges, 1985), 50.

62. Office of Civil Rights, U.S. Department of Education, *Statement of Findings in Response to Complaint Filed by the Women's Law Project of Legal Assistance Foundation against Chicago Board of Education* (Washington, D.C.: Government Printing Office, 1986), 4–5.

63. Carew and Preston, *The Washburne Report,* 5.

64. Author interview with Charles Lutzow, December 23, 1989.

65. Carew and Preston, *The Washburne Report,* 5.

66. Ed Marciniak, *Washburne Trade School: Its Future in the Chicago Metropolitan Labor Market* (Chicago: Institute of Urban Life, Loyola University, 1986), 25.

67. Barry Cronin, "Union Pulls Out of Washburne," *Chicago Sun-Times,* October 10, 1986.

68. Author interview with Charles Lutzow, April 28, 1995.

69. Barry Cronin, "Washburne Minority Goals Peril Carpentry Program," *Chicago Sun-Times,* November 14, 1986.

70. *Chicago Sun-Times,* Barry Cronin, "Washburne Faces Carpenter Pullout," December 4, 1986, 8.

71. Green, "Vocational Education from a Black Perspective," 27–28.

72. Author interview with Charles Lutzow, December 23, 1989.

73. Author interview with Luke Helm, last principal of Washburne Trade School, March 6, 1995.

74. Author interview with Charles Lutzow, April 28, 1995.

75. Author interview with Toni Henle, researcher on the University of Illinois, Center for Urban Economic Development, February 24, 1995.

76. 1990 United States Census, EEO File for Cook County, Illinois.

Notes to Chapter 6

1. Timothy Bates, *Banking on Black Enterprise: The Potential of Emerging Businesses for Revitalizing Urban Economies* (Washington, D.C.: Joint Center for Political and Economic Studies, 1993), 2.

2. Judith Kerner Thompson and Jacqueline N. Hood, "The Practice of Social Performance in Minority-Owned versus Nonminority-Owned Businesses," *Journal of Business Ethics* 12 (1993): 205.

3. U.S. Department of Commerce, *1992 Economic Census: Survey of Minority-Owned Business Enterprises* (Washington D.C.: Bureau of the Census, 1996), 5, 8.

4. Ibid., 3.

5. Bates. *Banking on Black Enterprise,* 17.

6. Ibid., 12, 17.

7. Jan Crawford Greenburg, "Affirmative Action down but Not Out," *Chicago Tribune,* June 14, 1995, 1.

8. Michael Tackett, "Affirmative Action Ruling Challenges 30 Year Trend," *Chicago Tribune,* June 13, 1995, sec. 1, p. 17.

9. Bates, *Banking on Black Enterprise,* 1993.

10. Author interview with Cecil Troy, owner of Grove Fresh Orange Juice, November 4, 1988.

11. Samuel Doctors, ed., *Whatever Happened to Minority Business Development?* (Hinsdale, Ill.: Dryden Press, 1974), 112.

12. Chicago Urban League, "Statement on the Community Reinvestment Act before a Special Panel Convened by the Comptroller of the Currency," April 6, 1978, Federal Reserve Bank of Chicago.

13. Arthur Blaustein and Geoffrey Faux, *The Star-Spangled Hustle* (Garden City, N.J.: Doubleday, 1972), 80.

14. Author interview with Louis Caldwell, founder of the Negro Chamber of Commerce, April 7, 1989.

15. Harvard Sitkoff, *The New Deal for Blacks* (Oxford: Oxford University Press, 1978), 263.

16. Theodore Cross, *The Black Power Imperative: Racial Inequality and the Politics of Non-Violence* (New York: Faulkner Books, 1984), 268.

17. John McClaughry, "Black Ownership and National Politics," in The American Assembly, eds., *Black Economic Development* (Englewood Cliffs, N.J.: Prentice-Hall, 1969), 40.

18. August Meier and Elliott Rudwick, *CORE: A Study in the Civil Rights Movement, 1942–1968* (Urbana: University of Illinois Press, 1975), 51

19. Blaustein and Faux, *The Star-Spangled Hustle,* 51.

20. Ibid., 130

21. Ibid., 201–2.

22. "Federal Compliance to Minority Set-Asides," report by the Congressional Task Force on Minority Set-Asides, Honorable Mervyn M. Dymally, Chairman, to the Speaker of the U.S. House of Representatives, September 8, 1988, 66.

23. Daniel Levinson, "A Study of Preferential Treatment: The Evolution of Minority Business Enterprise Programs," *George Washington Law Review* 49, no. 1 (November 1980): 65.

24. Ibid., 66.

25. Ibid., 67.

26. Comptroller General of the United States, "Report to Congress on the Small Business Administration and the Office of Minority Business Enterprise" (Washington, D.C.: Government Printing Office, 1973), 1.

27. Ibid., 2.

28. Major Thomas Jefferson Hasty III, "Minority Business Enterprise Development and the Small Business Administration's 8(a) Program, Past, Present, and (Is There a) Future?" *Military Law Review* 145 (summer 1994): 1–112.

29. Government Accounting Office, *The SBA 8(a) Procurement Program—A Promise Unfulfilled* (Washington, D.C.: Government Printing Office, 1981), 7.

30. Author interview with Diane Bast, the Heartland Institute, April 12, 1989.

31. Press Release by Michael Cardenas, Administrator for U.S. Small Business Administration's 8(a) Program, May 1, 1981, from the Appendices to Hearings before a Subcommittee of the Committee on Government Operations, House of Representatives, 97th Congress, 1st session, March 28, 1981, 419.

32. See "Federal Compliance to Minority Set-Asides," 73–74, as one example of where fraud is pointed to as an ongoing problem.

33. Hasty, "Minority Business Enterprise Development," 52.

34. Author interview with Manuel Rodriguez, founder of the Hispanic American Construction and Industry Association, Chicago, March 29, 1989, and Percy Hines, former director of the Contractors Division of the Chicago Economic Development Corporation, March 6, 1989.

35. Lawrence Tell, "Minority Firms Aim for $5.2 Million Piece of Public Works Pie: Local Contractors Quarrel with New Federal Programs," *Chicago Reporter* 7, no. 4 (April 1978).

36. Levinson, "A Study of Preferential Treatment," 75.

37. *City of Richmond v. J. A. Croson,* 488 U.S. 469 (1989), 12.

38. Ibid., 13.

39. Levinson, "A Study of Preferential Treatment," 77.

40. Hasty, "Minority Business Enterprise Development," 27.

41. Author interview with Philip Clark, former director of affirmative action, Department of Public Works, City of Chicago, March 1, 1989.

42. Author interview with Hermaine Wise, director of contract compliance, Purchasing Department, City of Chicago, under Mayor Jane Byrne, April 3, 1989.

43. Kenneth Mladenka, "Blacks and Hispanics in Urban Politics," *American Political Science Review* 83, no. 1 (March 1989): 165–91.

44. Timothy Bates and Darrell Williams, "Preferential Procurement Programs and Minority-Owned Businesses," *Journal of Urban Affairs* 17, no. 1 (1995): 7.

45. Minority Business Enterprise Legal Defense and Education Fund, *The Effects of* Richmond v. Croson *and Similar Attacks on Federal, State, and Local M/W/DBE Programs Nationwide*, report published April 1994, 40.

46. Author interview with Anthony Robinson, president of MBELDEF, September 12, 1995.

47. Udayan Gupta, "Cash Crunch: For Black Entrepreneurs, Raising Money Is Often the Biggest Hurdle," *Wall Street Journal*, February 19, 1993, R4.

48. Bates and Williams, "Preferential Procurement Programs and Minority-Owned Businesses," 7.

49. Ibid.

50. Author interview with W. T. Luxion, chief operating officer of Wil-freds Construction Company, September 11, 1995.

51. Author interview with Taylor Cotton, executive director of Black Contractors United, August 30, 1995.

52. Author interview with W. T. Luxion, September 11, 1995.

53. Bates and Williams, "Preferential Procurement Programs and Minority-Owned Businesses," 7.

54. Judith Crown, "Minority Firms Already Report Drop in Business," *Crain's Chicago Business*, August 7, 1995, 32

55. Janice Franke, "Defining the Parameters of Permissible State and Local Affirmative Action Programs," *Golden State University Law Review* 24 (spring 1994): 391.

56. Paul Sonn, "Fighting Minority Underrepresentation in Publicly Funded Construction Projects after *Croson:* A Litigation Strategy," *Yale Law Review* 101 (May 1992): 1578.

57. *City of Richmond v. Croson*, 488 U.S. 469 (1989).

58. Ibid.

59. Ibid., 32 of the majority opinion.

60. Ibid., 31 of the majority opinion.

61. Mitchell Rice, "Government Set-Asides, Minority Business Enterprises and the Supreme Court," *Public Administration Review* 51, no. 2 (March–April 1991): 120.

62. Sonn, "Fighting Minority Underrepresentation," 1577.

63. Nina Munk, "Fighting over the Spoils," *Forbes*, August 15, 1994, 50.

64. Author interview with Margaret Simms, Joint Center for Political Studies, August 10, 1995.

65. Author interview with Amy Crow, director of affirmative action, Greater Chicago Water Reclamation District, August 17, 1995.

66. One of the principal examples is Philadelphia, which has had its program rejected three times.

67. Author interview with Lawrence Rosenthal, deputy corporation counsel, City of Chicago, August 17, 1995.

68. Author interview with Evangeline Levinson, former director of minority procurement, Chicago Board of Education, August 16, 1995.

69. Author interview with Anthony Robinson, September 12, 1995.

70. Munk, "Fighting over the Spoils," 50.

71. Walter Dellinger, assistant attorney general, "Memorandum to General Counsels," issued by the U.S. Department of Justice, Office of Legal Counsel, June 28, 1995.

72. Ibid.

73. *Adarand Constructors, Inc. v. Peña*, 63 U.S.L.W. 4523 (U.S. June 12, 1995).

74. Ibid.

75. *Affirmative Action Review: Report to the President*, July 19, 1995, 6.

76. Michael Tackett, "Court Ruling on Bias Tricky for Democrats," *Chicago Tribune*, June 14, 1995.

77. Author interview with Anthony Robinson, September 12, 1995.

78. Judith Crown, "Quota, Unquota: Contractors Feel the Pinch," *Crain's Chicago Business*, August 7, 1995, 32.

Notes to Chapter 7

1. William Julius Wilson, *The Truly Disadvantaged: The Inner City, the Underclass, and Public Policy* (Chicago: University of Chicago Press, 1987), 109.

2. *The World Almanac and Book of Facts, 1995* (Mahwah, N.J.: Funk & Wagnalls, 1994).

3. Stokely Carmichael and Charles Hamilton, *Black Power: The Politics of Liberation in America* (New York: Random House, 1967), 46.

4. Ibid.

5. Martin Luther King, Jr., *Where Do We Go from Here?* (New York: Harper & Row, 1967), 148.

6. Ibid., 7

7. Quote is taken from James Cone, *Martin & Malcolm & America: A Dream or a Nightmare* (Maryknoll, N.Y.: Orbis Books, 1991), 235.

8. "Dr. King Plans Sweeping Demand for an Open City," *Chicago Daily News*, June 8, 1966; "Dr. King's Big Gamble," *Chicago Daily News*, July 9, 1966, both from the Chicago Urban League files, box 116, folder 12, University of Illinois, Chicago Archives.

9. Author interview with Rev. Leonard DeVille, former assistant pastor, Fellowship Missionary Baptist Church, October 25, 1988.

10. "The 1971 Expo," from the personal files of Dwight McKee, former youth director of Operation PUSH.

11. Author interview with Rev. Alvin Pitcher, one of the founding Breadbasket ministers, March 12, 1992.

12. Author interview with Cecil Troy, founder and owner of Grove Fresh Orange Juice and founding board member of Operation Breadbasket, November 4, 1988.

13. Author interview with Dwight McKee, October 13, 1988.

14. Author interview with Rev. Alvin Pitcher, March 12, 1992.

15. David Garrow, ed., *Chicago* (Brooklyn, N.Y.: Carlson Publishing Co., 1989), 203.

16. Author interview with Alvin Robinson, insurance broker, November 2, 1988.

17. Author interview with Roscoe Morgan, Chicago firefighter, June 20, 1992.

18. Author interview with Cecil Troy, November 4, 1988.

19. Author interview with Alvin Pitcher, March 12, 1992.

20. Author interview with Cecil Troy, November 4, 1988.

21. "The 1971 Expo."

22. Garrow, *Chicago*, 211.

23. Barbara Reynolds, *Jesse Jackson: America's David* (Washington, D.C.: JFJ Associates, 1985), 179–80.

24. Author interview with Alvin Boutte, former president of Indecorp, October 18, 1988.

25. Barbara Rose, "Indecorp, Shorebank Merger Talks," *Crain's Chicago Business*, July 12, 1993.

26. Author interview with Independence Bank executive, October 18, 1988.

27. Barbara Rose, "Indecorp, Shorebank Merger Talks," *Crain's Chicago Business*, July 12, 1993.

28. Barbara Rose, "New Banking Era Jolts African-American Lender," *Crain's Chicago Business*, July 19, 1993.

29. William Raspberry, "PUSH vs. Nike: Serious Issues or Hocus-Pocus?" *Chicago Tribune*, August 30, 1990.

30. Mike Royko, "No, Nike's Still Not Shaking in Its Boots," *Chicago Tribune*, October 2, 1990.

31. Steven Strahler, "Higginbottom Sees Clout Lost in Fatal Fire," *Crain's Chicago Business*, January 29, 1996.

32. John Kass and Jerry Thomas, "Daley Hits Gang-Linked Voter Drive: Mayor Criticizes Urban League's Role," *Chicago Tribune*, February 16, 1996, sec. 2, p. 2.

33. Nancy Weiss, *The National Urban League, 1910–1940* (New York: Oxford University Press, 1974), 180.

34. Author interview with Taylor Cotton, former director of the Affirmative Action Division and executive director of Black Contractors United, March 7, 1996.

35. Eddie Williams, "Black Political Progress in the 1970s: The Electoral Arena," in Michael Preston, Lenneal J. Henderson, and Paul Puryear, eds., *The New Black Politics* (New York: Longman, 1982), 75; Joint Center for Political and Economic Studies, *Black Elected Officials: A National Roster* (Washington, D.C.: Joint Center for Political and Economic Studies Press, 1991), 1.

36. James H. Lowery and Associates, *Developing a Minority and Women Owned Business Enterprise Program*, study prepared for the Honorable Harold Washington, Mayor of the City of Chicago, March 1985, 3–12.

37. Ibid.

38. I obtained this information when I was hired as a consultant by the Sawyer administration to assemble the documentation needed to support the continuation of the existing set-aside.

39. U.S. Bureau of the Census, *Survey of Minority and Women Owned Business Enterprises* (Washington, D.C.: Bureau of the Census, 1987).

40. Author's personal knowledge.

41. John Kass, "Daley Calls for an End to Racial Politics: Mayor Defends Black Supporters," *Chicago Tribune*, December 15, 1994.

42. Ann Marie Lipinski, "Edgar Campaign Ties Benefit Black Groups," *Chicago Tribune*, February 4, 1991.

43. Byron P. White, "Black Voters Get Less of Edgar's Time," *Chicago Tribune*, September 25, 1994.

44. James Hill and Blair Kamin, "CHA Chief Lowers Cabrini Cost Estimate," *Chicago Tribune,* June 29, 1996.

45. John Kass, "Council Groups Unite against Daley on Tax," *Chicago Tribune,* February 19, 1993.

46. John Kass, "Cop Exam Frustrates Aldermen: Results of Hands-off Test Create Friction during Council Hearings," *Chicago Tribune,* August 12, 1994.

47. Stevenson Swanson and Sabrina L. Miller, "Hard Cash from Concrete Waste," *Chicago Tribune,* January 15, 1996.

Notes to Chapter 8

1. Patrick Reardon, "Survey Finds Optimism a Growth Industry in City," *Chicago Tribune,* August 20, 1996, 1.

2. Jeff Bailey and Calmetta Y. Coleman, "Despite Tough Years, Chicago Has Become a Nice Place to Live," *The Wall Street Journal,* August 21, 1996, A1.

3. See Donald L. Miller, *City of the Century: The Epic of Chicago and the Making of America* (New York: Simon & Schuster, 1996), for an excellent description of the early growth of Chicago suburbs.

4. Gary Orfield and Carole Ashkinaze, *The Closing Door: Conservative Policy and Black Opportunity* (Chicago: University of Chicago Press, 1991).

5. Elliott D. Sclar and Walter Hook, "The Importance of Cities to the National Economy," in Henry Cisneros, ed., *Interwoven Destinies: Cities and the Nation* (New York: W. W. Norton, 1993), 62, 67.

6. John McCarron, "City Needs Fixing, Not Yuppie Bashing," *Chicago Tribune,* July 11, 1993, Business Section.

7. Bailey and Coleman, "Despite Tough Years, Chicago Has Become a Nice Place to Live," A1.

8. Author interview with Art Lyons, executive director of the Center for Economic Policy Analysis, July 17, 1996.

9. Ellen Shubart, "Adding More Beef to Yards' Revival Bond Issue Will Advance Redevelopment," *Crain's Chicago Business,* August 1, 1994.

10. Ibid.

11. Author interview with Art Lyons, July 17, 1996.

12. Ibid.

13. Arthur Lyons et al., *Reducing Property Taxes to Promote Industrial Development: Does It Work?* Prepared for the Comptroller of the City of Chicago, July 1988, 50.

14. Ibid., 51.

15. Malcolm Bush, Anna Maria Ortiz, and Ann Maxwell, *Tracking the Dollars: State Social Service Spending in One Low Income Community* (Chicago: Woodstock Institute, 1996), 19.

16. Woodstock Institute, *The 1990 Community Lending Fact Book* (Chicago: Woodstock Institute, 1992).

17. Author interview with Spruiell White, program officer for the community initiatives program at the John D. and Catherine T. MacArthur Foundation, June 5, 1996.

18. Author interview with Steven Alexander, former deputy commissioner of the Department of Economic Development under the Washington and Sawyer administrations, August 27, 1996.

19. National Congress for Community Economic Development, *Changing the Odds: The*

Achievements of Community-Based Development Corporations (Washington, D.C.: National Congress for Economic Development, 1991), 2.

20. Randy Stoecker, "The Community Development Corporation Model of Urban Redevelopment: A Political Economy Critique and an Alternative" (http://www.scn.org./lPcds/cdc01.htm), 2.

21. Ibid., 6.

22. Author interview with Wanda White, executive director of the Community Workshop on Economic Development, June 2, 1996.

23. Arthur Blaustein and Geoffrey Faux, *The Star-Spangled Hustle* (Garden City, N.J.: Doubleday, 1972), 116.

24. For a fuller discussion of Nixon's anti-urban policies, see John Mollenkopf, *The Contested City* (Princeton, N.J.: Princeton University Press, 1983), 126.

25. Stoecker, "The Community Development Corporation Model of Economic Development," 4.

26. Author interview with Leon Finney, former executive director of The Woodlawn Organization, December 3, 1988.

27. Ibid.

28. Mercer Sullivan, *More Than Housing: How Community Development Corporations Go About Changing Lives and Neighborhoods* (New York: Community Development Research Center, New School for Social Research, 1993), 104–5.

29. Quoted in ibid., 8.

30. Nicholas Lemann, "The Myth of Community Development," *New York Times Magazine,* January 9, 1994, 27–31, 50, 54, 60.

31. Author interview with Mary Nelson, executive director of Bethel New Life, June 13, 1996.

32. Ibid.

33. Mitchell Sciridoff, "The Seeds of Urban Revival," *The Public Interest,* no. 114 (Winter 1994): 92.

34. Comments by Gary Stern, president of the Federal Reserve Bank of Minneapolis, "Resolving Conflict: The Fed's Role in Community Reinvestment Act" (http://woodrow.mpls.frb.fed.us), 2.

35. John Schmeltzer, "Streamlined System on Community Lending: Activists Pleased, Though Data Plan Dropped," *Chicago Tribune,* April 20, 1995.

36. Speech by Dick Rosenberg, chief executive officer of Bank of America, Dallas, Texas, August 17, 1995, 3.

37. Sharon Stangenes, "A Boost for Loans to Poor," *Chicago Tribune,* November 3, 1993.

38. Speech by Dick Rosenberg, Dallas, Texas, August 17, 1995, 4.

39. John Schmeltzer, "Moves to Better Housing: Banks Respond to U.S. Pressure for Reinvestment in Urban Areas," *Chicago Tribune,* April 30, 1995.

40. Jacqueline Simmons, "Home Prices Soar in Unexpected Places," *Wall Street Journal,* February 13, 1996, A2.

41. Author interview with Shawn Peterson, staff member for U.S. Congressman Floyd Flake, June 14, 1996.

42. Editorial, "Don't Starve the Housing Machine" *Chicago Tribune,* July 27, 1995.

43. Author interview with Alton Bathrick, former senior vice president of Robert W. Baird and Co., investment bank in Milwaukee, June 17, 1996.

44. Ibid.

45. Ronald Grzywinski, "The New Old-Fashioned Banking," *Harvard Business Review,* May–June, 1991, 94.

46. Julia Ann Parzen and Michael Hall Kieschnick, *Credit Where It's Due: Development Banking for Communities* (Philadelphia: Temple University Press, 1991), 50.

47. "Community Development Corporations," May 26, 1995 (http://www2.ari.net/home/poverty/m9516/html).

48. Author interview with Alton Bathrick, June 6, 1996.

49. Marilyn Marks Rubin, "Can Reorchestration of Historical Themes Reinvent Government? A Case Study of the Empowerment Zones and Enterprises Communities Act of 1993" *Public Administration Review* 54, no. 2 (March–April 1994): 161–69.

50. Author interview with Wanda White, June 2, 1996.

51. Rubin, "Can Reorchestration of Historical Themes Reinvent Government?"

52. Nik Theodore, "How Effective Are Enterprise Zones?" in Marya Morris, ed., *Public Investment* (Chicago: American Planning Association, 1994), 2.

53. H. Lee Murphy, "Cities: Don't Give It All Away; Incentives Prove to Be Poor Lures Survey Shows," *Crain's Chicago Business,* March 21, 1994.

54. Theodore, "How Effective Are Enterprise Zones?" 2.

55. Michael Porter, "The Competitive Advantage of the Inner City," *Harvard Business Review,* May–June 1995, 69 (reprint no. 95310).

56. David Osborne and Ted Gaebler, *Reinventing Government: How the Entrepreneurial Spirit Is Transforming the Public Sector* (New York: Penguin Books, 1992), 19.

57. Rubin, "Can Reorchestration of Historical Themes Reinvent Government?"

58. Author interview with Mary Nelson, June 13, 1996.

59. Author interview with Spruiell White, June 5, 1996.

60. Author interview with Wanda White, June 2, 1996.

61. Author interview with Spruiell White, June 5, 1996.

62. Author interview with Wanda White, June 2, 1996.

63. Flynn McRoberts, "Funds Set for Urban Renewal: Losing Bidders Hit Empowerment Zones," *Chicago Tribune,* March 7, 1996.

64. Author interview with Wanda White, June 2, 1996.

65. Author interview with Congressman Bobby Rush (D-IL), June 13, 1996.

66. Marilyn Gittell, Janice Bockmeyer, Robert Lindsey, and Kathe Newman, *The Urban EZs: Community Organizations and Community Capacity Building* (New York: Howard Samuels State Management Policy Center at CUNY, 1996), 21.

67. Author interview with Alton Bathrick, June 6, 1996.

68. Julie Bennett, "Franchising along City Streets May Soon Rival the Boom in Suburban Malls," *Crain's Chicago Business,* August 1, 1995.

69. Porter, "The Competitive Advantage of the Inner City," 57.

70. Author interview with Mary Nelson, June 13, 1996.

71. Paul Merrion, "Getting Inner City Groceries off the Shelf; Financing Help Could Jump-Start Southside Site," *Crain's Chicago Business,* October 3, 1994.

72. Anthony Taibi, "Banking, Finance, and Community Economic Empowerment: Structural Economic Theory, Procedural Civil Rights, and Substantive Racial Justice," *Harvard Law Review* 107, no. 7 (May 1994): 1530.

73. Author interview with Shawn Peterson, June 14, 1996.

INDEX